Winners and Losers in Globalization

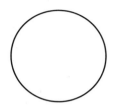

Guillermo de la Dehesa

Winners and Losers
in Globalization

Blackwell
Publishing

© 2006 by Guillermo de le Dehesa

BLACKWELL PUBLISHING
350 Main Street, Malden, MA 02148-5020, USA
9600 Garsington Road, Oxford OX4 2DQ, UK
550 Swanston Street, Carlton, Victoria 3053, Australia

First published 2006 by Blackwell Publishing Ltd

1   2006

Library of Congress Cataloging-in-Publication Data

Dehesa, Guillermo de la.
    Winners and losers in globalization / Guillermo de la Dehesa.
        p. cm.
    Includes bibliographical references and index.
    ISBN-13: 978-1-4051-3382-1 (hard cover : alk. paper)
    ISBN-10: 1-4051-3382-1 (hard cover : alk. paper)
    1. Globalization—Economic aspects.   I. Title.
HF1359.D45 2006
337—dc22

                                                  2005015449

A catalogue record for this title is available from the British Library.

Set in 10/12.5 pt Dante
by Graphicraft Limited, Hong Kong
Printed and bound in India
by Replika Press

For further information on
Blackwell Publishing, visit our website:
www.blackwellpublishing.com

Contents

Foreword

Paul Krugman

Globalization is a subject that stirs uncommonly strong emotions. Perhaps this is because globalization, by taking the economic system beyond the boundaries of any one state, in effect forces us to decide how we really feel about the invisible hand. If we regard markets as basically a good thing, then the power of globalization to produce wealth – in particular, its power to lift poor countries rapidly into the modern world – can move us to excited praise. If, on the other hand, we are basically distrustful of markets – if we are initially grudging about allowing even a domestic economy to be driven by individual self-interest – then the prospect of a market system that has moved beyond any one government's ability to control fills us with dread.

Because the global economy is such a fraught issue, those who try to make sense of it are often challenged on their credentials. If an economist writes about globalization, he may be accused of lacking knowledge of the real world. If a businessman writes, he may be accused of lacking an understanding of the larger forces at work – or perhaps of thinking only of profits, not of human needs. If a politician writes about it – well, who trusts politicians? Almost everyone who has tried to say something sensible about the phenomenon has some weakness of knowledge or credentials that at least potentially makes his opinion suspect.

But once in a while you get someone like Guillermo de la Dehesa – that is, someone whose knowledge and experience crosses the usual boundaries, who cannot be impeached on the usual grounds. Mr. de la Dehesa earns a living as a highly successful banker; he surely cannot be accused of not understanding the real world. But he is no mean economist; for many years he has been a major voice on European and international economic issues. I first got to know him through the high-level economic conference circuit, both the European branch centered around such organizations as the Centre for Economic Policy Research, where he is now chairman, and the international financial branch centered around such organizations as the Group of Thirty. But that's not all: Mr. de la Dehesa has extensive experience in government and has established a reputation as someone who is prepared to run professional, even personal risks on behalf of democracy and justice. And he has always been a strong voice, in particular, for those less lucky than himself – which means that he can be trusted to deal fairly with the fact that globalization produces losers as well as winners.

In other words, he is someone whose motives you can trust, and whose breadth of knowledge and experience are rare in this or any other area.

I don't expect this book to settle the debates over globalization: there is too much real uncertainty about the issue, and anyway there are too many people firmly committed to their views to be shaken by any argument or evidence. But perhaps Guiillermo de la Dehesa's excellent book can lower the temperature and give us all a better sense of what this new global economy is really all about.

Introduction

Globalization has not only become one of the most fashionable words for politicians, businesspeople, union leaders, and economists alike, but it has also turned into a scapegoat word for everything that is going wrong in the world. For many politicians and citizens in developing countries, globalization is the guilty party in financial crises and contagion as capital invested in promising economies is withdrawn quite suddenly at the first sign of economic or political weakness. For many unions and political parties in the developed world, globalization stands accused of destroying jobs and increasing income inequality as international competition brings with it "social dumping" from countries with low wages and inhuman working conditions. Many governments blame globalization for a rapid loss of national sovereignty, as they perceive that states and governments become powerless before the irresistible rise and influence of financial markets and multinational corporations. This set of attitudes has come to be known as "globaphobia," and it reached a climax in December 1999 with the failure of the Seattle summit of the World Trade Organization (WTO) to launch the so-called Millennium Round of trade liberalization and it has continued at every meeting of the IMF, World Bank, G7, APEC, or even at Davos, but fortunately with decreasing levels of virulence. Protests today are less frequent and more organized through political or direct channels and some have been diverted to other issues like the Iraq war.

Many politicians on leftist and rightist positions criticize globalization while actually benefiting from it. Barely differentiated attacks on globalization come from conservative thinkers such as Britain's John Gray and left-minded intellectuals such as William Greider in the US. Nevertheless, the overwhelming majority of economists presently defend the globalization process in general, although some question the desirability of financial globalization or the need for a true international governance of its process. The

Indian economist Jagdish Bhagwati (1998 and 2004), a fervent proponent of free trade and globalization, who opposes the liberalization of short-term capital flows, is, perhaps, the most outstanding of these. Bhagwati believes that free capital movements inevitably trigger financial crises that may eventually turn opinion against trade liberalization, which he considers essential for growth and convergence between countries. He considers that trying to impose the total freedom of capital flows in developing countries, as the IMF and the US Treasury did, for a while, was a grave mistake, because most developing countries did not have the quality of institutions and financial regulation and supervision to deal with the huge amount of short-tem capital inflows, and suffered a major financial crisis, starting in Asia and spreading to the rest of the developing world. In the meantime, those Asian countries which did not open to capital inflows, asuch as China and India did much better and wheathered the crisis. He blames the "Wall Street–Treasury Complex" for that, and hails the IMF decision of pulling back and rectifying the mistake, albeit too late (Bhagwati, 2004)

Other economists of great prestige and repute such as Paul Krugman (1999a) and Barry Eichengreen (1999a) defend both trade and financial globalization but favor the selective and temporary introduction of controls on short-term capital inflows to avoid crises. Paradoxically, another respected economist, Nobel Prize laureate Maurice Allais (1999), opposes both the liberalization of capital flows (and with it free-floating exchange rates) and the globalization of trade, placing himself oddly in the anti-globalization camp.

Finally, another Nobel laureate, Joseph Stiglitz (2003) who, in principle, is not against globalization, strongly opposes the way the IMF, the World Bank, the WTO and other international organizations interpret globalization and implement their policies in the developing countries. He has taken a very hard line against the IMF, for the wrong policies imposed to some countries under its programs, and against the so called "Washington Consensus Principles," which he considers to be in some cases ill defined and in others worsely implemented by many countries, under the misguided influence of IMF "neo-liberal" advising. In any case, only a very small group of economists disagree with globalization, but many more are not happy with the way globalization proceeds, without worldwide governance institutions to supervise and control it.

In this book, I will attempt to present the reader with a technical, objective and dispassionate analysis of the globalization debate, detailing its economic effects on individuals, businesses, governments, and nation-states.

I will assess its impact on both labor markets and financial markets, on global economic growth and on income distribution and on real convergence between different national economies. Objectivity and empirical evidence are crucial if we are to illuminate such an emotionally charged debate between the apparent few *globaphiles* and many *globaphobes*. So this is a simple review of the best theoretical and empirical research published on the different issues of globalization, which I hope will be accessible to readers unfamiliar with economics.

Let me say from the outset that, on the whole, globalization will be positive for growth and for world convergence, although the costs and benefits will not be distributed evenly. There are winners and losers as in all processes of economic change. I do believe, though, that the former are far more numerous than the latter.

On the one hand, globalization is improving economic efficiency and boosting productivity and economic growth, by acting in unison with the latests waves of technological innovation. But, on the other hand, it also tends to fragment production processes, labor markets, political entities, and even societies. It combines the beneficial effects of innovation and dynamism with the negative impact of financial crises or other kinds of shocks. It should be stressed again, though, that the former effects are far more important than the latter.

In this respect, neither *globaphobia* nor *globaphilia* seem entirely justified. Globalization is neither a limitless source of benefit to humanity, as some claim, nor is it guilty of all the ills for which it is held responsible. In economics nothing is absolute and everything is relative. The globalization process in which we are immersed has relatively much more positive than negative consequences for the world economy as a whole. Nevertheless, if we are to avoid again widespread rejection by society, it is crucial that we attempt to minimize the negative effects for specific countries or individuals that may be affected negatively or even excluded from globalization. Such a wholesale rejection occurred in 1914 during the 44-year phase of globalization, an experience which showed, after two world wars and a great depression, that halting its process is a far less attractive alternative for everybody.

In reality, the main losers of globalization are now those peoples and countries which are not able to join the globalization process and are left behind, mainly by not having credible institutions: political, legal, economic, or social. On the contrary, the main winners are those which benefit from having been able to open to it attracting foreing trade, capital and

technology. Therefore, the main losers are not the "victims of globalization" as is often said by some ill-informed pundits, but the "victims of the
lack of globalization."

It is a fact that markets and companies lead globalization to a far
greater extent than governments. This is a positive development after many
decades in which the opposite situation prevailed. Both markets and governments are necessary and also tend to have failures when leading, but
markets tend to correct them faster and better than governments. But this
change of leadership also generates contradictions, which will have to be
dealt with. One of these is that markets develop through a complex process of individual decision-making, whereas democracy is a product of collective decisions endorsed by majorities. Another is that markets develop
more efficiently where there is less government intervention. Yet society
seeks greater economic security and social stability with globalization
based on rules that prevent social disintegration, and chooses governments
that guarantee social protection and cohesion. As Daniel Cohen (1999) points
out: "present day globalization and technology are an unfinished revolution. They lack specific social regulation. Until a new global framework
of social rules is developed, the present unrest will continue."

These questions were discussed at the Davos summit in January 2000
where both British Prime Minister Tony Blair and US president Bill
Clinton made outstanding contributions. For Blair there is a great opportunity in the new century to create an open world economy and a global
society. But this will only be possible if the unprecedented opportunities
that globalization creates for people's welfare are combined with a strong
ethical base and mutual responsibility to prevent countries or individuals
from being excluded. This means an international commitment to help those
affected by debt, genocide, or environmental problems. Unlike last century, concludes Blair, the twenty-first century will be a battle for pragmatic
ideals not for ideological dogma.

Clinton's evaluation of the globalization process is similar. According
to him, it is essential that workers and families in both developing and developed countries reap the rewards of globalization. Industrialized countries
must ensure that the poor and those disadvantaged by change are not left
behind and that all workers have access to the benefits of education and
professional training in the application of new technologies. Leaders of developing countries must narrow the gap between rich and poor and ensure
that governments and institutions are open and transparent. This is essential for attracting the foreign investment needed to improve growth rates

and tackle social problems. There is a limit to what the industrialized economies can do to help those developing countries that do not take the necessary measures. They can, however, reduce their debt burden, trade with them, invest in them, and support education and training policies. Blair and Clinton's Davos speeches, I believe, sum up quite clearly the opportunities and challenges posed by globalization.

I am grateful to my friend, the great economist Paul Krugman, for providing the introduction to this book, which has been written during weekends and holidays where I found the time and, I hope the inspiration, for this task of trying to bring such an important economic debate to as wide an audience as possible.

What Is Globalization?

Globalization is a dynamic process of liberalization, openness, and international integration across a wide range of markets, from labor to goods and from services to capital and technology. It is not a new process but, rather, has unfolded gradually since the middle 1950s and it will take many years yet to finally reach completion, if politics permits. Nor is this the first wave of globalization. Between 1870 and 1914 a similar process occurred which was nearly as intense as this one. The twentieth century began with global market integration and this was resumed several decades later, but only after a sinister relapse in the globalization process that coincided with two bloody world wars, the spread of communism and fascism and the Great Depression. The latest phase of globalization looks likely to be more durable. The first wave lasted only 44 years and ended violently with the First World War while the present period is already surpassing 50 years and has more solid foundations than the first.

It can only be hoped that this globalized era does not end as badly as the previous one since that would again mean a retreat from peaceful economic competition under market rules, to political and military competition and armed conflict. This would be a tragic denouement. There are winners and losers in both cases but the losers in the former do not also lose their lives, although some could be severely disadvantaged by the process. In the final analysis, globalization is based upon freedom: the freedom to trade with the rest of the world and capitalize on each country's comparative advantage; the freedom to invest where returns on capital are greatest, within a tolerable level of risk, and the freedom to set up shop in the country of one's choosing, whether as a business to reap higher profits or larger market share, or as an individual seeking better wages and/or working conditions.

Not paradoxically, business economists have been the first to use the term globalization. One of the first to use it was Theodore Levitt (1983) in his work on the globalization of markets. Levitt described a process in which the concept of production, based upon product cycles, was being replaced by a new concept of global marketplace. In the first stage, new products were sold in the most developed countries until they became obsolete. From then on they were restricted to the less developed economies until they disappeared from the market. In the second global stage, the same product is sold throughout the world using the same methods and techniques. This reduces costs and harmonizes consumer tastes on a global basis.

Michael Porter (1990) also used the term globalization to differentiate a so-called multinational company from what he termed a global one. A multinational corporation is one that operates in several countries but makes no attempt to unify its operations from a strategic standpoint. The global company, on the other hand, pursues a world strategy with perfect co-ordination and integration between different national operations, generating synergies and allowing the whole to become far greater than its parts.

Kenichi Ohmae (1990) went a step further and defined the global company as one which has entirely abandoned its national identity, operating as a denationalized entity on a world scale. Consequently, the supervision of the nation state is basically irrelevant for this type of company, whose R&D activities, financing strategies, and human resource policies are also played out on a global stage. A typical example would be Nestlé, a Swiss company with just two Swiss nationals amongst its top ten executives. The rest are from five different foreign countries. Nestlé is present in 150 countries yet its activity in Switzerland is relatively insignificant.

The primary agents of globalization, then, are the big multinational corporations, both financial and non-financial, established in many or most countries. They raise trade and capital flows between regions and integrate markets on a global basis. However, these companies are only able to drive globalization thanks to a series of technological advances and political decisions that allow them the freedom to do so.

What are these determining factors in the globalization process? The first, undoubtedly, is technology. The development of new technologies in transport and telecommunications has led to a spectacular fall in costs.

Ocean freight costs per short ton, in 1990 US dollars, have come down to less than $30 in 2000, having been $100 in 1930. Average air transportation revenue per passenger mile has been reduced from $100 in 1930 to $10 in 2000. Moreover, jet air shipping and refrigeration have changed the status of goods that had previously been classified altogether as not tradable internationally, such as perishable fish, live lobsters, fruits, vegetables, and flowers. The cost of a three-minute telephone call from New York to London, for example, was $300 in 1930, $50 in 1960 and is now a few cents of a dollar. Satellite charges have come down from $100 of 1990 in 1975 to less than $1 in 2000. The cost of processing information by computer plunged from $100 per second in 1975 to a cent in 1995. Today, the cost is just $0.001 per second. The number of Internet users as a percentage of the total population has gone up from 1 percent in 1990 to 14 percent in 2000 as an average in the world, but up to 55 percent in the US, to 45 percent in the European Union, to 37 percent in Japan and to 18 percent in Emerging Asia (IMF, 2005).

The same can be said for road, air, or maritime transport. The cost of ocean transport as a percentage of the price of wheat has come down from 80 percent in 1830 to less than 10 percent today. Not only has the price of transport fallen; so has the importance of commodity trade in the world economy. The transport of raw materials and unprocessed food products has been replaced to a large extent by finished manufactured goods that are made with lighter materials and so occupy less space. In other words, the products traded today have a greater unit value and the cost of transport has fallen, reducing the ratio of the former to the latter. All of which has radically diminished the natural barriers of time and space between countries, and decimated the cost of sending goods, services, people, capital, technology, or information from one to another. The world size is shrinking as economies internationalize and become increasingly interdependent.

The second factor is the liberalization of the exchange of goods, services, and capital. This has taken place at a multilateral level via the General Agreement on Trade and Tariffs (GATT), the World Trade Organization (WTO), the Organization for Economic Cooperation and Development (OECD), and the International Monetary Fund (IMF), and has been strengthened by a plethora of unilateral, bilateral, and regional agreements between different national and regional authorities. As a consequence, average tariff rates have come down, between 1980 and 2000, from 30 percent to 12 percent in developing countries and from 10 percent to 4 percent in industrial countries. Global trade of goods and services has gone up from 20 percent of GDP in the early 1970s to about 55 percent of GDP in 2003 (IMF, 2005).

The depth of globalization

All this does not mean that the globalization process has yet assumed massive dimensions. On the contrary, there is still a long way to go. One of the simplest ways of measuring the extent of globalization in goods and services is by comparing the relation between external trade and output in each country. Although this proportion has grown constantly since the mid-1950s (i.e., the volume of international trade has risen much more rapidly than national output), it is still barely above its level a year before the outbreak of the First World War. The share of exports in world output reached a peak in 1913 that was not surpassed until 1970. In 1913 Japan, for example, was a more open economy than it is now. Then, the sum of Japanese exports and imports represented 30 percent of GDP. Today, it represents 22 percent. The UK has become more open. Britain's trade–GDP ratio has risen from 47 percent to 57 percent. France, Germany, and the USA have also increased the international exposure of their economies. Their trade–GDP ratios are now 51 percent, 69 percent, and 26 percent, respectively.

Obviously, the greater the size of a country or region, the smaller it is its trade to GDP ratio. While in countries such as the US, the European Union, and Japan, the ratio is between 22 percent and 26 percent, countries such as Holland, Belgium, or Ireland have ratios well over 100 percent. Spain, my own country, has undergone a radical transformation. In 1918 the sum of Spanish exports and imports represented 24 cent of GDP. In 1959, during the period of autarchy under the Franco dictatorship, it had fallen dramatically to 9 percent. Since then the ratio has soared to close on 60 percent, above countries such as France and Italy. As a whole, the volume of world trade has increased sixteen fold since 1950 while world GDP has only increased five fold. This trend toward larger openness has been helped by the lowering of tariffs and other barriers to trade. At the peak of the previous globalization episode, in 1913, average effective tariffs in Europe which were around 12 percent, are now less than 5 percent for the OECD countries, thanks to the GATT rounds, after having reached 22 percent in the 1930s. Nevertheless, their tariff dispersion is very large, being much higher in agricultural produce and in labor-intensive manufactures, which are making it very difficult for developing countries to access OECD markets.

Another way of measuring the globalization process is by observing price convergence between different national economies for goods and services that are identical or homogeneous. In an entirely globalized world economy, prices for the same goods should be exactly the same everywhere, once local taxes and transport and insurance costs are excluded. However, the present reality is a long way from this perfect state. Arbitrage, defined as the activity of buying an item in a place where it is cheap and simultaneously selling the same item where it is expensive, should drive prices to equality. Its failure to do so perfectly is a source of repeated surprise to economists. Often the explanation is that the commodities in question are not in fact identical. Brand names matter as well as marketing, retailing, warranties, and customer service. Exchange rates are also part of the culprit for the price difference. Nevertheless, these price differentials are a larger surprise in the case of non-differentiated non-branded commodities.

The fact is that there are still notable divergences between countries, even within the European Union. The pre-tax price of exactly the same model of car, for example, can be found to be up to 30 percent higher in some EU countries than in others. This occurs either because distribution in one country is more efficient than in others, because national tastes are different and there is a clear bias in favor of nationally produced vehicles, or because consumers have been unable to compare prices. Whatever the reason, multinationals discriminate in their pricing strategies between different countries and are able to obtain higher average profit margins for the same model. The euro introduction is slowly tending to close this gap as the existence of a single currency makes comparison of prices for goods and services far easier.

Markets between countries are less integrated than national markets, even when the countries in question share a border. The volume of cross-border trade between Canada and the US, for example, is twenty times smaller than inter-provincial trade in Canada, despite the existence of a 4,000 km long border and the near absence of trade barriers. The fact that they both have a different currency may help to explain their preference for national goods and services.

The integration and globalization of financial markets has increased faster than the trade in goods and non-financial services, thanks mainly to technological advances. Yet the process is still far from complete. One way of measuring the extent of financial globalization is by observing net outflows from countries that export capital because they have a surplus of savings, i.e., those with current account surpluses on their balance of payments, and net inflows of those that import capital because thay have a savings shortage and so have a current account deficit. During the first phase of globalization from 1870 to 1914, capital exports from the UK were 5 percent of GDP as a yearly average, and reached 10 percent in some years. In the last few years, Japan, with the largest current account surplus in the world, has only exported capital worth 3.5 percent of its GDP. The average net outflow from OECD economies is just 2.5 percent of GDP.

Another way of measuring financial globalization is by comparing foreign direct investment with national direct investment. In OECD countries today, FDI is equivalent to 6 percent of national investment while in the UK during the first 13 years of the twentieth century FDI was equal to all national investment. Only in the last few years, in large developing countries such as Mexico, Brazil, and China, has FDI been able to reach up to 20 percent of net national investment.

Nevertheless, if measured by the amount of the total foreign assets and liabilities of the different countries, financial globalization has increased at a fast pace. In 1970, industrial countries' foreign assets were 25 percent of GDP and foreign liabilities were 28 percent of GDP; today they have increased to 210 percent and 225 percent of GDP respectively. In emerging market countries, during the same period, foreign assets have increased from 9 percent of GDP to 72 percent and foreign liabilities from 27 percent to 95 percent of GDP (IMF, 2005).

Nor has there been a total convergence of interest rates (controlling for exchange rate risk) on a global basis as should occur in an entirely globalized financial system. In other words, exchange rates have not responded to or fully compensated the spreads between short-term interest rates (as we would expect from the interest rate parity theory), nor long-term spreads between inflation rates (an assumption of the purchasing power parity theory). As a consequence, interest rate convergence has been slow and volatile, but in the right direction. For the major OECD countries real interest rate dispersion has been coming down from a standard deviation of 12 percent in the 1940s and 1950s to that of 1 percent in the 1990s (IMF, 1997).

Nevertheless, financial globalization is advancing at a satisfactory pace. Between 1980 and 2003, while world real GDP has grown at an annual average rate of 3.5 percent, the exchange of bonds and shares has grown, in real terms, at an annual rate of 25 percent. Foreign exchange transactions have grown at an annual rate of 24 percent and international loans have increased at a rate of 8 percent. Meanwhile, foreign direct investment has risen at an annual rate of 9 percent and trade in goods and services at an annual average rate of 7 percent. If financial globalization continues to proceed at this pace, the process could be completed within 25 years, while trade globalization may take more than 40 years, provided nobody places obstacles in the way of liberalization and the Millennium Round of the WTO goes ahead as planned, which is not yet the case today.

Globalization and asymmetry

One of the biggest problems for globalization is that while market integration for goods, services, and capital advances at a lively pace, labor markets are barely integrated at all. Robert Reich (1991) asks "Who are we?" and reaches the conclusion that in a world where most factors of production (capital, technology, production plants, capital goods) can be shifted from one country to another, except for non-tradable land, the only truly national factor is labor, which can globalize only very slowly or, in some cases, not at all. For this reason, the "we" in Reich's question are workers. Everything else is going global.

Labor mobility between OECD countries has stagnated in recent years and it advances slowly between developed and developing countries. This has led to an increasing divergence between per capita income in different countries and regions given that migration is the quickest, but not the optimal, way of equalizing income across countries. In the first wave of globalization between 1870 and 1914, more than 60 million people emigrated from Europe to America and a total of more than 100 million migrated globally out of an average world population of 1500 million; that is, migration accounted for 6.7 percent of the total. Today's migration flows are much smaller as a proportion of the total population. Immigrants represent close to 200 million out of a world population of 6,100 million; that is 3.3 percent, half that in the previous globalization. This slow integration between labor markets is a result of immigration control, on the one hand, and cultural, linguistic, and educational barriers, on the other. In 2000, the stock of migrants as a percentage of world population was almost 3 percent. The largest stocks of legal immigrants were in Oceania, with 19.1 percent of total population, in North America with 13 percent, and in Europe with 7.7 percent. The lowest stocks were in Latin America, with

1.1 percent, in Asia, with 1.4 percent, and in Africa, with 2.1 percent of total populations. In 2000, 7 percent of the population of the EU countries was foreign born, and out of 27 million non-nationals, 10 million came from other EU countries and 17 million from developing countries. In the United States 35 million – the 12.6 percent of the total population – were immigrants, most of them from Latin America.

Nevertheless, it is very likely that immigration into the OECD countries will rise significantly in the coming years in view of the problems posed by its increasing ageing population. In 2004, the median age of the OECD population was 39 years, and it is likely to reach almost 50 years by 2050, while, in the developing countries, median age will go up only from 24 years now to 35 years in 2050 (United Nations, 2005). This trend will make it more necessary than ever to have an international organization that tries to guide the increasing migration flows as well as their different contractual systems and the proper treatment of migrants in the countries of destination.

Despite all this, the present phase of globalization has more solid foundations than the former period at the beginning of the century. Then, far fewer countries were part of the process. Never before have so many economies been open to global trade and finance flows than now, after the liberalization of the former communist economies. Technological advances in telecommunications mean that global companies are more integrated than ever and that the market can integrate consumers and producers faster through the Internet. Technology has also powered the development of financial markets, speeding up transactions, settlements, and payments to an extraordinary extent. Daily transactions in foreign exchange markets, for example, have risen from $15 billion to $3 trillion, a 200-fold increase in just 30 years. While net capital flows, as we have seen, have not increased from their levels at the beginning of the twentieth century, gross flows of foreign exchange, bonds, deposits, and stocks have risen exponentially, all thanks to increases in velocity and integration facilitated by information technology.

Present-day globalization is also far more widely institutionalized than the first wave. The existence of international organizations like the WTO, the IMF, and the OECD as well the development of multinational corporations and global financial entities, all make it much more difficult to reverse the process.

Bordo, Eichengreen, and Irwin (1999) go further and argue that the world we live in today is radically different from that of the early twentieth century partly because political systems are more democratic and, therefore, allow greater representation of citizens' interests but also because the character of globalization itself has changed. Integration is broader and deeper than a hundred years ago. International trade represents a greater proportion of output and both trade and investment now reach sectors such as retailing, and public and private services that were localized and closed in the years before the First World War. Financial integration is far greater and far more profound than then, despite the fact that FDI has still not reached previous levels. Finally, these economists believe that the evident tensions in the process of trade liberalization and financial instability should not be too great a cause of concern now since they were similar or greater at the beginning of the century, despite lower levels of globalization than those which we enjoy today.

Globalization and Economic Growth

To gauge the impact of globalization on growth, we have first to look at economic theory and then at various empirical studies on the question, including those by the OECD (1998b), the World Bank (1987) and the IMF (1997). The WTO has recently carried out an extensive analysis on this issue, which I intend to review in some detail. I will first explain the effects of trade globalization on growth and then go on to discuss international capital flows, or financial globalization.

Trade globalization and growth

Theoretical models

What does growth theory tell us about international trade? What follows is a quick overview of neoclassical and endogenous growth models. Traditional neoclassical models such as that of Robert Solow (1956 and 1957) and Trevor Swan (1956) consider that capital accumulation, the main growth motor, is financed almost completely by domestic saving. While countries can borrow money abroad, this is provisional. Therefore, the level of savings in an economy plays a decisive role in its growth performance. Countries, that save more, can invest more and, therefore, grow more quickly. These models are based on the assumption that returns on investment tend to diminish as capital accumulates, i.e. as the stock of capital, increases. As a result, returns on investment tend to be lower as a country gets richer and has a greater stock of capital. This means that, in the long run, there will be a convergence of income per capita between countries, provided they have reached a certain level if income, known as a "steady state."

These models, however, identify two factors that can prevent this convergence of income per capita from taking place. The first is that productivity and income from the factors of production (capital and labor) are different from one country to another. These differences are, basically, a result of differing levels of human and physical capital. Those countries where workers are more and better educated and trained tend to have higher productivity and income than others. Other variables that affect productivity are current public spending, which reduces long-term growth rates, and public spending on education and infrastructure, which boosts long-term growth; the inflation rate which is negatively correlated with growth; the legal status of contracts, positively correlated with growth and the development of the financial sector and foreign trade liberalization, are both positively correlated with growth (Robert Barro, 1998).

The second factor is that per capita income has a direct positive effect on the intensity of physical capital in the economy and, consequently, an indirect effect on the savings rate. The differences between savings rates in different countries are so enormous that they have a clear effect on differences in per capita income. The poorest African countries have internal savings rates of 5 percent of GDP while some southeast Asian economies register up to 40 percent savings rates. While these differences persist, growth and long-run per capita income convergence will not be possible. Only those countries, which improve human capital, defend property rights, have higher-quality institutions and public policy and higher saving rates, will manage to grow faster and converge.

In these models, trade liberalization can indirectly boost economic growth. In fact, any policy that increases economic efficiency by achieving a better allocation of resources will increase growth. Trade liberalization is one of these. It will also, therefore, have a lasting positive effect on savings and investment, as Richard Baldwin (1989) has shown in his analyses of the European single market.

This positive impact of international trade on growth is a dynamic version of Keynes's famous multiplier effect, a mechanism by which state investment can boost output to a greater degree than the initial injection of capital by stimulating the economy and creating jobs, when there is a relatively high level of unemployment. Trade liberalization generates greater economic efficiency since it reallocates productive resources toward those sectors with a greater comparative advantage. Consequently, it increases productivity and, as a corollary, raises wages and per capita income, as Alan Deardoff (1974) has shown. A good example of this is the opening of the economies of Asia to foreign trade. National savings and foreign investment shifted to those industries that expanded thanks to liberalization, and gave a substantial boost to their growth rates. Once an economy has restructured and is fully integrated into the world trading system, the effect on growth begins to fade, but this generally occurs at a higher level of income. Empirical analysis shows that economies that are more open to foreign trade usually post higher growth rates than closed economies. As Michael Porter (1990) has shown, international competition makes firms more open to innovation and to the assimilation of foreign technology, while closed economies lack the necessary stimuli to innovate and raise their productivity.

Empirical analysis by Edward Denison (1962), based on growth accounting, showed that 50 percent of US growth was attributable to the accumulation of factors of production, capital and labor. The other 50 percent was the product of a residual deriving from technical progress, considered to be exogenous in the neoclassical model. This came to be called the Solow residual, after the US Nobel Prize winner Robert Solow. This residual of technical progress was made up of technological innovation, human capital and the way production is organized. Here too the exposure to foreign trade had a positive effect. All of these factors led to an increase in the productivity of capital and labor above that of simple accumulation, and this analysis created an incentive to develop new models capable of explaining with greater precision the growth process.

The new models of endogenous growth created by Romer (1986), Lucas (1988), Rebelo (1991), Grossman and Helpman (1991a), and Aghion and Howitt (1998) introduced three fundamental innovations to the postulates of the neoclassical models. On the one hand, they consider technical progress to be endogenous and not exogenous, by which they meant that it is dependent on policy initiatives designed to boost investment in education, training, research and development; improved tax conditions for the factors of production; greater openness; and an increase in foreign trade. At the same time, they argue that there may be constant or even increasing, and not diminishing, returns on investment as the capital stock increases, i.e. that increases in the return on physical and human capital are greater than proportional as a result an increase in its stock.

Finally, they introduce the assumption that scientific technical knowledge is a special factor, not only because it creates externalities which benefit the other factors of production but also because it generates greater increasing marginal returns.

The implication of these models is that the per capita income of different countries does not necessarily tend to converge in the long term toward a "steady state" or equilibrium because not all of them have acquired technological knowledge in the same degree or the same fashion. The result is that those countries with worse endowments of physical and human capital at the outset might never converge with the more developed economies, which have a greater capital stock, thanks to the increasing returns to scale of this stock and the positive externalities derived from scientific and technical knowledge for the rest of their factors of production.

What does international trade contribute to growth in these new models? It contributes quite a lot, as a matter of fact, because the endogenous relationship between productivity and technical progress is not only determined by policies to improve the latter, but also by market forces. These, in turn, as we have seen, are determined, to a substantial extent, by exposure to foreign trade, and by the process of "learning by doing." As Kenneth Arrow (1962) showed, international trade plays a determining role too in "learning by doing," (i.e., that people get new ideas by using old ones and that invention is incidental to normal production activity), which is a key determinant of productivity and growth.

In the first place, we can establish a connection between endogenous productivity gains and market forces through the process of "learning by doing." The more a country manufactures a good, the better it becomes, both in quality and cost. The examples of microprocessors, mobile phones, PCs, automobiles or aircraft leave little room for doubt about this. Their quality and capacity has risen, and their price fallen as experience is accumulated.

International trade affects this process in two ways. On the one hand, learning is faster and more thorough in those industries which are in expansion and slower in contracting sectors. The net effect will depend on productivity gains. If these are greater in the expanding sectors than the productivity losses in contracting industries, the net effect is positive. International trade determines, through the process of comparative advantage, which sectors or products are in expansion and which in decline, ensuring that efficiency and productivity are greater in industries in expansion.

On the other hand, international trade promotes the diffusion of technology, enabling countries to learn not only through their own specialized experience in production and the exploitation of their comparative advantage, but also through the diffusion of technology from their trading partners. Those who specialize in high-technology goods and services benefit from international trade by increasing sales and international market share. Those who specialize in traditional mature industries, benefit by importing high-technology goods and services, in which productivity increases rapidly, at much lower prices. This means they reduce their payment for imports of technological goods and the diffusion of these increases. Consequently, everybody benefits in terms of higher growth, specialization and exchange.

In the second place, some endogenous growth models consider investment in research and development, a key part of so-called technical progress, as the motor of growth (Grossman and Helpman, 1991b). Trade and international competition force companies to devote more resources to R&D in new production processes and new products in order to maintain and extend their competitive advantage. These new processes and products are then protected via patents which give exclusive, if temporary, rights to production and commercialization, so that investment in R&D can be recovered, and so that there are incentives to continue research and commit more investment to research. Economic integration and globalization through trade and international investment enhances business interest in R&D and encourages governments to increase investment in education and basic research. Liberalizing trade also increases the size of markets in which a firm competes and therefore the potential profit to be made as a result of developing a new product or process, as well as the benefits from learning and innovation in other countries. Work by Robert Barro and Xavier Sala i Martin (1995) comparing two countries – one developing, the other developed – sheds some light on this area. The developed economy innovates and the developing economy simply copies the innovations of the first. Growth in the developing country will depend on the cost of imitation and on its initial stock of knowledge. Provided the cost of imitation is less than that of innovation, the developing country will grow faster than the developed economy. As Maurice Obstfeld and Kenneth Rogoff (1996) have pointed out, the cost of imitation is closely linked to the degree of openness of the developing economy. The more open the economy, the greater the likelihood of gleaning new ideas which are being developed in the rest of the world and the lower the cost of imitation.

To sum up, trade liberalization can stimulate innovation and growth by stimulating the diffusion of technology and knowledge, learning processes, and investment in R&D. The final result, however, will not always be equitable. Paul Romer (1990) and Gene Grossman and Elhanan Helpman (1995) explain how international trade tends to make smaller economies with an initial handicap in technology, specialize in traditional productive activities that yield slower growth and lower productivity. Larger economies, on the other hand, or those well endowed with scientific and technological resources, are able to extract far greater benefits from international trade and so achieve faster growth rates, this is called the "scale effect."

Empirical evidence

Several empirical studies have tried to apply these models to economic reality. First of all, economists searched for correlations between trade liberalization and economic growth. Most of these studies do indeed find a positive correlation between exports and GDP growth (Michaely, 1977; Krueger, 1978; Feder, 1983; Romer, 1989; DeLong and Summers, 1991; Edwards, 1993; and Rodrik, 1993). There is a problem, however. Trade flows are actually a poor indicator of the openness of an economy. In general, small countries export and import a greater proportion of their GDP than larger economies. This is because their own production is generally less competitive given that there are few economies of scale or because natural resources are scarce. However, studies that compensate for the size of different economies also show positive correlations between trade openness and growth. Shirquin and Chenery (1989) show that the growth premium from trade liberalization varies between 0.2 percentage points per year for big exporters of manufactured goods and 1.4 percentage points per year for smaller producers of primary goods.

Other studies (Balassa, 1985; Leamer, 1984; Edwards, 1992) calculate the degree of openness by comparing the difference between actual exports and potential exports, (determined by applying a model from trade theory) and reach the conclusion that the net difference between the two is positive. The smaller the difference between actual and potential exports, the greater trade openness and the faster economic growth should be.

Another method used by economists (Sachs and Warner, 1995) involves the creation of an index of openness based on several criteria such as the importance to trade of non-tariff barriers, average customs rights, the difference between the official and black market exchange rates and the importance of state-owned trade companies. They conclude that open economies grow between 2 and 2.5 percentage points faster than closed economies.

Other economists have used the difference between domestic and international process to gauge the impact of trade openness on growth (Barro, 1991; Dollar, 1992; Easterly, 1993; Lee, 1993). They reach the obvious conclusion that those countries where the difference between internal and external price differences is narrower, grow more rapidly because they benefit from lower costs and prices, which makes them more competitive. The narrower the difference, the greater the countries trade openness since international trade tends to bring the prices of traded goods and services into line, provided they are homogenous. Besides, as Harrison (1995) points out, there appears to be a virtuous circle between trade liberalization and growth. Periods of fast growth encourage trade liberalization and liberalization lifts the growth rate.

Some studies show that positive correlations are greater in those countries with average or high-income levels than in those with low incomes (Michaely, 1977; Ram, 1985). However, these studies are now rather dated and what they actually appear to show is that economic policy in middle and high-income countries is more coherent and sustained. Later studies (Matin, 1992) show that the correlation is not hugely different between developed countries and sub-Saharan Africa. Why do open economies grow faster? For some economists (Levine and Renelt, 1992) the answer is that trade liberalization increases the rate of investment as businesses bid to become more competitive. Others (Balasubramanian, Salisu and Sapsford 1996) argue that openness raises the quality and the productivity of investment in dynamic sectors because liberalization allows a country to attract greater levels of foreign investment and this has a greater impact on growth. Other studies highlight the propensity of foreign trade to induce technology transfer. Many imports appear to be instrumental in the diffusion of technologies, as David Coe and Elhanan Helpman (1995) have shown, discovering that domestic factor productivity is positively influenced by the R&D spending of trading partners, weighted by imports. Finally, for Keller (1997) the externalities deriving from foreign spending on R&D are substantial. This comes from the fact that it is invested in a specific branch of production and tends to improve national productivity, not only in this branch but also in other related sectors either upstream or downstream in the chain of production. As we have seen earlier, the effects of technology diffusion are enormously important in endogenous growth models.

Some research emphasizes the role of imports, Wacziarg (2001) and Lee (1995) because, contrary to popular intuition, theory suggests that imports can be as important as exports in stimulating long-term growth.

Therefore, most of the evidence is based on case studies or on regression analysis. The problem with case studies is that they are difficult to replicate and are affected heavily by country idiosyncrasies and with regressions; the main problem is endogeneity among the variables used. Most measures considered as the best for accounting for the degree of openness, such as the ratio of the sum of imports plus exports to GDP, are, unfortunately, closely linked to the level of income, because the numerator and the denominator are linked to the GDP growth.

Thus, Rodríguez and Rodrik (1999) have analyzed many of these empirical studies in a recent article and identified serious weaknesses and technical deficiencies. They conclude that evidence of a relationship between trade liberalization and growth is still vague and ambiguous. They also ask why there is a need for such a huge amount of empirical work to prove that openness favors growth. The likely answer, they say, is that no one has proved able to give clear, convincing proof that such a relationship exists. They cite a series of microeconomic studies, however, which show conclusively that the causal relationship between trade openness and growth is, in fact, the other way round. The most efficient firms are those that choose to export and causality seems to progress from greater productivity to a greater export volume. They also argue that faster economic growth does not necessarily mean greater welfare, nor vice versa. Some trade policies can boost growth but undermine welfare, others act as a brake on economic growth but not on welfare.

It is true that simultaneity and endogeneity are a concern. Bradford and Chakwin (1993) argue that causality runs from investment to growth and exports, but a correlation may emerge simply because exports are a component of GDP, rather than because of any extra contribution that trade makes to growth. The best way to deal with it is through trade shares as predicted by the "gravity model" due to Leamer and Levinson (1995), which have used Newton's physics on the gravitational attraction between two masses, which establishes that the gravity between two objects is proportional to their mass and inversely proportional to their distance. Therefore, bilateral trade between two countries is proportional to their respective GDP and inversely proportional to the distance between them.

Frankel and Romer (1999) by using such a model, show that, looking at the ratio of imports plus exports as a share of GDP in a cross-section of 100 countries from 1960 to 1998, the effect of openness on growth is even stronger when it is corrected by simultaneity. The impact of openness on income per capita is of the order of 0.3 over a span of twenty years, that is, when trade increases by one percentage point of GDP, income increases by one-third of a percent over twenty years. Nevertheless, Lee, Ricci and Rigobon (2004) using similar data but a different procedure to solve for the problem of endogeneity: "heteroskedasticity," which uses instrumental variables that move the variances instead of the means, find that most measures of openness have a positive effect on growth, even when controlling for the effect of growth on openness, but that the effect is small, once it has been corrected by reverse causality and the effect of other economic and policy distortions that are correlated with openness, such as the black market premium used by Rodríguez and Rodrik (2001).

More recent work by Wacziarg and Horn-Welch (2003) criticizes also the previous conclusions achieved by Rodríguez and Rodrik, showing that, by updating the Sachs and Warner methodology and using the new PPP data on income levels by Heston, Summers, and Aten (2002) during the period 1950–98 the results are very positive: countries that have liberalized their trade regimes have experienced, on average, increases in their annual rates of growth of the order of 1.5 percentage points compared with pre-liberalization times, and the post-liberalization increase in investment rates was between 1.5 and 2 percentage points, confirming past findings that liberalization works to foster growth in part through its effects on physical accumulation.

Despite the relative validity of some sceptical empirical research, it is widely recognized today that none of the most reputed economists defends the opposite thesis: that trade protection is good for growth. Some are more convinced of the openness–growth correlation, while others are more sceptical about it, although mainly about the size of the positive causal effect, but the majority stand by the positive, causal relationship, including extremely reputable economists such as Joseph Stiglitz (1998), Anne Krueger (1998), Robert Barro (1998), Jeffrey Sachs and Andrew Warner (1995), Paul Krugman and Maurice Obstfeld (1991), Maurice Obstfeld and Kenneth Rogoff (1996), and Jeffrey Frankel (2004), to name only but a few.

The clearest conclusion, perhaps, is that of T. N. Srinivasan (1999) who criticizes the methodology used in many of the empirical studies, but who adds, nevertheless: "The fact, that a large number of studies, using different data and methodology, reach the same conclusion about the relationship between trade openness and growth, which are, at the same time, consistent with their previous reasoning, suggests that they deserve serious consideration whatever the doubts about their conceptual and statistical defects."

There are a number of studies of static microeconomic costs of protection by tariffs, quotas, and other trade barriers. Patrick Messerlin (1999) has estimated that the European Union trade distortions impose a cost as high as 7 percent of EU GDP. The WTO uses a simple evaluation of protection vis-a-vis international trade, in terms of the cost to the consumers. It considers that every trade barrier raises import prices and national costs of production, restricts consumer choice, and lowers quality. These barriers act as a tax, says the WTO, so their elimination is the equivalent of a tax cut. The Uruguay Round of the GATT is considered to be the equivalent of a $214 billion yearly tax cut, which is almost 1 percent of world GDP. The WTO forecasts that the new Millennium Round will imply a further tax cut, or a further increase in disposable income for consumers, of $400 billion. It is perhaps worth stressing that a percentage point increases in world GDP growth is of tremendous importance. An increase from 3 to 4 percent, for example, would double world income every 17.5 years instead of every 23.3 years, a decisive difference for the world economy. One study made jointly by the IMF and the World Bank (2002) shows that a total liberalization of world trade will reduce the losses of disposable income, through lower costs of imports, and of export revenue by $ 700 billion annually.

Financial globalization and growth

The next question that we need to consider is the relationship between finance and economic growth, and between financial liberalization or openness and growth. As we will see later in the chapter, Wendy Dobson and Pierre Jacquet (1998) have studied these relationships and have tried to quantify them empirically.

Theory

In principle, the global integration of capital markets offers several potential benefits: Countries can share risks via international portfolio diversification; capital is allocated to the most productive locations and consumption can be smoothed across time periods in response to shifts in macroeconomic fundamentals. Unfortunately, world financial integration is still very small, although is has been increasing very fast since the 1980s. According to Aizeman, Pinto, and Radziwill (2004) on average, 90 percent of the stock of capital in developing countries is self-financed, and this fraction was surprisingly stable throughout the 1990s, confirming the pioneer work by Feldstein and Horioka (1980).

In general, economists have also tended to disagree about the role of finance on economic growth. For instance, on the one side, Robert Lucas (1988) dismissed finance as an "over-stressed" determinant of economic growth while Joan Robinson (1952) argued that "where enterprise leads, finance follows." Their views were that finance does not cause growth, it only responds to demands from the real sector. But, on the other side, Merton Miller (1988) argued that "the idea that financial markets do not contribute to economic growth is a proposition too obvious for serious discussion."

Nevertheless, a more recent survey made by Ross Levine (2004) shows that the large majority of the theoretical and empirical analyses available demonstrate a strong, positive correlation of the financial system and long-run economic growth. The reason is that there has been, since the 1990s a new and large body of theoretical and empirical research which has added further dimensions to that relationship, such as the effects of finance on reducing information and transaction costs; its positive effects on saving rates, investment decisions, and technological innovations; its important connections with political, legal, regulatory, and institutional frameworks; and its beneficial effects on incentives, income distribution, and poverty alleviation. Levine does not address, unfortunately, the same issues in relation to growth and international finance, such as cross-border capital flows and the importation of financial services.

The literature on the positive relationship between finance and growth goes back to Joseph Schumpeter (1911) who assigns a key role to credit as a motor of innovation and entrepreneurship. Without financial intermediaries, economic actors are restricted to a situation of self-financing, which is sub-optimal, since they have no capacity to borrow when investment opportunities offer greater returns than the cost of credit or when they are subject to temporal shocks.

Subsequent literature has been divided into two tendencies. The first (Stern, 1989) focuses exclusively on real factors affecting growth and gives no direct role to finance. The second tendency, established by Gurley and

Shaw (1955) concentrates on the financial system. Since the 1980s, a period marked by banking and financial crisis, the second interpretation has become more relevant.

Adherents of each tendency have contrasting viewpoints on the relationship between finance and growth. For Nicholas Stern and his followers, faster growth makes for a more efficient financial system, an inverse relationship. For the other school, the financial system plays a fundamental role in economic development, a direct causal relationship. Logically, as Raymond Goldsmith (1969) has argued, causality between finance and growth runs in both directions. There is a dynamic interaction between the two. Some countries have slow growth and repressed financial systems; others have developed financial systems and experience high growth. Between the two, there is a range of mixes of the two.

Ronald MacKinnon (1973) and Gurley Shaw (1973) studied the so-called problems of financial repression in developing countries. In many of these countries, capital accumulation, the mainstay of economic growth, is low, and returns on real and financial assets are often negative. For this reason it is a mistake to consider growth in relation to the accumulation of homogeneous capital because returns are diverse. Rather than allowing the financial markets to decide which investment is efficient and what the price of capital should be, the state intervenes directly to establish interest rate controls, determining how credit is allocated and preventing financial markets from mobilizing resources and allocating them in the most efficient fashion. This is financial repression. As a result, the level of national savings is low and its allocation to investment projects is inefficient. All this hinders growth.

Marco Pagano (1993) points out three transmission channels through which financial development can positively affect long-term growth. The first is through an increase in the proportion of savings directed into investment. Greater competition in the financial sector reduces transaction costs charged by financial intermediaries. This reduces the volume of savings that are lost in intermediation. Development of the banking system and capital market, then, is absolutely crucial for growth. The second channel is via an increase in the marginal social productivity of capital. A developed financial market is able to effectively gather information on debtors and investment projects. More and better information lowers transaction costs but it also ensures that savings are channeled into the right investment project. Furthermore, as financial intermediaries are able to diversify their investment portfolios they will be more prepared to invest in higher-risk projects that offer greater returns, previously starved of capital. At the same time, developed financial systems allow investors to diversify and share risk with intermediaries, be they banks, insurance companies, or capital markets. This makes higher-risk investment possible in new technology, which raises productivity and growth. Finally, greater access to information reduces savers' liquidity risk since banks can group the liquidity risk of depositors, lessen their need to invest in liquid assets and raise their participation in productive investment projects.

Pagano's third channel between financial development and long-term growth is the increase in the private savings rate. This transmission route is ambiguous since a developed financial system can also reduce the level of savings. On the one hand, it may reduce liquidity restrictions for private savers enabling them to save less (unless, of course, they borrow to save rather than consume). On the other, families with insured investments in financial markets may decide to save less. In other words, both personal insurance and credit can reduce savings rates and, in turn, slow long-term growth just as business credit and stock markets can raise investment and growth. There is no ambiguity at the other end of the scale. Repressed, underdeveloped financial systems do tend to reduce the level of savings and long-term growth rates.

The relationship between international finance and growth has also been the object of a growing number of studies. Paul Krugman (1992) made a review of most of this work: Neoclassical growth models suggest that international capital market integration plays no important role in growth. The abundance of external capital flows is irrelevant when explaining differences between growth rates, according to these models. Not even substantial levels of capital inflows make much difference to growth rates, since they are based on the assumption that returns on capital are diminishing. If poor countries have less efficient production functions and lower capital returns, then the neoclassical method of quantifying growth inevitably reduces the role of capital flows since, as we have seen, the Solow residual explains half of growth while the other half is attributable to the accumulation of capital and labor, and the relationship between both factors of production.

In the 1960s, Hollis Chenery and Michael Bruno (1962) and Ronald McKinnon (1964) developed the so-called "two-gap" theory, which showed that developing countries' growth rates are subject to two constraints. The first is the country's capacity to save and invest. The second is its ability to earn foreign exchange to finance the imports necessary for higher growth. Capital inflows help overcome both constraints since they complement internal savings with foreign savings and also provide scarce foreign exchange. But a necessary condition for this to occur is disequilibrium in the developing country's markets. If there is excess supply in labor markets a capital inflow will boost investment and labor demand and reduce unemployment. If there is excess demand in foreign exchange markets, it will be more difficult to obtain important currencies. In that case, capital inflows can clear the market and reduce the constraint on the import of goods necessary for growth.

Paul Romer (1986) and Robert Lucas (1988) took the next step by developing the idea of endogenous technical progress and increasing returns to the accumulation of physical and human capital, which meant that long-term growth could be explained almost entirely as a result of capital accumulation, eliminating the need for the Solow residual. This accumulation generates external economies in such a way that the elasticity of output to capital increases its share of GDP. Because of this, the social return on capital is greater than the private return, since there is a spillover effect into the rest of the economy, not just into the profitability of an investment. In such a case, any capital inflow to a developing country will raise the growth rate to a far greater extent than the pessimistic estimates of the neoclassical models.

As Krugman (1992) points out, if capital accumulation is subject to external economies and increasing returns, as Romer and Lucas argue, those countries with greater capital endowments will enjoy comparative advantage in those sectors which are intensive in capital and highly productive. This implies that the profitability of capital will be greater in countries with greater capital stock than those that have accumulated less. The corollary of this is striking: capital will tend flow from poor countries to rich, not the other way around as the neoclassical model would lead us to believe. This means, of course, that greater freedom of capital flows would not enhance the convergence of income levels between countries but, in fact, cause divergence.

Luiz de Mello (1997) criticizes these analyses and notes the impact of foreign direct investment (FDI) on growth in the context of endogenous growth models. De Mello understands FDI as a mixture of stocks of capital, knowledge and technology and describes several ways in which it can positively affect growth. In the first place, FDI is an important source of human capital and of technological change for developing countries since it facilitates the use of more advanced technologies by national firms and gives them access to knowledge and skills that raise the productivity of workers. In the second place, FDI boosts growth rates by promoting the incorporation of new technologies and new inputs in the production function of the developing economy. Not only in firms directly affected by the investment but also in other businesses through the spillover effect and its externalities. These transfers of knowledge and technology generated by FDI lead to innovation in processes and so allow firms to apply the knowledge transferred via FDI in the production of the same goods. This boosts productivity and growth. The same thing happens in so-called quasi-FDI, such as leasing contracts, licences, franchises, management contracts and even joint ventures. Coe and Helpman (1995) reach an identical conclusion when they show that capital goods imports are also a vehicle for technological change in the importing country. Finally, FDI heightens competition in an economy, forcing less efficient firms into bankruptcy and encouraging more efficient firms to invest in physical and human capital in order to remain competitive.

In all these models, FDI has positive effects wherever there are externalities that allow the rate of social returns to be higher than private returns, even where returns to capital are not increasing.

However, the positive effects of FDI will only be significant if the country in question has crossed a so-called "development-threshold," as Blomstrom et al. (1993) and Borensztein et al. (1995) have shown. These economists argue that a receiving country must have a high enough level of human capital in terms of education and training and good enough physical, institutional, and legal infrastructures, to make the investment worthwhile. If this is not the case, the effects will barely be appreciated, since the country will not offer a high enough return on the investment nor will it be able to absorb the transfer of knowledge and technology. This raises the obvious question of causality in empirical work on the relationship between FDI and growth. Is it FDI that determines growth, or growth that determines higher or lower levels of FDI? The answer depends to a large extent on the factors that determine FDI. If these are closely associated with growth in the receiving country, we can say that the growth precedes FDI. Experience shows that in large economies, such as China, Mexico, Brazil, or Argentina, with extensive consumer markets, a good geographical situation, adequate human capital, and adequate infrastructure, growth conditions FDI. In economies such as Chile, however, where markets are smaller and more open, FDI plays a determining role in the growth of output and productivity and precedes long-term growth.

Finally, southeast Asia is a clear example of the role played by capital inflows in conditioning growth. As Barry Bosworth et al. (1995) and Alwyn Young (1994) have shown, most of the growth in these countries is attributable to capital accumulation rather than improvements in factor productivity. This finding challenges neoclassical pessimism vis-a-vis the poor contribution of capital to growth (because of diminishing marginal returns to the capital stock). It also shows that foreign savings in the form of capital inflows have been crucial to Asian growth although an excess of capital inflows was the cause of the 1997–8 crisis in that region's fixed exchange rate systems and the inefficient allocation of this capital. As a general principle in economics, all that is abundant tends to be wasted or, at least, not employed efficiently. Paul Krugman (1994) and Alwyn Young (1994) were the first to warn that southeast Asia could not continue to grow eternally by a simple accumulation of factors of production, labor, and capital, unless productivity was increased, since this would trigger a crisis similar to that which occurred in Russia and the countries of Central and Eastern Europe.

Empiricial evidence

Most empirical studies show a positive relation between capital inflows, the liberalization of world financial markets, and growth. Levine and Renelt (1992) discover a very robust correlation between investment and growth. The same conclusion is achieved by Dani Rodrik (1999), who sees the source of growth as a self-reinforcing process, between expanding productive capacity, and the private profitability of investment. Financial liberalization is a vital precondition for this process to be set in motion.

Daniel Cohen (1993) bases his empirical analysis on a set of assumptions. External financing can be of help to a poor country but this depends on why the country is poor. If that is because the initial conditions are poor, foreign financing can be very useful to boost growth. If the problem is a low level of human capital, external finance can raise it. If it is because productivity is intrinsically low, external financing can also be of use, but only if the marginal productivity of capital is high enough. Assaf Razin and Chi-Wa Yuen (1993) argue that taxes on income from capital, together with the principle of residence, can explain variations in per capita income growth rates between different countries. The higher the tax, the lower growth.

The surveys made by Ross Levine (1997 and 2004) and his book with Demirgüç-Kunt (2001) compile the most substantial body of evidence to the effect that financial development is an important determinant of a country's short-run growth rate and long term convergence in growth rates. Phillipe Aghion, Peter Howitt, and David Mayer-Foulkes (2004), using the Schumpeterian growth theory, extend the previous work allowing the possibility of different long-run growth rates, in a cross-section of 71 countries over the period 1960–95, and find out that financial constraints inhibit technological transfers and that financial development, both in the domestic market and attracting FDI, helps growth and convergence through technological tranfers and productivity growth more than through capital accumulation, confirming most studies about the importance of productivity growth and technical progress in long-term convergence.

Finally, Bekaert, Harvey, and Lundblad (2004) find out that financial liberalization alone, that is, moving from segmented to financially open countries, contributes to 30 percent of the total increase in growth after liberalization of a sample of 95 countries in the 1980s and 1990s, after controlling for other elements which also have had a positive impact on growth. For them it is not just that the existence of capital markets is important for growth prospects, but it is also crucial that these capital markets be liberalized to allow foreign investors to participate and diversify their risk but also to permit local investors to diversify their portfolios across borders.

Dobson and Jacquet (1998) go a step further and try quantitative estimations of the benefits of financial liberalization. They estimate that global liberalization of financial services over a 10-year period under the Millennium Round of the WTO would mean gains of $1.3 trillion for business, households, and governments in the shape of lower capital costs, better services and a wider choice. Francois and Shuknecht (1999) conclude from a longitudinal analysis of a wide sample of countries that the transition from a closed financial system to an open one can imply increases in economic growth rates of between 1.3 and 1.6 percentage points per annum.

A study by John Williamson and Molly Mahar (1998) establishes a clear difference between simple capital account opening and the wider process of financial liberalization. The latter includes not only the removal of capital controls but also the establishment of competitive interest rates, the creation of banks and other financial institutions, and the privatization and independence of these. The benefits of a thorough financial liberalization ·

are much greater than a mere opening to capital flows since they mitigate the destabilizing impact that these flows have. However, recent experience makes it abundantly clear that the liberalization and globalization of capital markets is not by any means devoid of problems. Financial crises are more frequent. Intense capital inflows often give rise to financial bubbles and the sudden withdrawal of capital causes crisis and contagion in other countries. Moreover, many countries are excluded from external financing because they have not reached the development threshold. These are questions that will be discussed in chapter 9.

Historical experience shows that periods of globalization have yielded faster per capita GDP growth rates than periods of protectionism. From 1820 to 1870 average annual per capita GDP growth in developed countries was 0.9 percent. Between 1870 and 1913, the first wave of globalization pushed the average up to 1.4 percent. Between 1914 and 1950 the rate fell to 1.2 percent and between 1950 and 2000 it has risen to 3 percent.

By way of conclusion let me quote two extracts from outstanding economists on trade liberalization and capital:

First, David Greenaway (1998) who writes: "A highly protectionist and distorted trade regime is a necessary and sufficient condition for slow economic growth. A liberal and open trade regime is a necessary but not sufficient condition for fast growth. Trade liberalization in itself will not take an economy onto a new growth path. It can help substantially but must be compatible with other reforms in economic policy and needs to be sustained and sustainable."

Second, Jeffrey Sachs (1997) has written: "Global capitalism is surely the most promising institutional arrangement for worldwide prosperity that history has ever seen. Long-cherished hopes for convergence between rich and poor regions of the world may at last be about to be realised. But the world will need wisdom and stamina to reap the potentially vast benefits. The world must be prepared to deal honestly and boldly with the laggard regions, paying special attention to the acute and unresolved problems of tropical development. And the world must learn how to manage an open, rule-based system, on the basis of shared principles that cover nearly the whole earth."

Globalization, Real Convergence, and Income Distribution

In principle, in a very simple way, it can be said that economic prosperity is associated mainly with technical progress, which allows for faster productivity growth and therefore for higher wages and profits. Globalization then is a very important mechanism to develop and transfer technical progress around the world. Trade liberalization helps developing countries to learn and adapt new technologies through a better knowledge of the embodied technology in the goods and services that import from developed countries. Capital liberalization, allows larger foreign direct investment inflows into developing countries, which are not only related to more job creation and higher wages but also to the transfer of knowledge and technology to the local workers. The international liberalization of labor flows allows migrants into developed countries to acquire more knowledge through skill improvement, education, and learning by doing in the job, which can be transferred, later own to their own countries of origin. Therefore, globalization can help world convergence, not only through the possibility of developing countries to import and export more and to obtain inflows of locally scarce capital, but also through increasing knowledge and faster technological transfer.

History

In the period before the first industrial revolution (mid-eighteenth century), the per capita income in Western Europe was only 30 percent higher than that in China or India (Bairoch, 1993; Maddison, 1983).

The divergence between per capita income in what we now call the North and the South began with the industrial revolution (Baldwin and Martin, 1999) (Maddison, 2001) and not because of the colonial exploitation. This revolution set off a process of industrialization in Europe that stimulated growth enormously, while income in what are now the developing countries stagnated (Baumol, 1986; Baumol, Nelson, and Wolff, 1994). At the same time, international trade began to take off.

Great Britain, the pioneer of the industrial revolution, experienced rapidly increasing growth. Between 1700 and 1760 it grew by only 14 percent; between 1760 and 1820 by 34 percent and between 1820 and 1870 by 100 percent (Maddison, 1983). Although these figures have been subsequently reduced by Crafts (1995) and Maddison (2001), no one disputes the upward trend in Great Britain. Meanwhile, during the nineteenth century, per capita income in India stagnated, according to Maddison, or fell, according to Braudel (1984) and Bairoch (1993). The reason for this lay in the combination of the industrial revolution and international trade. Great Britain was transformed from an overwhelmingly agricultural economy into the leading world industrial power. The proportion of its labor force employed in industry rose from 18.5 percent in 1700, to 29.5 percent in 1800, to 47.5 percent in 1840, and in the same period it became a net importer of foodstuffs and a substantial exporter of industrial goods (Crafts, 1989). Meanwhile, the underdeveloped world experienced the opposite transformation. India went from being a net exporter of manufactured goods to a net exporter of primary products. In the seventeenth century the Indian textile industry was the world leader, in quality, volume of production, and volume of exports, but in the nineteenth century more that 70 percent of the textiles consumed in India were imported, principally from Great Britain (Cohen, 1997).

It was the industrial revolution that subsequently enabled the first wave of globalization to take place, based as this was on a reduction in the cost and increasing velocity of transport, reducing the distances between countries.

The expansion of railway networks between 1820 and 1850 and the growing use of steam in maritime transport between 1840 and 1870 were the principal driving forces behind this process (Hugill, 1993). In 1830, the fastest sailing ship took 48 days to make the crossing between Liverpool and New York, and 36 on the return trip. After 1840, steamships took 14 days in either direction. From 1870, the introduction of much lighter and stronger steel hulls reduced the time even further, as well as the cost of the coal used. By 1860 most important cities were already linked by telegraph.

In addition, London had already become the center of international financial intermediation, which facilitated the financing of buoyant world trade, and investment in the construction of railways, ships, and factories throughout the world.

In short, the first wave of globalization further widened the gap in per capita income between one group of countries and the other, which had begun to increase with the industrial revolution and was consolidated through the expansion of world trade and international investment. The principal cause of this divergence was the parallel industrialization of Europe and deindustrialization of the rest of the world, which was accelerated by the expansion of world trade (Baldwin and Martin, 1999). In 1750 the third world accounted for 73 percent or world manufacturing production. Later, its share fell to 50 percent in 1830, and just 7.5 percent in 1913 (Bairoch, 1982).

As a result, a number of countries, including Canada, Germany, Belgium, Denmark, France, Sweden, Switzerland, Italy, and Argentina, converged with Great Britain in per capita income terms, while by the end of this first wave of globalization, in 1913, the United States had managed to surpass her. Other countries, such as Spain, fell back slightly during this period and, finally, the countries of the third world, some European countries, such as Portugal and Hungary, and Japan, were clearly left behind. In 1850, before the first wave of globalization began, the difference between the richest countries (Great Britain, Australia, and Switzerland) and the poorest for which statistics are available (China, India, and Pakistan) was 4 to 1. By the end of that wave, in 1913, the difference had grown to 10 to 1. In other words, between 1750 and 1913 the difference in per capita income had increased almost ten-fold (Maddison, 1991).

The second wave of globalization, which began in 1950 and is still underway, has had the opposite effect. The North has deindustrialized and the South has industrialized. Industrial employment in the OECD countries has fallen considerably, except in Japan. In 1950, the average for industrial employment in Europe stood at 41 percent of the total. By 1998 this figure had fallen to 28 percent and today is lower than 24 percent. The newly industrializing countries in Asia have moved in the opposite direction and increased their percentage of industrial employment, from 14 percent to 27 percent, while developing countries such as India and China have reached of figures of between 10 percent and 20 percent.

Both trends have increased since 1980, when globalization began to accelerate. Trade between the North and the South is now made up mainly of manufacturing goods. Today 60 percent of Northern exports to the South are manufactures, as are 60 percent of Southern exports to the North. In general the manufactures exported by the North are capital and technology intensive while those exported by the South are labor intensive.

This change is due principally to the activities of multinational companies and their growing direct investment in many developing countries. They have located labor-intensive manufacturing in these countries, to take advantage of lower wage levels, and have reorganized their production from the local factories making the whole product, to "the global factory." This locates each part of the production process wherever it is cheapest or most convenient and final assembly in one plant in the group. As a result of this, "global factory" (Flamm and Grunwald, 1985) the combined local sales of all US multinationals overseas, through their affiliates, are three times greater than US exports, and the local sales of multinationals through their affiliates in all countries exceed total world trade by 30 percent. This means there has been an increasing industrial delocalization to developing countries.

During this fifty-year-plus period of globalization the US economy has grown by an average of just 2 percent a year, but the other OECD countries, especially Japan, have had faster growth and have therefore been able to close the income gap with the United States. Some developing countries – the newly industrialising countries (NICs) – have also taken an important step towards convergence with the United States and Europe because of their extremely high growth rates, especially the Asian NICs. However, many African, Latin American and Asian countries have had lower growth than the United States and, because of their frequently higher population growth rates, in some cases their per capita incomes have fallen.

In other words there has been a certain amount of convergence in per capita incomes among the rich and some intermediate countries (the NICs), and also some convergence at lower levels of income among the poor countries. This is what Danny Quah (1996) has referred to as "twin peaks convergence" or "convergence clubs," in which the income levels of the relatively rich and relatively poor countries gravitate together within each group, even though the distance between the two groups remains or widens. In terms of the neoclassical growth model (Solow, 1956) it is as if there are two "steady states" at two different levels, one for rich and upper-middle income countries and another for low and lower-middle income countries.

Nevertheless, this "twin-peaks" theory has been refuted, at least partially, by other economists (Sala i Martín, 2002a, 2002b; Bhalla, 2002) who have shown that world poverty, both in absolute and relative terms, has been reduced notably since the 1980s where the process of globalization has been faster, and that world personal income distribution has improved slightly in the same period. While world income distribution has improved, on average, between countries, (but not in all cases) some countries, mainly those that have not been able to reap the benefits of globalization, have failed to converge. By contrast, it has worsened slightly within countries, mainly due to the fact that China and India, which have opened quicker to globalization since the 1990s, have been growing faster than most developing countries but also have increased their internal level of inequality, at least temporarily, due to the fact that coastal areas have grown faster than internal regions and that cities have grown faster than rural areas and also due to the financial crises that some countries suffered in Asia and latin America.

This empirical evidence seems to be at odds with some other studies. According to the UNDP, United Nations Development Program (1999) in 1960 the difference between the average per capita income in the OECD countries and in the poorest countries was 30 to 1, and in 1997 it had grown to 74 to 1. In other words it had more than doubled. However, this report has made a very serious methodological error at comparing income distribution among countries. It considers that countries such as Luxembourg and Brunei, with negligible populations, have the same weight than India and China, with 1,300 and 1,100 million inhabitants respectively. If every country is weighted according to its population, the result is completely different, given that China, India and the southeast Asian countries, which represent around 40 percent of the world population, have grown much faster than the OECD countries since the 1980s, which represent less than 15 percent of the world population. Nevertheless, while the world average income distribution has improved, the standard deviation around the mean is still very high. While the countries of southeast

Asia have a per capita income today that is more than seven times greater than in 1960, and have therefore managed to converge rapidly with the OECD countries, the income of the poorest countries has stagnated since 1970 and in some ex-communist and African states it has fallen. Japan and the South Korea have gone furthest towards closing the gap with the United States. Korea, for example, increased its per capita income more than ten-fold between 1965 and 1995.

Obviously, real convergence is not always the same thing as a narrowing income distribution; this can worsen even though convergence has taken place. Changes in income dispersion or inequality depend on the relative importance of convergence and the effects of "shocks" or instability which affect economies individually or in groups, and tend to increase the dispersion of per capita income (Barro, 1997).

There are two different methods of measuring convergence that give rise to two different types: "beta" and "sigma" convergence (Barro and Sala i Martín, 1995). The first occurs when per capita income or output in the poorest countries grows faster than in the richest countries over the long term. The second occurs when the dispersion of per capita income across all countries reduces over time (i.e. when the standard deviation of the logarithm of per capita income or output falls over the long term). Beta convergence is a necessary but not a sufficient condition for sigma convergence. There can be a general beta convergence and still be increasing dispersion. As we have seen, between 1950 and 1997 beta convergence took place among the developed countries and the NICs, and also among poor and lower-middle income countries, but the gap between the per capita income of some of the richest and some of the poorest grew considerably, i.e., there has been no sigma convergence in certain cases.

Nevertheless, it should be stressed that, although poverty in the world has been significantly reduced, its absolute and relative levels are still intolerable in a world of increasing prosperity and it should be a matter of urgency to reduce them. Although global personal income distribution between countries has improved, it has worsened in some cases, notably in sub-Saharan Africa, and there has been an increase in inequality in some countries, notably in Latin America and the ex-communist countries. But inequality has increased in some OECD countries, notably in the US and the UK. In the United States the average difference in earnings between a shopfloor worker and the chief executive of the average large companies multiplied by almost six between 1990 and 1998, and on average it reached more than 400 times in the 500 largest US corporations! (*Economist*, 2003)

This is the result of the large returns on capital produced by the recent financial bubble and by the widespread use of stock options as a way of remunerating the top executives of companies. The richest 1 percent of US families own 39 percent of the assets of the whole country, i.e. 2.7 million people own 39 percent of the net worth of 270 million Americans. In Europe, for the moment at least, income distribution has not worsened to the same extent, except in the United Kingdom, which has been slightly less inegalitarian than the United States. In Latin America and parts of Asia, financial and currency crises have impacted very negatively upon the income of the poorest families, while the richest ones have been able to cushion their negative shock or have got even much wealthier by keeping their savings in dollars. Finally, as mentioned earlier, the developing countries that have grown faster in recent decades and have been able to reduce notably their levels of poverty, such as China, India and the South East Asian countries, because they have globalized faster, have Increased their levels of inequality, given that urban areas have developed faster than rural areas and areas close to the sea or navigable rivers have also grown faster than areas in the interior of those countries. This is a natural and temporary phenomenon of the earlier phases of growth, which later tends to diminish and eventually benefits the entire population.

This situation immediately raises two questions. To what extent is globalization responsible of gap between the per capita income in some of the rich and poor countries? Is this trend likely to continue in the future?

Other factors determining convergence

In answering to these questions various factors have to be taken into account. Firstly, in analyzing changes in the per capita income or output in different countries, the numerator of this ratio, i.e. GDP or national income, and the denominator, i.e. population, both have to be considered. If population grows more quickly than GDP, per capita income or output falls. The recent United Nations Population Fund report (UN, 2001) analyzes world population trends between 1960 and 1999. In 1960, out of a total population of 3 billion, 2.1 billion or 70 percent lived in developing countries. By 1999 the population of those countries had risen to 4.8 billion, out of a total of 6 billion, i.e. to 80 percent of world population.

Africa, with an average fertility rate of over five live births per woman, is the area where the population has increased the most. There are 767 million Africans today, almost three times as many as in 1960. Asia, the most populous region, has more than doubled its population in this period, reaching a total of 3,600 million. The same has happened in Latin America. In contrast, the population of the rich countries has grown by only a small amount since 1960: by 50 percent in the United States and 20 percent in Europe during this 40-year period. The projections made by the UNFPA show that by the middle of the twenty-first century the total world population will have reached almost 9,000 million, 23 percent of them will be living in Africa, compared to 9 percent in 1960; 55 percent in Asia; 9 percent in Latin America, and 13 percent in the OECD countries. Europe, which had 20 percent of the world's total population in 1960, will see its share fall to less than 7 percent in 2050.

This means that one of the greatest determinants of the widening income gap between some rich and some poor countries has probably been the difference in population growth rates. The low annual European rate (0.5 percent) between 1960 and 2000, combined with a 3 percent annual economic growth rate, meant that its per capita income grew by 2.5 percent. In Africa, on the other hand, economic growth has barely been able to keep up with a population growth rate of 4 percent, resulting in a stagnant per capita GDP. A similar, though slightly better, situation can be found in Latin America, where economic growth has just exceeded the average population growth rate of 3 percent a year, so per capita income has increased slightly. Finally, Asia, with a population growth rate of 2.5 percent, has managed to almost double its per capita income because it has experienced the highest economic growth since the last 1960s. Convergence has therefore been far greater, especially in China, India, Korea, and southeast Asia, where an average annual GDP growth rate of 7 percent has more than doubled per capita GDP.

According to the projections made by the United Nations Population Fund (UNPFA, 2000), population growth will be enough by itself to ensure that the gap in per capita incomes in some countries will widen significantly over the next fifty years, unless there is a decrease in the fertility rate in poor countries and an increase in the rich countries, or there is massive migration from the former to the latter. Migration is likely, given that, for example, Europe will have lost 70 million people by 2050 while Africa may well have gained more than 1.2 billion. These enormous imbalances in population and income can only be resolved through migration. By 2050 more than 30 percent of the European population will be over 70 years of age, while 40 percent of the African population will be under 20 and the shortage of working age population in Europe will have to be compensated by immigration from Africa, Latin America and Asia. Central and Eastern European countries will lose an even greater proportion of their populations than the European Union, therefore, immigration from that region will be low. Without this immigration, the fiscal situation in Europe will become unsustainable, because there will be fewer than two economically active Europeans for each retiree. So will the corresponding situation of unemployment and relative poverty in the poor countries.

The second source of inequality that has to be taken into account is technology. The recent wave of developments in information technology, biotechnology, and genetics will also have a negative effect on world income distribution, at least in the medium term.

On the one hand, biotechnology and biogenetics will lead to a substantial increase in life expectancy in the developed countries, with people living to almost 100 years of age on average by 2050. This will further complicate the fiscal problems of those developed countries, such as Japan and the European Union, that are facing a decrease in population. These technologies may also bring a solution to the problem of hunger in other parts of the world, with the result that the population in developing countries will grow even more because life expectancy will increase. The AIDs pandemic, which has increased mortality rates in Africa, will probably also be arrested or reduced.

At the same time, as I will explain in the next chapter, information technology will allow highly skilled workers to increase their productivity and their real earnings, while those with lower levels of skill will be confined to poorly paid unskilled jobs or face unemployment. The low levels of education and human capital in poorer countries make it difficult for them to absorb the information technologies that are diffusing quickly through rich countries, where they will lead to increases in productivity and their standard of living.

The third element that has to be taken into account in understanding differences in per capita incomes is geography. The geographical location of a country plays a part in determining its future. A study of global patterns of development between 1965 and 1990, carried out by the Harvard Institute for International Development (HIID) under the direction of Jeffrey Sachs (1997), demonstrated on average that landlocked countries tend to grow at a slower rate than those situated on the coast. The lack of an exit to the sea reduces growth rates by 0.79 percentage points because it increases transport costs and price of imports, especially for mountainous countries. Those situated in the tropics tend to grow 1.3 points less that those in temperate zones, reflecting the costs of an inferior climate, health problems, and a less-productive agriculture. It is difficult to escape from the poverty trap in the tropics because the majority of workers are employed in low-productivity agriculture. Only Hong Kong and very small tropical countries such as Singapore have become rich because they have been able to specialize in services and manufacturing. As Sachs observes, "air conditioning is probably the greatest leveller of labor productivity in industry and services." Other tropical countries in southeast Asia have taken off thanks to industrialization in the last few decades. Those which have not industrialized have generally stagnated, though this does not mean that agriculture cannot be the basis for take off in a tropical country. The island of Java is an example. Malaysia, swapping rubber for palm oil, is another. So is the northern Thailand. The negative effect of the tropics on health by itself reduces growth by another 0.8 percentage points compared to temperate countries, according to this study.

Finally, the policies adopted in different countries have also been a cause of economic divergence. Southeast Asia has emphasized openness to international trade based on manufacturing exports, fiscal rectitude that has avoided budget deficits, and the promotion of education and training. This has generated rapid growth and allowed the countries in question to catch up to a far greater extent than others in Asia, Africa, and Latin America, which followed closed import substitution models, or indulged in less austere fiscal expansion.

It is very important to bear all these factors in mind because the three surprising, but quite robust, empirical regularities concerning economic growth detected by the pioneering work of Nicholas Kaldor (1961), and subsequently updated by Paul Romer (1989), seem to remain still valid. The first is that growth rates and capital–labor ratios are almost constant over the long term, not only in individual countries but in the world as a whole. The second is that capital tends to represent a constant share of a country's aggregate production. The third is that growth and accumulation are highly variable between countries for the reasons already cited. In other words, it seems to be possible, according to these regularities, for real convergence to take place in the long term.

What does seem to be clear is "conditional" convergence, which states that the lower the starting point of per capita GDP, in relation to its long-term steady state, the higher the growth rate. This proposition is derived from the assumption of diminishing returns to capital in the neoclassical model. Economies with less capital per worker in relation to their long-term capital–labor ratio tend to have higher returns and therefore faster growth. This is known as "conditional" growth because the level of the steady state of capital and output per worker depends, in the Solow and Swan model, on the savings rate, the rate of population growth and the structure of the production function; characteristics that vary between different economies. Other economists include other sources of variation, such as the quality of institutions, government policies, and human capital (Acemoglu and Robinson, 2000) (Acemoglu, Johnson, and Robinson, 2002) (Engerman and Sokoloff, 2000, 2005) (Rodrik, Subramanian, and Trebbi, 2002).

This conditional convergence is held to reduce income differences between countries by about 2 percent or 3 percent a year, which means that it would take between 25 and 35 years to reduce initial differences in per capita income between two countries by half (Barro and Sala i Martín, 1992; Mankiw, Romer, and Weill, 1992).

How might globalization improve or worsen this situation?

Theory: two opposing accounts

As we saw in the previous chapter, there are two different accounts within economic theory about the effects that globalization has, directly, on growth and, indirectly, on convergence: one more optimistic and one more skeptical (De la Dehesa, 1995). As I have also made clear, by definition, globalization involves the increasing mobility of goods and services, and factors of production such as capital and technology, except labor, which is still much less mobile although its mobility has also been increasing faster in the last few years.

The optimistic account

According to neoclassical models – of international trade and the mobility of capital and technology (Heckscher–Ohlin: Ohlin, 1933), and of growth (Solow and Swan, 1956) – the mobility of goods, services, and capital, and the process of economic growth should lead to increasing convergence in per capita income.

In the Heckscher–Ohlin model, international differences in income, as well as international specialization, are the result of differences in factor endowments. Countries with better capital–labor ratios, or better skilled to unskilled labor ratios, tend to have higher productivity and therefore higher incomes than those with lower ratios.

Market integration and the mobility introduced by globalization tend to reduce differences in per capita income. This mobility means that capital and skilled labor will tend to move from rich countries, where they are more abundant and cheaper, to poor countries, where they are scarce and more expensive, while unskilled labor will tend to move from poor to rich countries. This will lead to a gradual equalization of factor endowments between countries, and therefore of their prices, in accordance with the factor price equalization theorem (Samuelson, 1948 and 1949). The same can be said about the equalization of factor prices through international trade in goods and services (Mundell, 1957). Rich countries will specialize in capital and skilled-labor intensive products and services, that they will export to poor counties, and these will specialize in lower skilled-labor intensive products that they will export to rich countries. In other words, the movement of factors of production can take a direct form in which they flow from one country to another, or an indirect form through international trade, because the movements of goods and services is a substitute for the movement of capital, labor, and technology. International trade acts as a substitute for the lack of labor mobility. This is the theoretical origin of the desperate call advanced by many developing countries governments that "trade is better then aid."

Equally, the traditional neoclassical growth theories formulated by Solow and Swan predict a long-term trend towards the convergence of per capita incomes because, as I have already explained, they are based on the assumption that capital accumulation is subject to decreasing marginal efficiency. When a country is poor and its capital stock is small, each successive addition to that stock generates lower marginal increases in output. This is where the idea of beta convergence originates because, as a result of the marginal efficiency of accumulable factors of production, poor countries tend to grow more quickly than rich ones; a situation that, assuming identical levels of technology, preferences and knowledge, will lead to a gradual equalization of incomes in the long term. The introduction of capital and labor mobility into these models tends to accelerate the process of convergence as both of these factors of production tend to move in the right direction. Capital will seek higher marginal productivity in poor countries, and labor higher salaries in rich countries. This is the more optimistic account of the link between globalization and convergence.

However, these explanatory models of globalization and the integration of the world economy lost some of their validity in the 1980s, especially the former, for a variety of reasons:

The skeptical account

Firstly, the standard Heckscher–Ohlin model is based on a series of assumptions that are not normally to be found in reality. Transport costs are not zero; production functions are not identical in all countries; there are economies and diseconomies of scale; markets are segmented and oligopolistic instead of functioning according to perfect competition; trade is becoming predominantly intra-industrial or intra-firm (within the same industry or firm) and not inter-industrial (between agriculture, energy, industry and services); tastes are not identical although they are slowly tending towards homogeneity; there are more than two factors of production; there are clear differences in productive efficiency; and, finally, economies of scale and external economies also play an important differential role.

On the one hand, the production functions of rich countries are usually more efficient because their workers are better trained and are equipped with larger amounts of capital and technology. In other words, total factor productivity is greater in rich countries; that is why they are richer. If this is the case, it may be that the patterns of international trade in goods and services are determined by differences in productivity and not by differences in factor endowments. A clear example of this is "Leontief's paradox" (Leontief, 1953): In the post-Second World War period, when per capita income in the United States was already higher than in other industrialized countries, Leontief showed that US exports were consistently somewhat less capital intensive than its imports. US comparative advantage was determined by technology more than by capital intensity, which gave rise to the paradox that its technological leadership was more evident in sectors with apparently moderate capital intensity than in those with a high capital–labor ratio. The same is true today, in a more pronounced way, in the export of high-technology services by the most developed countries. This leads to the conclusion that there is no universal tendency towards the equalization of factor prices through international trade.

The same can be argued with respect to the free movement of capital. In a hypothetical world in which all countries have the same technological level, the trade in goods and services is a substitute for the movement of capital and labor, as explained above. However, if some countries are more efficient and productive than others (a much more realistic assumption), it will not be the case. Moreover, the logical outcome in this situation is for the opposite to occur: capital moves from poorer to richer countries rather than the other way round. The low-wage advantage of poorer countries can be more than compensated for by their low productivity, making convergence unviable.

Equally, the same can also be said about the movement of labor. It may be, and in fact it is the case, that the mobility of highly skilled workers is much greater than that of the unskilled. They act in the same way as capital, in the sense that, attracted by higher salary differentials, they move from poor to rich countries rather than the other way round. The "brain drain" from poor countries is an example of this. Today 50 percent of those employed in the high-technology industries in Silicon Valley come from India or China.

In addition, the Heckscher–Ohlin model of international trade assumes decreasing or constant returns to scale and the absence of external economies. However, both forms of cost savings are very important in practice. On the one hand, firms in developed countries are larger (they include the majority of multinationals) and closer to minimum efficient scale than those in less developed countries, so they are more competitive in international markets (Neven, 1990). On the other hand, external economies mean that firms in the same sector tend to locate near each other, forming clusters (Porter, 1990), because they benefit from lower information and technology costs and the availability of specialized labor, etc. In other words, on the one side, economies of scale lead to the concentration of production in more efficient plants and larger firms and, on the other side, external economies due to the concentration of these plants in the same locality. As Krugman (1991b) points out, globalization can lead to national clusters becoming global because the integration of world markets provokes increased business concentration and greater specialization. Clearly, territorial concentration will usually take place within or near large final markets. This implies the concentration of production where large high-volume, high-income markets are to be found, i.e. in the developed countries, rather than the movement of factors of production to countries with lower wage costs but at a greater distance. In the end everything depends on whether the savings from the scale and concentration of production, together with savings on transport costs, compensate for the costs of congestion in more developed countries plus the savings that could be made on labor costs by relocating in a developing country. In other words these two sets of cost savings can act either as centripetal or centrifugal forces in the distribution of productive activity between developed and developing countries (Krugman, 1998a).

Secondly, neoclassical growth models are slowly being replaced by the new "endogenous growth" models, which were originally formulated by Romer (1986) and Lucas (1988) and are based on different assumptions. The first, as we saw in the previous chapter, is that technological progress is not an exogenous residual but is endogenous and the product of the search for competitive advantage based on policies to foment education, training, innovation, and technology. The second is that returns to physical and human capital, particularly the latter, are increasing to scale rather than decreasing or constant, in other words, that the rate of return on the capital stock can increase marginally with each addition to that stock. The third is that scientific knowledge does not simply generate externalities that increase the productivity of other production factors but also relatively higher marginal productivity.

The implication of these new models is that countries do not converge on a steady state. Instead poor countries with smaller endowments of physical capital, human capital, and technology may never converge with the rich counties. Only those poor countries that manage to achieve a fast accumulation of their stock of human capital have any chance of convergence. As Giuseppe Bertola (1999) points out, the choice between neoclassical models and endogenous growth models is very important because they have very different views on the role that market and economic policy should play. The economic policy has a much smaller role in the former than in the latter, where its main role in promoting physical and human capital, and R&D, is decisive.

From the point of view of these endogenous growth models, globalization means that the mobility of capital may increase income differences because it will flow to wherever the marginal productivity of capital is greatest. According to these models, this will be in the more advanced countries and those with the largest capital stocks. Robert Lucas (1990) asks himself why there is not a greater flow of capital from rich to poor countries when marginal returns should be, by definition, higher in the second than in the first, since capital is scarcer. He comes to the conclusion that, apart from political risks, which are very important, there are two other factors that restrict the flow. The first is the difference in levels of human capital between some countries and others, which go a long way to compensate for the differences in the marginal productivity of capital. The second is the restriction on the entry and exit of capital in many countries or the limits on portfolio investment in some developing countries.

Nor will the mobility of labor by itself necessarily lead to convergence because the utility of emigration is not unrelated to the share of capital in the production function. As the amount of capital increases, the share of labor and wages tends to fall, and the benefit of moving from one country to another reduces in relation to its cost.

If the transfer or mobility of technology is introduced into these models, convergence only takes place if the costs of imitation for developing countries (which, fundamentally, imitate innovations made in developed world) are lower than the costs of innovation in the most advanced countries. This is more likely to be the case for less technologically advanced products and processes that are easier to imitate (Grossman and Helpman, 1991a). This is the more skeptical theoretical account of the whether globalization will be able to increase convergence. From this point of view, globalization will widen the gap between those countries and individuals who are able to adapt to the new situation and the new technologies, and those who are not (Fitoussi, 1997).

Finally, as it has been demonstrated in chapter 2, the international trade "gravity models" (Leamer and Levinson, 1995) show the importance of distance in exchange and in globalization in general, due to the cost of transporting goods and sometimes services. The countries further away from the main markets receive lower prices for their exports to those markets and pay higher prices for the imports from them. This is another reason why they have a lower rate of growth and they have more difficulties to converge with the countries close to the center.

Some hopeful models

Despite all this, Richard Baldwin and Phillipe Martin (1999) argue that we should not lose heart. There is an analytical framework that, in line with Romer and Lucas's endogenous growth theory and Krugman's new economic geography, can explain the growing divergence that exists today but also holds out hope of convergence taking place in the future. Baldwin and Martin analyze two regions with the same initial conditions (North and South) and four growth phases. In the first phase, pre-globalization

(1750–1870), transport costs are very high, there is little trade, and industry is primitive, undynamic, and divided between North and South. The dispersion of industry itself contributes to the lack of dynamism because it reduces contact between entrepreneurs and prevents the diffusion of any innovations that are or may be made. In addition, the lack of competition means there is no incentive to innovate or make technological improvements so world growth is slow.

In the next phase (1870–1913), when transport costs begin to fall quickly, international trade increases and the centripetal forces of concentration, according to Krugman (1998), leave the existing distribution and dispersion of industry in a delicately balanced state. As both regions are identical, whichever takes the first step (most of the time, a matter of luck and often the result of a fortuitous event) is the one that begins to take off, in this case in the Northern region, and immediately finds itself in a virtuous circle. Its greater per capita income gives it a bigger market, which attracts more investment, and this in turn increases the size of its market further, so the circle feeds on itself. Industry in the North benefits disproportionally from an increase in innovation and industrialization, which in turn leads to the disappearance of industry in the South when it cannot compete with Northern exports. As a result the North increasingly specializes in industrial goods and the South in foodstuffs and primary products. The industrialization of the North and the deindustrialization of the South generate a widening gap in per capita income levels between the two.

In the first wave of globalization between 1870 and 1913 the reduction in the cost of exchanging goods internationally is much greater than the reduction in the cost of exchanging ideas and innovations.

In the third phase (1914–60) the costs of transporting goods continue to fall until they reach their natural limits, and the cost of exchanging ideas begins to fall because of the development of telecommunications. This opens the way to the fourth phase, when the second wave of globalization takes place.

In the present globalization phase (1960 and beyond), the costs of transporting ideas fall far enough to make the North–South, center–periphery division unstable, thanks this time to centrifugal forces (Krugman, 1998a). Entrepreneurs and innovators in the South, who now have easy access to Northern technology, and much lower labor costs, begin to close the gap and initiate their own take off. Industrial investment flows to the South, income increases, as does the size of the market and it enters into its own virtuous circle. The North suffers because of competition from the South and increasingly specializes in services to compensate for its increasing deindustrialization. Gradually the per capita incomes of the two regions converge.

In other words, we find ourselves in a phase when globalization and the growing exchange of ideas and innovations may provide the definitive impulse behind the industrialization of the South and its convergence in per capita terms with the North, which gives some hope for the future.

A similar point of view is expressed by Venables and Limao (1999) by integrating the Heckscher–Ohlin model of International Trade with the Von Thunen (1826) pioneer model of spatial analyzis. International trade is both determined by the productive factor endowment and the distance of the periphery from the central locations or main markets of more developed countries. The interaction of geography and endowments will tend to divide the world in economic zones: countries close to the center may specialize in transport-intensive activities, as it has been happening in the center of western Europe for many years. Moving further out, countries become more diversified producing more goods and trading more of them, as it happened in the European periphery. Still further out, countries may become import substituting (replacing some of their imports from the center with local production) as occurred for a while in some Latin American and Asian countries. At the extreme, most peripheral countries could be autarkic. The longer the distance from the center, the lower the real incomes of the countries.

The trade pattern of every country will then be a mixture of the factor endowment and the factor intensity of the goods it produces and the transport intensities of its exports, derived from its distance to the center. As globalization means a strong reduction in transport costs on all activities, it is the same as moving all countries closer to the center and, therefore, tends to raise incomes. However, it also tends to turn the terms of trade against non-central countries. On balance, globalization produces convergence of incomes given that countries closer to the center tend to experience a welfare loss due to the fact that the factor intensity endowment effect will be still larger than the transport intensity effect, causing negative terms of trade changes (for instance, Mexico) and those further out tend to experience a welfare gain, because the transport-intensity factor is much less important the further they are from the center (for instance, China).

Moreover, when a new activity needs to be located its final decision will depend on the transport intensity and the factor intensity of the new product compared with the existing intensities. If it has a low transport intensity and a high labor intensity it will definitely be located in the more peripheral countries, but even if the new product has a high transport intensity it can also be located in the further periphery, given that the costs of remoteness are already incorporated in the factor prices of these countries, increasing their attractiveness. This model is confirmed by the present trend of outsourcing and offshoring of production to further-out countries, given the increasing reduction of transport costs, mainly in the service sectors and light manufacturing.

Similar results are achieved by Fujita and Thisse (2003), who find that income inequality among countries falls with globalization when looking at the effect of the spatial fragmentation of the value chain and consequently of delocalization of production in developed and developing countries. They use a model of imperfect competition, which takes into account both skilled and unskilled labor and two units of production: the headquarters and a single far away relocated plant, in which, the headquarter uses skilled labor and the plant uses headquarter services and unskilled labor. They find out that that fragmentation of production, one of the main engines of globalization, due to the falling of trade and communication costs, contributes to the narrowing of the gap between rich and poor countries. The reason is that the fragmentation of production is harmful for both skilled and unskilled workers in the headquarters in the developed country and is beneficial for the workers of the plant in the developing country. Even though the nominal wage of the skilled workers at core is unaffected, they suffer because an increase in the local price index and because the fall in the communication costs make real operating profits lower than before.

Another recent model by Redding and Schott (2003), following previous research by Hanson (1998) and Redding and Venables (2001), ties up a country's human capital accumulation to its distance from global economic activity and shows that the higher the trade costs, the lower human capital accumulation and per capita income. If skill-intensive sectors are relatively trade cost intensive and are characterized by stronger increasing returns to scale, being located in the economic periphery can reduce the return to skill, reducing the incentives for investing in capital accumulation, and reducing the per capita income. Firms located in remote locations pay higher trade costs on both their sales to final markets and their purchases of imported intermediate inputs, and, therefore, they have less value added available to remunerate domestic factors of production and less incentive for investment in human capital accumulation, the contrary to firms located close to the center of global production and markets. If the costs of transporting, trading, exchanging information and monitoring fall further with better infrastructures, technology, and the acceleration of globalization, they will have a chance to reduce their gap in income per capita with the countries close to the center.

In this more optimistic vein, and according to Mathew Slaughter (1997), there are three ways that international trade can contribute to real convergence. The first is through Samuelson's (1948 and 1949) factor price equalization theorem, which, as explained earlier, states that a country taking part in free trade will tend to equalize the price of its factors of production with the rest of the world. However, there are a number of problems with this theorem. The first is that it describes the outcome of a situation in which free trade and a steady state in equilibrium already exist, but this says nothing about the process of trade liberalization. This presents a problem because the literature on convergence is concerned with a process of convergence towards a steady state. Edward Leamer (1995) has developed a factor price equalization theorem, which captures the idea that freer trade will lead to the convergence of factor prices in different countries. He calls it the "factor price convergence theorem." It states that, as countries eliminate barriers to free trade, the equalization of the price of goods will tend to eliminate differences in factor prices.

Another problem with Samuelson's theorem is that it only holds under certain strict assumptions, such as there being no barriers to trade and technology and where preferences are identical in all countries. However, these strict assumptions are not found in reality, so a convergence in the price of goods may take place without there being a similar convergence in factor prices (Slaughter, 1995b).

A third problem is that both theorems deal only with the convergence or equalization of the price of factors of production, but per capita income is determined by a combination of both the price and the quantity of factors: i.e., it is the sum of income from labor and from capital. This means that even if factor prices converge, per capita incomes might diverge if the factor endowments among countries also diverge. International trade cannot eliminate differences in endowments of labor and capital, only differences in their price. Rassekh and Thompson (1996) have demonstrated this very clearly.

The second way in which international trade can affect per capita income is through its role as an intermediary in the flow of technology. If this flow tends to be from more advanced to less advanced countries, the trade through which it takes place will tend to raise the price of factors of production in the less advanced countries, because improved technology implies that all factors of production have a greater marginal physical productivity and therefore a higher price (Dollar, Wolf, and Baumol, 1988) and Rosenberg (1980). But the same problem arises here. Per capita income also depends on the endowments of capital and labor and if these diverge too much between countries, there will be no increase in the convergence of per capita income.

The third way is through trade in capital goods. When a country imports capital goods it improves its capital endowment or stock, its productivity and, therefore, its per capita income. This will only occur, however, if factor prices, in contrast with the previous two ways discussed, are converging or diverging more slowly than the capital endowment is growing.

Chui, Levine, and Perlman (1999) examine the welfare gains from North–South trade and their distribution using an endogenous growth model adding the Vernon's product-cycle theory. They find two mechanisms by which openness may increase world growth and welfare for both the North and the South. The first is through specialization in which trade sees the North devoting more resources to innovative R&D. The second is through knowledge spillovers, which enable the South to progress into higher stages of development. However, this second channel has an ambiguous effect on world growth. In stage II when the South only copies and does not innovate (Vernon's product cycle emerges), increased spillovers reduce the incentive to innovate in the North and long-term world growth falls; but as spillovers increase further, the South enters stages where it begins to innovate and world growth increases. Despite this negative effect of transition from phase I to phase II, all our tade equilibria yield higher growth rates and welfare than the autarky regime even when the South is in its copying stage of development. Therefore, they find out that world integration should be accompanied by a strenghthening of international property rights which have the effect of encouraging innovation and discouraging copying in the South.

Finally, a paper by Richard Baldwin and Phillipe Martin (2003) shows that within the context of endogenous growth models and new economic geography models, growth in the form of innovation can lead to catastrophic spatial agglomeration à la Myrdal or à la Krugman, but this may change if capital mobility can be taken into account. Spatial agglomeration of economic activities can be consistent with delocation of firms to poor countries, through capital mobility and technology spillovers.

The conclusion to be drawn from the all the above is that international trade can stimulate convergence in per capita income if it improves not only the price of factors of production but also their endowments and the innovation spillovers to developing countries.

However, international trade is not the only important element in convergence. According to Solow's neoclassical model, savings and investment rates are also fundamental. So are endowments of human capital, R&D, and technology according to Romer and Lucas's endogenous growth models. Demographic changes are very important as well, due both to the mobility of factors of production (migration) and changes in fertility and mortality. So too, are international transfers of capital, such as cohesion and structural funds, which played such an important part in the convergence of Ireland, Spain, and Portugal within the European Union (Ben David and Papell, 1996).

Only by taking these elements into account can we understand the positive empirical findings made in studies of the link between international trade and the convergence of per capita income by Sachs and Warner (1995), Dollar (1992), Edwards (1993), Ben David and Papell (1996), and Williamson (1996). Not doing so can lead to negative correlations, such as those of Fiekele (1994) or ambiguous ones, such as those of Rodrik (1992).

Globalization, understood as the combination of increased international trade and the growing free movement of capital and technology, can contribute to convergence as long as it increases the diffusion of technology and the dissemination of ideas (Dollar, Wolf, and Baumol, 1998; Rosenberg 1980), and appropriately directed capital flows (Lucas, 2000), in such a way that, as Baldwin and Martin (1999) suggest, the current globalization process provides the definitive impulse behind industrialization in the South, deindustrialization of the North and, finally, the convergence of per capita income between the two. I will look at this process in more detail in the next chapter.

Globalization, Employment, and Labor Markets

The globalization process, like all processes of change and heightened competition, has important consequences for the distribution of economic activity around the world in accordance with the comparative advantage of countries and their firms. This redistribution inevitably leads to changes in the generation of employment and unemployment, to how labor is remunerated, i.e. the level and distribution of wages, and to the shares of capital and labor in total GPD. These three processes are of great importance to understand the impact of globalization on labor markets.

In principle, using a standard theoretical framework (De la Dehesa, 1999e) globalization opens the world to international competition and induces a better allocation of labor, capital, and technology by allowing each competing country to specialize its production according to its relative comparative advantages in the factors of production. Developed countries have a clear comparative advantage in the supply of products and services intensive in capital, technology, and highly qualified labor and a comparative disadvantage in those intensive in less qualified labor. Therefore, in those countries, the demand for capital, technology, and more qualified labor increases while the demand for less qualified labor decreases. This shift of the demand curve to the left increases the probability that less qualified workers end up with relative lower salaries or even unemployed, increasing the probability of entering into a situation of structural unemployment in that segment of the labor force, if labor markets are rigid.

The contrary happens in developing countries, where the demand for both less qualified and qualified labor increases, given that local and foreign firms, which have invested in the country, are able to compete more favorably in international markets. This shift in developed countries is even bigger given that the supply curve of less qualified labor tends to have a less steep slope than that of more qualified labor, thus, the number of unemployed of lower skills tends to be larger than the number of skilled workers who find new jobs. There are two reasons for this asymmetry. The first one is that trade unions, which tend to have a higher affiliation of less qualified workers, oppose a reduction of wages of their affiliates as a response of their lower demand, thus generating a higher unemployment rate. The second is that unemployment subsidies tend to be larger, as a proportion of their wages, among less qualified workers than in more qualified workers, and therefore the former will have a temporary lower incentive to look for a new job. The end result will depend of the slope of both supply curves, the lower the slope of the curve, the higher the effect of the shift of the demand curve on reducing wages or generating unemployment.

But, on the other hand, globalization generates also a reduction of unemployment since it makes the demand for labor more sensitive to labor costs and, therefore, it makes more costly, in employment terms, for trade unions to press for higher wages. There are two reasons for this to happen. The first one is that the increase in international competition reduces the market power of national industries and thus for employment to react more rapidly to shifts in the labor costs. The second one is that the higher international mobility of capital allows for the firms to react to changes in labor costs relocating production where labor costs, that is, wages weighted by productivity, are more competitive. Under this more sensitive response by firms to labor costs, trade unions are obliged to be less aggressive in pressing for higher wages, given that the cost in terms of employment are now much higher.

These shifts in the demand for different levels of labor qualification are provoked by three channels of competition due to globalization: First, through increased trade, that is, workers of developing countries with lower labor costs compete indirectly, through cheaper exports, with the workers of domestic firms in developed countries. Through foreign direct investment, that is, firms relocating the most labor-intensive parts of their production of goods and services to developing countries looking for lower labor costs. Third, through migration, that is, workers of developing countries migrating to developed countries and competing locally with the domestic labor force for employment.

Globalization, economic activity, and delocalization

In the first place, and paradoxically, the growing integration of markets, brought about by globalization, has led not to the agglomeration of production in a few locations, but to the disintegration of the production process by locating different layers of the value chain in different geographical locations and in different countries. The production of goods and services in all countries now incorporates productive activity that takes place elsewhere (Feenstra, 1998). Firms find it pays to relocate more and more of the production process. Part of it may stay in their home country while part moves abroad to exploit the comparative advantage of each country. This is known as vertical specialization, in which countries specialize in different stages of the value chain (Hanson, 1996) (Hummels, Rapoport, and Yi, 1997).

This is a radical change from the traditional form of vertically integrated production, known as Fordist production, exemplified by the automobile industry. Various prominent economists have referred to this change and to the idea that production can be internationally disaggregated. Bhagwati and Dehejia (1994) call this process "kaleidoscopic comparative advantage"; Krugman (1996a) uses the phrase "slicing the value chain"; Leamer (1996) prefers the more widely accepted concept of delocalization, while Antweiler and Trefler (1997) call it "intramediated (rather than intermediated) trade."

Delocalization mainly involves labor intensive activities, though it increasingly includes other forms. Two clear examples are the Barbie doll (Tempest, 1996) and Nike sports shoes (Tisdale, 1994).

The raw materials for the Barbie (plastic and hair) come from Taiwan and Japan. It is assembled in Indonesia, Malaysia, and China. The moulds and the paint for decorating it come from the United States. China supplies the cotton cloth for its clothes. The dolls are exported from Hong Kong at a price of 2 dollars per unit. This includes 35 cents for the Chinese labor and 65 cents for the materials, with the remainder going to transport costs, administration, and profits. The dolls are sent to the United States where they sell for 10 dollars, of which 1 dollar goes in profit to the design company, Mattel, and the rest goes on transport, marketing, and distribution. Despite the delocalization and disaggregation, therefore, the majority of the value added still originates in the United States. The dolls are sold all over the world at a rate of two per second and Mattel enjoyed sales worth a total of 1.4 billion dollars in 1995 from this source alone.

Another well-known example is that of Nike sports shoes. Almost 75,000 people are employed in Asia making the fabric and other parts of Nike shoes, although only a small proportion are employed directly by the company. The rest are employed in Korean and Taiwanese owned factories that have supply contracts with Nike. Nike has 2,000 employees in the United States and generated 360 million dollars in sales in 1993. Since then the figure has tripled.

The delocalized activities of these firms form part of a long "value chain" which includes the whole range of productive and commercial activities, from design and quality control to distribution to retailers. In contrast to traditional theory on the "internationalization" of multinational companies, which I discuss in the following chapter, these companies farm out a large part of their production because the cost advantages of delocalized production are greater than the transaction costs this generates. The naive American consumer may think these products are "made in the USA" because the brand name is American, but they are the product of many different factories and workers in many different countries.

The same is true for many other US and European companies. Half of IBM's work force is outside the US. General Electric is the largest private employer in Singapore, where a total of over 100,000 people work for the company producing or assembling electronic components to be sent to the United States. At the start of the 1990s, some 20 percent of the production from US's companies was carried out by non-US citizens outside the United States (Feenstra, 1998).

As a result of this process, industrial activity in the OECD countries has fallen from 30 percent of GDP in 1960 to less than 20 percent in 2000 and it is still falling. Industrial employment has fallen from 28 percent in 1970 to 17 percent in 2000 and keeps falling.

Despite this irreversible trend, the idea persists throughout the developed world that industry is the most important economic activity for an "industrialized country" (as developed countries have traditionally been called) to be involved in, and that, paradoxically, producing goods is much more important than inventing them, controlling their advertising and brand name, or financing and transporting them.

The atavistic idea exists that factory production is essential and therefore closing a steelworks or a car plant provokes a political crisis. But cutting tens of thousands of jobs in Wall Street banks is not seen as traumatic. Equally, opening a chemical plant is treated as a great achievement, even though it creates only a limited amount of employment, but opening a large shopping center or call center, creating hundreds or even thousands of jobs, attracts much less attention.

This is, probably, the result of recent history. The western democracies were able to defeat Germany in two world wars because the "American industrial machine" produced tanks, planes, and artillery on a massive scale. In the developed countries, industry has been the traditional source of employment for "young men with lots of muscle and little else" (*Economist*, 1998).

Industry is considered special because it is believed to provide higher growth, better jobs, more export earnings and greater technological progress than any other activity. However this is not in fact the case. A family might own two or three cars, fridges, dishwashers and washing machines over the years, but as it becomes richer it spends an increasing amount of its income on health, education, insurance, investment, leisure, culture, tourism, and many other services, from telephony to cleaning. As the demand for these services grows, the workers employed in them get higher wages, for doing more interesting jobs than working in a factory. Young people in the developed world today prefer working in services, from telecommunications to the Internet, and from transport and tourism to biotechnology and health (*Economist*, 1998).

Brown and Julius (1993) show that the same thing is happening to industry in OECD countries today as has happened to agriculture in the course of the twentieth century. At the start of the century 68 percent of all employment in Japan was in agriculture; in the United States the figure was 44 percent; and in Britain it was 20 percent. Today the last figures have fallen to 5.3 percent and 2 percent respectively. However, not only have these countries not got poorer, they have got richer because industry and services have created more productive and better paid jobs than those in agriculture. The poorest countries in the world have 80 percent of their population employed in subsistence or low-productivity agriculture. That is the reason they are so poor. The reverse of this picture is to be found in the continual increase of service employment in the developed countries. In the United States the figure today stands at 74 percent of total employment; the average for the OECD countries is 64 percent

percent and 65 percent for the European Union. Only in Japan is it slightly less at 62 percent (OECD, 1999a).

It is now the turn of industry and it is very likely that in a few decades time, industrial employment in the OECD countries will have fallen to less than 10 percent of the total. We should not worry that industry, first the labor intensive industry and then much of the rest, is gradually being delocalized to other countries. We must get used to the idea that production is becoming disaggregated, with some parts of it being delocalized to wherever it is more profitable and also the idea that whole industries will be shifted to developing countries, as has happened in shipbuilding and steel production since the 1980s. We have to forget the idea of mass industrial production by one company, in one country and in one plant. Production has become a process that takes place in many plants, in many countries and by many companies. So far, ownership of the product, control of the brand name, and design, quality control, marketing, and financing have all remained in the hands of companies in the developed countries. In time, highly competitive firms will slowly begin to emerge, as happened in Japan and later Korea, and they will be able to compete on equal terms with industrial companies in the developed world. In fact, Korea and Taiwan, the first countries in East Asia to take over from Japan as centers of industrial production, began to deindustrialize in the late 1980s in favor of other countries in southeast Asia such as Thailand, Malaysia, Indonesia, the Philippines, and Vietnam. In the context of globalization, every country will be able to exploit its comparative advantage in an increasingly integrated market. Gradually, the Asian, European, and Latin American NICs, and others that will emerge in the future, will increase their share of world industrial production, while the developed countries will further increase their share of services. They will specialize more and more in the production and export of services while the NICs specialize in the production and export of manufactures. In 1997, 30 percent of world trade was in services and 54 percent of the 500 leading companies in the world, according to the list produced by *Fortune* magazine, were service companies (Hufbauer and Warren, 1994). In short, the deindustrialization of the developed countries cannot be seen as a symptom of failure in their manufacturing sectors or in their economies as a whole. On the contrary, deindustrialization is a general characteristic of economic development in advanced economies and is closely related to improvements in the standard of living. International trade has not played a large part in this process, but it has been reflected in the figures for net manufacturing exports, that have fallen further in Europe and the United States than in Japan. The most important factor has been the increasing demand for services as populations as have grown richer, and this has meant there has been a generalized trend towards deindustrialization in the developed world (Ramaswamy and Rowthorn, 1991).

None of this is to deny there can sometimes be problems of adjustment associated with deindustrialization, in specific manufacturing sectors or in the economy as a whole. It may be that, in the short term, the service sector cannot absorb all the labor freed from the manufacturing sector, because world economic growth is not strong enough, because due to institutional rigidities in the service sector or in the labor market, or because the investment needed to expand the service sector takes time to appear.

However, economists who have studied the process empirically have not been alarmed. For example, Robert Lawrence (1994) has analyzed imports by US multinationals as a way of measuring delocalization and he comes to the conclusion that these imports are not yet high enough to have an effect on national employment or wages. Similarly, after measuring delocalization by looking at foreign direct investment abroad by multinationals, Paul Krugman (1995b) finds this is still too low to change the pattern of employment and wages.

On the other hand, Robert Feenstra (1998) disagrees. He measures delocalization not simply by taking into account imports by US multinationals but also the imports of intermediate and final goods used in these companies' production processes or sold under their brand name. He shows that the United States is importing a growing proportion of its intermediate goods, in the form of capital goods or consumer goods at an intermediate or advanced stage of production, to which value is added in the United States. The fact that intermediate capital and consumer goods increased from 10 percent of total US imports in 1925 to 50 percent in 1990 and to 60 percent today, and that they are imported in and increasingly finished form, means that the process of delocalization has gone much further than it appears by measuring final imports by multinationals or their foreign direct investment. According to Audet (1996) this phenomenon is even more pronounced in countries such as Canada, France, Germany and the United Kingdom, so its effect on the level of productive activity and employment may be even greater in Europe, especially in more labor intensive manufacturing such as clothing, shoes, and toys.

Since the 1990s, the outsourcing and offshoring of services to developing countries is creating an enormous amount of attention and concern by politicians and the media in developed countries, because of the fear of job losses (UNCTAD, 2004). Research, by Mary Amiti and Shan-Jin Wei (2004), has studied this issue in depth, concentrating on business services and the computing and information service trade. They ask the following questions: Has service outsourcing exploded in recent years? How does it compare with the level of previous material outsourcing? Who are the biggest outsources of sevices to the rest of the world? Who are the biggest insources of services from the rest of the world? And finally: Are services outsourcing producing big job losses?

They show, first, that service outsourcing has been steadily increasing but is still at very low levels. For example, in the US, imports of computing and business services as a share of GDP were only 0.4 percent in 2003 from 0.1 percent in 1983 and 0.2 percent in 1993, according to the IMF balance of payments data. Second, exports of these services are greater than imports, in the US and other developed countries, and that their net surplus has been increasing in recent years, showing that trade in services is very similar to trade in goods: a two-way street increasingly dominated by intra-firm or intra-industry trade. Third, although the US is, in value, the largest outsourcer of computing and business services with $41 billion, followed by Germany with $39 billion, when scaled by GDP, its proportion of outsourcing type of trade is very low compared with the rest of the world. The US is ranked only 117th in the world. The UK is 85th. China is ranked 99th, before the US. The countries with the highest ratio of imports of business services to GDP are Ireland, Angola, the Republic of Congo, and Mozambique – small economies. India and China, which are considered by the media as the largest recipients of service outsourcing they are ranked 11th and 8th in total outsourcing in value terms, just after the most developed countries.

Fourth, the US is also the biggest insourcer of business services with $59 billion, followed by the UK, Germany, France, and the Netherlands, while those countries perceived to be the absolute biggest insourcers in value terms, such as India and China, are ranked 6th and 14th. The UK and the US are the biggest net insourcers followed by Hong Kong, India, Singapore, China, and France. Russia, Italy, Korea, Indonesia, Japan, and Germany the biggest net outsourcers. In terms of GDP the largest insourcers are small countries like Vanuatu, Singapore, and Hong Kong – all exceeding 10 percent of GDP. India is a larger insourcer than the UK (3.8 percent of GDP versus 2.4 percent respectively) and China is slightly ahead of the US (0.8 percent of GDP versus 0.6 percent of GDP respectively).

Fifth, material outsourcing is much larger than service or intangible outsourcing and it has been going on for a much longer time. Finally, outsourcing of services has no negative effect on employment either in manufacturing industries or service industries. Both authors take the case of 69 manufacturing industries and 9 service industries in the UK as an example, and look at correlations between employment and outsourcing, using a first and a second period lags, by comparing the top five fastest and top five slowest sectors in employment growth and their associated growth in service outsourcing. They find a positive effect, though not robust across industries and specifications, but there is no negative effect in any of the manufacturing industries. This result does not mean that workers do not lose their jobs in some manufacturing firms, but they tend to be able to find another job in another firm within the same industry classification. In service industries, using the same methodology, the positive net effect is small and the only negative effect, also small and not robust, is with a two period lag.

Globalization, trade, and wages

In the 1970s, a fundamental change took place in the US labor market and in the remuneration levels of its workers, as Mathew Slaughter (1999) explains. Firstly, average real wages began to fall. In the century prior to 1973, real hourly wages had grown by an average of 1.9 percent per year. Since 1973 they have fallen by an average of 0.4 percent a year. Those who have suffered most have been lower-paid workers, whose real wages have fallen by more than 20 percent in some cases. On the other hand, higher-paid workers have experienced a considerable increase in their hourly incomes, especially managers and chief executives, and especially when their earnings from stock options are taken into account.

Second, there has been growing wage inequality between higher- and lower-skilled workers. Between 1979 and 1994, the gap between the real incomes of the skilled workers in the ninth decile (the highest paid) and the median increased from 1.73 times to 2.04 times, and that between the median and those in the first decile (the lowest paid) increased from 1.73 times to 2.13 times and continues to do so today. Inequality has not only increased between workers with different skill levels but also between those in the same occupation and with the same level of skills: The better paid have increased their earnings more than the lower paid. The so-called "residual" inequality, that measures differences between groups according to gender, race, education and experience, has also increased.

Although inequality has not increased to the same extent in other OECD countries, the phenomenon has been the same, except in the United Kingdom where the earnings inequality has grown considerably, and Canada, Germany, and Finland, were it has reduced slightly or stayed the same. In general, there has been less wage inequality in Europe, but a greater increase in unemployment, except in the United Kingdom where both rose temporarily. This lower inequality seems to be the result of institutional rigidities in the labor market. Theoretically, the cause of these changes can only be an increase in the supply of lower-skilled workers compared to the higher-skilled, or an increase in the demand for the latter compared with the former.

However, the relative earnings and employment prospects of higher-skilled workers have improved even though their relative supply has increased. If labor markets function flexibly, earnings can only rise at the same time as an increase in supply, if demand increases at a faster rate.

In fact the demand for skilled workers in the advanced economies has increased in two ways: first, *between* industries because output in those employing more unskilled workers has decreased while it has increased in those employing skilled workers, and second and more importantly, *within* industries. In general, firms tend to demand more skilled than unskilled workers and this has increased their relative wages (Berman, Bound, and Griliches, 1994; Katz and Krueger, 1998). In countries where wages are fixed in a relatively flexible way in decentralized labor markets, such as the United States and the United Kingdom, the decrease in the demand for unskilled labor and the increase in the demand for skilled labor have led to an increase in the wage gap between the two groups. In countries where there has been less or non-existent wage dispersion, because of rigidities in the labor market and the welfare state, there has been a sharp increase in unemployment among unskilled workers.

However, it is important to note that the dispersion of individual earnings among full-time workers is only one way of measuring inequality. Others take into account individual earnings across the whole population of working age, or family incomes. According to these measures, earnings inequality among US workers is similar to that in European countries (OECD, 1996a). This is because the negative effect of greater wage dispersion among US workers is compensated for by the positive effect of higher employment rates. In other words, the effect of the greater inequality is not as costly in economic terms for the US economy as the effect of unemployment for the European economy, though both are very costly in social terms.

It is also important to note that the comparative dispersion of gross earnings from wages is different form that of disposable incomes because of differences in systems of taxation and social transfers in each country. Taxes on labor are much lower in the United States but so are unemployment subsidies. The opposite is the case in Europe.

What could have been the cause of these changes in the demand for the different types of worker, and the wage inequality and/or unemployment resulting from them?

Most studies have emphasized the role of technological change, on the one hand, and that of international trade, capital movements and immigration, on the other; in other words, technology and globalization, which go hand in hand.

International trade and wages

Let us start with international trade. How can this affect wages? Competition from low-cost imports reduces the profitability of the firms that compete with them. They then reorient their production toward more profitable products. In other words, international trade gives rise to changes in domestic demand for factors of production. The import of products from countries where they are produced with more intensive use of cheaper, less productive, unskilled labor will tend to reduce the prices of these products and the profitability of their production, compared with the price and profitability of skilled labor-intensive products, so firms will reorient their production towards these. Since the supply of factors of production is fixed, this will entail a variation in their price and, above all, a fall in the relative earnings of lower-skilled workers. The most important factor in this link between foreign trade and wages is not so much the volume of goods imported or exported, as the *price* at which they are exchanged. This is the essence of the famous Stolper and Samuelson (1941) and Samuelson (1948 and 1949) theorem, which states that relative changes in the price of imports affect the price of the factors of production, increasing the return to some and decreasing it to other. Wages tend to increase for labor used intensively in sectors whose relative prices increase, and vice versa.

What needs to be analyzed therefore is whether the prices of goods in the OECD economies have changed in a way that indicates competition from imports from developing countries has reduced the relative earnings of low skilled or unskilled workers.

There is little evidence to confirm this link. In fact, various studies show the opposite, i.e. that during the 1980s and 1990s the price of goods produced using higher-skilled labor have fallen in relation to the price of goods produced using lower-skilled labor. This is shown by Lawrence and Slaughter (1993) and Sachs and Shatz (1994) for the United States, Neven and Wyplosz (1996) for the European Union, and Saeger (1996) and Slaughter and Swagel (1997) for the OECD and a whole.

Other empirical studies, such as those by Leamer (1998) and Baldwin and Cain (1997), show that, in the case of the United States, the relative prices of goods in skilled-labor intensive sectors fell in the 1970s, but they find no clear trend in the 1980s. Mathew Slaughter (1999) provides a detailed overview of these empirical studies.

Studies have also been carried out that take volume as well as price into account, and come to the conclusion that the impact has been small in both the United States (Revenga, 1992) and in Europe (Neven and Wyplosz, 1996). Despite the increasing importance of developing countries in the world economy and world trade, they account for just 20 percent to 40 percent of merchandise imports in the OECD, which is the equivalent of between 3 percent and 8 percent of GDP. In other words, neither their volume not their impact on prices have been large enough, at least up to now, to account for more than a small part of the wage dispersion, the increase in unemployment, or the shift in demand towards higher-skilled workers. This does not mean that the impact has been negligible for those workers at the bottom of the wage distribution who have been most affected. A European or US worker producing toys, textiles, or shoes in competition with Chinese workers whose wages are a tenth, and whose productivity is only slightly lower, stands little chance of keeping her job in the medium term unless he or she agrees to a pay cut.

Another way of measuring the impact of trade on wage dispersion is through "factor content" (Sachs and Shatz, 1994; Wood, 1994). This is established by calculating how much skilled and unskilled labor is used in the production of a country's merchanize exports and how much would have been used had it produced its imports. The difference between the two is taken to represent the impact on the demand for each type of labor, compared with the demand that would have existed in the absence of international trade. Both Sachs and Shatz, and Wood reach the conclusion that the demand for labor in industry falls as a result of trade, but to a greater extent in Wood's (1995) analysis. However, this form of measurement has been severely criticized (Freeman, 1995; Lawrence, 1994; Leamer, 1994; Deardoff and Hakura, 1994).

This debate about the impact of trade on wage inequality has brought labor market and development economists into conflict with their colleagues who specialize in international trade, as William Cline (1997) and Mathew Slaughter (1999) have shown.

International trade specialists believe that trade influences wages through the price of imports and exports. Although both developed and developing countries benefit from trade, the lowest-skilled workers in developed countries may lose out because the relative prices of the products they make are forced down by competition from goods imported from developing counties. Labor market economists believe that international trade affects labor markets in developed countries negatively through the volume of trade rather than prices. Importing goods from developing countries is the equivalent of importing the labor used in their production. In other words the import of unskilled labor intensive goods is the same as an increase in the supply of this labor in the importing country, and leads to a fall in the wages of these workers (Slaughter and Swagel, 1997).

Labor economists were the first to analyze this impact at the beginning of the 1990s, when they discovered that wage inequality was increasing, especially in the United States. The first studies, such as Bound and Johnson (1992), identified technological change as the most important factor responsible for this inequality, with trade and immigration some way behind. The same conclusion was reached by Mincer (1991) by Berman, Bound, and Griliches (1994) and by Minford et al. (1996). Other studies, such as Freeman (1991) give greater importance to the reduction in union membership and activity (between 15 percent and 40 percent).

Some labor market economists, however, believe that the impact of international trade and immigration are the main factors behind the decrease in relative wages among the low skilled. Borjas, Freeman, and Katz (1997) find that international trade and immigration account for 40 percent of wage inequality in the case of low-skilled workers and 20 percent of the whole. Borjas and Ramey (1994) and Karoly and Klerman (1994) come to similar conclusions.

Adrian Wood (1995), a development economist, identifies the impact of international trade as the most important factor, using a model based on the factor content of Northern imports. According to his model, between a third and two-thirds of wage inequality is related to international trade, through the import of manufactures from developing countries.

Subsequently, international trade economists have fiercely criticized these studies, showing that trade has had some impact on unskilled labor intensive sectors but in general this has been small. Krugman (1995a) has calculated it to be, at most, no more than 10 percent of the total. Cooper (1994) also offers a figure of 10 percent, while Baldwin and Cain (1997) suggest between 9 percent and 14 percent. Krugman and Lawrence (1994), Lawrence and Slaughter (1993) and Sachs and Shatz (1994) suggest lower or minimal figures, based on the relatively small weight that manufacturing imports from developing countries have within total US imports and manufactures. Feenstra and Hanson (1996) find out that foreign outsourcing from the US to Mexico accounts for 15 percent of the skilled–unskilled wage gap in US workers, while technological upgrading accounts for 35 percent of this rise.

Many of the differences between the two groups of economists are due to the different methods and models used, the different periods under consideration and the different groups of workers that have been linked to trade and migration flows. A new approach to this issue has recently been made by Peter Neary (2002) who has developed a model of oligopolistic instead of monopolistic competition, where he assumes that firms are large in their own markets but small in the world economy as a whole. His results show that North–North trade is as important as North–South trade in affecting the higher demand of skilled workers over unskilled ones because many firms, only under the expectations of higher competition from others in developed countries, make defensive investments in technology which raise their relative demand for skilled labor and therefore achieves the conclusion that the distinction between trade and technology shocks to the labor market in the relative demand for skilled labor is misplaced.

Francois, Grier, and Nelson (2004) also depart from the trade and wages literature and its emphasis on North–South trade, and examine North–North trade and relative linkages between trade-based integration and relative wages in an Ethier-type (1982) division of labor model. North–North trade is still much larger in volume than North–South trade and therefore a better potential explanatory variable when attempting to understand the link between globalization and wages. They find out a positive relationship between trade and the skill premium. Interestingly, that relationship is weker than would be implied without taking into account the relationship between trade and total factor productivity (TFP). With it, the magnitude of the effect is larger than most estimates.

Technological change and wages

Empirical studies on the impact of technological change on wage inequality have been more convincing and have shown that technological change, which favors skilled workers, has been a more important factor than international trade. On the one hand, technological change is partly related to trade. Competition from imports can have a greater effect on wages if it leads firms to introduce technology that replaces unskilled labor. However, the causality can run the other way: i.e., technological advances effect the structure of production and therefore international trade flows. And the opposite might even occur: That, as international trade brings down the price of lower-skilled labor intensive goods and raises the price of skilled labor and capital, it is possible to imagine an increase in the relative price of the latter which creates an incentive to develop technology that replaces them (Rowthorn and Ramaswamy, 1997). On the other hand, Krugman (1994) has shown how the development of information technology has significantly increased the productivity and earnings of those workers who use it. Foreign trade may favor the spread of this technology and, indirectly, the higher-skilled workers who know how to use it. Haskel and Slaughter (1998) find ample evidence of a correlation between technological change and increases in the productivity and earnings of higher-skilled workers, and the same conclusion has been reached by Feenstra and Hanson (1998), by Baldwin and Cain (1997), by Leamer (1998), by Berman et al. (1994), and by Wood (1995). A clear illustration of the importance of technology for wage inequality is that there has also been wage dispersion and a relative decrease in the wages of unskilled workers in developing countries (Robbins, 1996).

A study by Timothy Bresnahan (1999) explains in detail how the use of computers has affected wage inequality. They have steadily reduced the demand for lower-skilled workers in administrative tasks and increased the demand, on the one hand, for higher-skilled employees to deal with clients and, on the other hand, for directors and managers who are able to identify and bring in business. In other words, they have reduced the back office of companies and increased the front office and management.

Nevertheless, it is also important to understand the link between trade, industrialization, new technologies and geographical concentration. Until recently, most research in international economics ignored the location of economic activity inside countries. That is, the fact that the majority of industrial firms are located in cities or heavy populated regions and produce goods for urban consumers. Only at the beginning of the 1990s did theoretical work in international trade begin to incorporate geography into trade models (Krugman, 1991b) and (Fujita, Krugman, and Venables, 1999).

Globalization and the spread of digital and telecommunication technologies have the potential to alter the way people live and work. If lower communication costs free individuals from having to work in the cities, then, advanced countries could eventually become de-urbanized. Furthermore, if globalization continues to change national patterns of industrial specialization, it could also reorient the location of economic activities inside countries. Recent theory is based on the idea that geographic concentration results from a combination of increasing returns to scale in production and transport costs, that is, the total costs of doing business in different locations. Increasing returns to scale imply that larger firms are more efficient than small firms, creating an incentive to locate production in a few plants. Transport costs imply that firms prefer to locate near the large consumer markets. The interaction of these two forces creates an incentive for industrial firms to locate together, which contributes to the formation and development of cities. But, as soon as countries liberalize trade, positive transport costs imply that firms will relocate towards regions that have better access to world markets. For instance, when Mexico decided to open up to international trade and to join NAFTA, its industry was heavily concentrated in the macro city of Mexico DF, after its opening, many industries move closer to their main market, that is, the US, locating closer to the Mexico–US border and leaving the DF (Hanson, 1996) Moreover, with the development of new communication technologies, many cities will lose employment, mainly in services, to the benefit of other areas with less congestion, better climeate and lower land prices, where the demand for skilled and unskilled labor will increase.

Financial globalization and wage dispersion

The other aspect of globalization that can have an affect on wage dispersion is the mobility of capital. In principle, capital movements and the price of imports can have identical effects on wages, as Robert Mundell (1957) was the first to demonstrate, using the standard Heckscher–Ohlin model. His theory works in the following way: an increase in trade between the high-wage United States and low-wage Mexico can have some negative effects on lower-skilled US workers, who have to look for work in sectors that previously employed few unskilled workers. Suppose that General Motors relocates one of its production plants on the other side of the Mexican border to take advantage of the cheaper labor, i.e. sets up a *maquiladora*. As there is now less capital in the United States compared to the supply of workers, wages will tend to fall there and rise in Mexico. In other words, low-paid workers in the United States are not only threatened by the import of goods produced by cheap foreign labor, but also by the fact that this labor is equipped with capital exported from their own country.

Another corollary of this theory is that the imposition of import controls will not avoid the convergence of factor prices, especially those of labor, when there is unrestricted capital movement. As capital seeks to invest wherever it is most productive, import controls provoke the export of capital that not only tends to equalize factor prices but at the same time eliminates the need for trade. Capital movements and trade are substitutes for each other and tend to have the same effect on wages (Obstfeld, 1998).

This theory supports the growing concern about foreign direct investment by multinationals, leading to the so called 'export' of jobs, and the subcontracting of services by national companies outside their borders, to which unions and politicians attribute the fall in domestic employment and wages.

Although, as I make clear in the following chapter on multinationals, this has occurred in some labor-intensive industries, it does not appear that firms in advanced countries have substituted national for foreign workers to any great extent (Slaughter, 1995a; Feenstra and Hanson, 1996a; Feenstra and Hanson 1996b).

This problem is linked to what has been referred to as "social dumping" by poor countries that exploit their comparative advantage, not only in cheap labor but also in non-existent social protection, wretched working conditions and excessive working hours. However, these have always existed and always will. Europe did the same during the industrial revolution (Engels, 1845); and, as Paul Krugman (1997a) points out, in many poor countries, a badly paid job is better than no job at all. This issue should be approached solely as a question of the defense of human rights and not as a protectionist argument. In any case, it is not now, and does not appear that it will, in future, become a serious problem for the developed countries, except in some very capital-intensive artisan manufacturing. Social dumping by the shadow economy within many developed countries, especially Europe, is much more important (De la Dehesa, 1994).

Another effect of capital mobility is that it can increase the extent to which workers have to bear the adjustment costs of instability or a fall in the real terms of trade (i.e. a fall in the price of exports compared to those of imports), which means that their spending power or real incomes are reduced since this has the same effect as a devaluation. The effects of a fall in real terms of trade cannot be absorbed equally by all the factors of production because capital moves freely and therefore its risk-adjusted rate of return tends towards world rates. Labor therefore has to absorb most of the impact of the fall in the price of its output (IMF, 1997). An increase in capital mobility can therefore result in increased wage instability in the face of external shocks. This, in turn, may lead to, either, increased wage dispersion, if the wages of unskilled workers are adjusted downwards more quickly than those of skilled workers, or, as has been the case in Europe, to an increase in unskilled unemployment, if there is a combination of real downward rigidity in wages and high capital mobility. In the latter case, in other words, the effects of fluctuations in real terms of trade will be reflected in the number of workers employed, rather than on their wages.

Another area where the free movement of capital can generate inequality is between those whose income is derived from capital and those whose income is from labor (Fitoussi, 1997) for two reasons. Firstly, because capital can be invested wherever it provides the greatest return and, if it is diversified enough, the beneficiaries of income, capital gains and profits from this capital can increase their average returns and decrease their average risk, either by delocalizing industry or services, or by investing capital in countries offering high returns, providing a certain segmentation in the market exists, as it does today. This gives them a great advantage over wage earners who are relatively immobile and vulnerable to the risks of recession in the country where they work or the delocalization of their workplace. Secondly, the mobility of capital and the Internet make it increasingly difficult to tax the owners of capital because it is difficult to track its origin and destination. As a result, since the 1990s, tax revenues from capital have fallen and those from labor have increased. In other words, the owners of capital have greater advantages, because of their mobility, than those whose only income is from labor.

Migration and wages

Finally, another aspect of globalization is the, still small, increase in immigration. The proportion of illegal immigrants in the US population has risen from 4.8 percent in 1970, to 6.2 percent in 1980, to 7.9 percent in 1990, and may now stand at almost 10 percent (Borjas, Freeman, and Katz, 1997). The growth has been similar in Germany and slightly less in France.

In 2000, approximately 180 million people were living outside their countries of birth, 3 percent of the world's population, compared with only 75 million in 1965, and its rate of growth has since been accelerating. The majority of these people moved from developing to developed countries.

One of the reasons for the limited increase in immigration over the last few decades could be income convergence. As earnings in poor countries increase, if the difference in wages between an advanced economy, which is a destination for migration, and a poor country, from which there is net emigration, falls to less that four to one, migration from the latter to the former diminishes or stops (Straubhaar, 1988). But since the 1980s, the large asymmetry in demographic trends between industrial and developing countries has more than compensated for the effects of income convergence.

Emigration is also closely related to international trade. As one diminishes the other increases because, as Mundell (1957) shows, international trade is a substitute for the movement of factors of production. Imports of unskilled labor-intensive goods from poor countries by developed ones are a perfect substitute for the migration of this labor in the same direction. As long as the workers in question have jobs in the exporting industries, they will have less incentive to emigrate and they will also be exporting their labor time embodied in the exported product. This is the equivalent of having employed it in the production a similar good in the importing country. For this reason emigration can have the same effect on wage inequality in developed countries as international trade.

Nevertheless, because immigrants tend to be less skilled than workers in the country of destination, they may have a negative effect on the wages and/or the employment of the least-skilled domestic workers in that country. However, empirical studies show that these effects are still small. Friedberg and Hunt (1995) have shown this for the United States and Zimmerman (1995) has done the same for Europe.

If, on the other hand, immigrants are higher skilled than the average domestic worker, as is the case of Russian Jewish immigration into Israel, this can lead to higher growth in the receiving country because their high level of human capital compensates for the initial decrease in the stock of per capita physical capital. In addition, the higher level of the new human capital tends to increase the returns on physical capital in the receiving country (Martin, 1996).

An interesting point of view of the effects of immigration is shown by Fredrik Anderson and Kai Konrad (2001). They start from the well established fact that there is a high marginal tax burden on human capital returns in most OECD countries and that, at the same time these countries spend a considerable share of their budgets on subsidized public provision of education. Governments tax the returns on human capital heavily because this tax base is rather inelastic at the time when the tax rate is chosen. At the time when individuals choose their human capital investment they anticipate the high tax rate burden and this prevents them from investing as much as they would like. Governments would like to commit to choosing lower tax rates than the ones they actually chose because they would yield better private investment incentives in human capital, but when the returns from those investments accrue, thirty years later, these investments cannot be reversed, and they feel tempted to tax them heavily. As they are aware of this hold-up problem that leads to underinvestment in human capital, they then try to subsidize education to overcome the problem it generates for its own "time inconsistent" tax policy.

The authors find out that globalization and a greater propensity to migration among skilled workers removes the hold-up problem of excessive taxation. If workers can migrate freely and if governments choose their taxes independently, the problem disappears because of tax competition, which reinstalls the correct private incentives for human capital investment, and no government corrective educational policy is needed.

Finally, there are other factors that affect wages and wage dispersion. In a very interesting study by Richard Freeman and Remco Oostendorp (2000) who have transformed the "October Enquiry" of the International Labor Organization into a consistent data file on pay in 161 occupations in over 150 countries from 1983 to 1998, the file shows that: Skill differentials vary inversely with the gross domestic product per capita. During the 1980s and 1990s they fell modestly in advanced countries, fell more sharply in upper middle-income countries and rised markedly in countries moving from communism to free market and in lower middle income countries. Wages in the same occupation vary greatly across countries measured by common currency exchange rates and purchasing power parity. Cross-country differences in pay for comparable work increased, despite larger world trade. They conclude that according to the new data file, the principal forces that affect occupational wage structures around the world are the level of gross domestic product per capita and unionization and wage-setting institutions.

Conclusion

What conclusions can we draw about the impact of globalization on deindustrialization, increased unemployment and wage inequality in the developed countries?

The available evidence so far shows that deindustrialization in the developed world should be seen as a natural part of the development process in advanced economies, both in the sense of an increasingly wealthy population demanding more and better services, and of technological progress centered on knowledge production rather than manufacturing.

There is much less evidence that globalization has had an impact on employment than politicians, workers and unions seem to think. Once again it is the development of information technologies that has had the greater impact on employment and wages in unskilled and administrative jobs. Most probably, the main reason for this is the high and increasing value that the demand for labor places on education. This has grown at a much higher rate than the supply, leading to wage inequality in more flexible countries, such as the United States, and unemployment for those with lower levels of education and training in more rigid ones, such as Japan and continental Europe.

Finally, there is more evidence on the link between globalization and wage inequality, especially in the United States and the United Kingdom, and on increased unemployment in continental Europe but there is still not a great deal. On average the empirical studies carried out suggest that technology has three times the impact of trade and immigration together. There is little evidence of the effect of capital movements on this inequality, but it may be relatively more important.

What measures can be taken to improve the employment prospects and relative incomes of lower-skilled workers?

In the short term, the most effective policy would be to increase transfers payments to lower-skilled workers through a tax increase on higher-skilled workers and the owners of capital. Transfers from wealthier to poorer workers are already taking place in various countries; transfers from capital owners are much more difficult to bring about because capital mobility makes it increasingly difficult to levy taxes. This high level of mobility, together with the competition to secure investment is in fact having the opposite effect.

Various suggestions have been made as to how to tackle these problems. At the time of German reunificiation, George Akerlof, Rose Yellen, and H. Hessenius (1991) suggested that subsidising the jobs of workers in East Germany would reduce their level of unemployment without increasing public spending, because this would pay for itself through a reduction in unemployment benefits. More recently, Edmund Phelps (1997) has proposed subsidies for the lowest-paid workers in the United States, the 125 billion dollar cost of which would be recouped through lower unemployment benefits and increased tax revenue. In relation to the high level of long-term unemployment in Europe, Dennis Snower and Guillermo de la Dehesa (1993) have suggested that workers could choose between receiving unemployment payments and transferring them temporally to a company that hires them. This system would not only avoid any extra costs on public spending, but also it would generate higher revenue in the medium term. Hans Werner Sinn (2004) shows that the best and cheapest way to defend the wages and social benefits of unskilled workers in developed countries against wage competition from immigrants is through wage subsidies to national unskilled workers, excluding, temporarily, the immigrants.

In the long term, the only effective policy is to increase the skill levels of low-paid and unemployed workers through a massive program of spending on education and training, especially in the new information technologies and knowledge-based services.

Globalization and the Size of Firms: Multinationals

Multinational companies are the main agency through which globalization is taking place, and globalization is in turn promoting the rapid development of multinational or global companies. In other words they feed off and reinforce each other.

Globalization and the development of multinational companies

The reason for this interrelationship is very clear. A study of companies in the European Union, by Kumar, Rajan, and Zingales (1999), concludes that they are becoming increasingly global; that globalization is a process which promotes the growth of large companies because to be successful and increase their market share they need a presence in the maximum number of countries. There is therefore a high and increasing correlation between the size of the market and the size of companies. According to the recent World Investment Report from the United Nations (UNCTAD, 2004) 61,000 parent multinationals, many of which are medium or occasionally small in size, have established more than 900,000 affiliates in all the counties of the world. Of these 61,000 parent companies, 50,000 are based in developed countries. Their affiliates have sales worth almost eight trillion dollars, i.e. the equivalent of the United States GDP or more than double the value of world exports, and these are growing at a much faster rate than exports, by between 20 percent and 30 percent. The affiliates of US multinationals alone sell three times as much in the countries where they operate, as total US exports. Despite this, the United States has a huge trade deficit. This paradox raises an interesting question. In a completely globalized world, counting transactions between residents and non-residents, such as imports and exports, in the balance of payments, loses a great deal of its significance. In the integrated European Union, transactions between member countries are classified as sales, rather than imports or exports, because they take place in the same market. Perhaps in the future, when globalization is much more advanced, it will become necessary to count international transactions in the balance of payments, not in terms of where the companies involved are located but in terms of their ownership. If that were the case today, the United States would have a huge surplus instead of its present large deficit, because the sales by its multinationals' affiliates would be included in the calculation.

The fact is that multinationals are currently responsible for two-thirds of world exports of goods and services and almost 10 percent of all domestic sales in the world. This gives some idea of their growing importance.

Multinational companies have a decisive influence on international trade not only because of the volume they generate, but also because they are radically changing its pattern: from one based on traditional inter-industrial trade to one based on intra-industrial or intra-firm trade. In other words, from one (inter-industrial) in which countries specialize in, and export, specific products in which they have an absolute or relative comparative advantage, and import others in which they do not have such an advantage, or that they need for consumption or to add value to their production or exports, to another pattern (intra-industrial or intra-firm) based increasingly on trade between parent companies and their foreign affiliates. In 1997, intra-firm trade represented more than 40 percent of total OECD country trade. Automobile companies, for example, design models in the parent company where they also control marketing, quality control, financing, and insurance, and produce parts in whichever affiliate is the cheapest or most convenient. They then assemble models in different countries according to local tastes, national or regional technical specifications, and the size of the market. This international division of labor creates an increasing amount of trade within each company, between its affiliates located in many different countries. Spain's principal imports and exports originate in the automobile industry and are accounted for, overwhelmingly, by half a dozen multinationals; through the trade between their plants in Spain, their subcontractors and their plants in other countries, as well as the parent companies.

The second way in which multinationals play an enormously important role in globalization is as a conduit for foreign direct investment (FDI). At the end of 1996 the total stock of FDI in production plants, machinery and real estate owned by multinationals outside their countries of origin amounted to more than three trillion dollars, equivalent to Japan's GDP. FDI has increased three times as quickly as domestic investment, though it still only represents the equivalent of 7 percent of the total domestic investment in the OECD countries.

The 100 biggest non-financial multinationals, of which 90 are from the "triad" of the United States, the European Union, and Japan, have an accumulated FDI of 1.8 trillion dollars, almost two-thirds of the total.

The third function of multinationals is the diffusion of technology around the world (Vernon, 1966 and 1974; Magee, 1977). Seventy percent of all the payments for royalties or technology made in the world are between multinationals and their affiliates.

Finally, it should not be forgotten that multinationals pay better wages to their employees and create more stable employment. In Turkey, for example, the wages they pay are 24 percent higher than those paid by local companies, and in the late 1990s they have increased their work force by 11.5 percent, while the local companies only increased theirs by 0.6 percent (*Economist*, 2000).

The most coherent explanation for the growth of multinationals is the existence of economies of scale (Dunning, 1958; Hymer, 1976; Buckley and Casson 1976) both in specialization, technology, and R&D, and in purchasing, advertising and experience, as well as economies of scope to take advantage of synergies among the above. These size-related savings make multinationals more efficient, less vulnerable to losing their independence and more able to absorb smaller competitors. There are exceptions: Boeing and Airbus, which dominate the commercial aviation market, are unusually large but nevertheless are not multinationals because they do not manufacture or subcontract in a large number of countries. Instead they are concentrated in a few plants.

Theory

The economic theory of multinationals (Caves, 1982; Ethier, 1986) sets out to explain why they organize production through affiliates in a large number of countries, instead of exporting directly from production plants in their home countries, when transport costs are falling rapidly. For example, why do US automobile multinationals produce in neighboring Mexico or Canada, or even Latin America, Europe, and Asia and not export directly from the United States?

The modern theory of multinationals divides this question into two parts (Krugman and Obstfeldt, 1991). The first is: Why produce in various countries and not in just one? This is known as location theory. The second is: Why is production in different countries controlled by the same firm and not by separate ones? This is known as internalization theory. The former explains why Mexico and Canada do not import cars from the United States and the latter why Mexican and Canadian industry is not independently controlled by national capital.

Location theory is easy to understand (Vernon, 1974; Dicken and Lloyd, 1990). The location of production is often determined by natural resources. For example aluminium smelting must be located where bauxite is available and electricity is cheap. Manufacturers of minicomputers or PCs have to locate their design and prototype production where there are science and engineering skills and a highly qualified workforce, such as in Massachusetts or northern California, and locate final assembly, the most labor intensive stage of production, where labor is cheapest, for example, in southeast Asia. Other determining factors are transport costs and trade barriers. The cases of Mexico and Canada are explicable less because of transport costs than because of quotas and other import barriers. When production is located in countries further away from the United States, such as South Africa or Australia, transport costs are a bigger part of the explanation, although these are falling. Location theory, therefore, is based on the same arguments as general trade theory.

Internalization theory is more complex (Coase, 1937; Williamson, 1975). Operations spread across several countries involve high transaction costs and multinationals exist because these costs fall substantially when they are internalized. Production from one affiliate is usually the input for another, and vice versa. Technology developed in one affiliate can be used in the others. It is cheaper to coordinate a large number of affiliates than to managed them separately. This does not mean that all transactions have to take place within companies. Components can be bought from and sold to other companies, and technology can be licensed. But most of these transactions are cheaper if they take place within the same company. There are two fundamental arguments as to why this is the case.

The first emphasizes the advantages of internalization for technology transfer. Although, from the economic point of view, technology is seen as useful knowledge that can be sold, licensed or franchised, there are problems in doing this. The knowledge needed to run a factory cannot be easily written down, packaged and sold because it consists of the knowledge and experience of a group of individuals. On the one hand, it is difficult for the buyer to know the value of the product, since knowledge is an intangible that is difficult to value. If the buyer knew its value, he or she would not have to buy it. Finally, not only intellectual property rights are hard to establish, but also, once a technology has been licensed, it can be easily copied, by other competing companies, when clear legal mechanisms do not exist to safeguard them. All these problems can be overcome if, instead of selling a technology to another company, an affiliate is set up and the technology transferred to it.

The second argument focuses on the benefits of internalization for vertical integration. If an upstream company produces a good that is used as an input by a company further downstream a number of problems may arise. The first is that if both companies have a monopolistic or oligopolistic position there may be a conflict over price: the former will try to maximize it and the latter to minimize it. There may also be problems of coordination if there are uncertainties over demand and supply. Finally, an excessive fluctuation in the price might represent a serious risk for one or other of the companies. It is possible to avoid or reduce the importance of these problems by vertically integrating both processes within the same company.

However, the evidence on internalization is not as clear as that on location, because it has not been as widely studied; since multinationals have only been in existence for a relatively short time, and both the speed of technological change and the environment in which they operate create uncertainty.

One fairly recent development in the operation of some multinational companies is outsourcing and offshoring: that is, the subcontracting of the services or part of production process to companies within, or increasingly outside, the multinational group and relocating them to other companies within the same country (outsourcing) or to other companies, owned by the parent company or through joint ventures with domestic companies in developing, or even other developed, countries (offshoring). New computer and telecommunication technologies allow greater control to be exercised over transaction costs and reduce the advantages of internalization.

Taken to its extreme, this process leads to the "virtual" company, and the disintegration or displacement of the production process analyzed in the previous chapter. This is a company in which the role of parent is reduced to the minimum leaving it with control over design, technology, quality, the brand name, marketing, advertising, finance, and distribution. The rest is subcontracted out in various countries, on long-term contracts for the supply of parts, components, and assembling, as well as external administrative, auditing, systems and services, either with companies owned by the parent or to non-owned foreign companies. Dell computers is one of the companies that most approximates to this model. The development of the Internet and the other information and communications technologies may lead to extremely important changes of this sort, in the near future, in the way multinationals are organized and operate.

One of the problems faced by multinationals is the cost of employing workers in different cultural, legal, educational, and linguistic contexts. Edward Lazear (1999) argues that these costs are offset by the benefits to be gained from employing complementary factors of production that can be found more easily or cheaply in other countries or cultures. The important thing is to instill in them the ideas of best practice and team-work, which will lead to a reduction in costs. To do this, a single working language is essential even if this means paying higher wages to bilingual workers, hence the widespread use of English worldwide.

Types of multinationals

Modern theory distinguishes between two types of multinational: vertical and horizontal. The former are those that distribute the stages of the production process geographically, according to the intensity of the factors of production used. Skilled labor-intensive activities are located where this is more abundant and therefore cheaper (in the advanced countries), as are lower-skilled labor-intensive activities (in the developing countries) and the same applies to natural resources or to capital. Different theoretical models for vertical multinationals have been constructed by Helpman (1984), Helpman and Krugman (1985), and Lall (1980).

Horizontal multinationals are multiplant enterprises that replicate essentially the same productive activities at a number of locations, taking advantage of economies of scale and reductions in transport costs. Models of this type have been developed by Markusen (1984) and by Lipsey

(1984). There has, recently, been an attempt to integrate the two models of multinationals in a "knowledge–capital" model (Markusen and Maskus, 1999), which is based on the idea that knowledge is geographically mobile and acts as an input for each multiproduction plant. Recent empirical evidence provides more support for the horizontal model (Brainard, 1997), although it also supports the knowledge–capital model. Vertical multinationals operate, to a greater extent, in countries that have different levels of development, with the center of operations situated in the most developed. Horizontal multinationals generally operate in similar countries with the center of operations in the country with the largest national market. The knowledge–capital model can be found in both types of situation: in similar countries and those with different endowments of skilled labor. In the latter case the center of operations is located in the country with the most skilled labor and the main production facilities are located in countries with the biggest market and/or the largest pool of cheap unskilled labor.

A clear distinction has also been made between plants located to produce locally for large national markets, and those located to produce for export, in which case labor costs are the determining factor.

Another important distinction is between multinational companies and global companies (Ohmae, 1990; Porter, 1990), i.e. companies with the majority of their production and work force located outside their home countries. On average, two-thirds of a multinational's production, and two-thirds of its workforce, will be in its home country. However, there are a handful of companies that have over 50 percent of their assets, sales and employees located abroad and can therefore be defined as global. These include Royal Dutch–Shell, Exxon–Mobil, Volkswagen–Audi, IBM, Bayer, ABB, Nissan, Elf Aquitaine, and Nestlé. Nestlé has 87 percent of its assets, 98 percent of its production, and 97 percent of its workforce located outside Switzerland. Clearly these are, in the main, companies whose parent is located in a small country or oil companies that inevitably have to locate most of their exploration, production, and refining plants in producing countries. The same applies to chemical and pharmaceutical companies that have to overcome barriers in the form of local health regulations, and automobile companies that have to avoid quotas and other trade barriers, especially in countries with large local markets. Peter Dicken (1998) strongly opposes Ohmae's idea of "denationalized" global companies. In his opinion all companies "belong" to a specific country and retain a close loyalty to it.

In an increasingly globalized world, those companies, which cross borders and try to serve the world market, are the ones that prosper most. Alternatively, a company will normally disappear when it is bought by a more successful rival. In other words, the growth of multinational companies is an obvious consequence of globalization and prosperity. Globalization means that competition is much fiercer, so only the most competitive companies survive and grow by merging with or buying their competitors. Once they have become large multinationals it is difficult for them to be displaced or bought. This can be seen from the fact that two-thirds of the 100 biggest multinationals today were in the same list ten years ago.

The development of large multinationals also obliges the companies they subcontract to, for parts and components, or even their own affiliates, to become multinationals themselves, because large companies require a homogeneous product near each of their plants. The same has happened to auditing firms, consultants, and commercial and investment banks. These have increasingly located in the same places as their large multinational clients.

Grossman and Helpman (2002) have looked at the main determinants of the choice of outsourcing versus FDI by multinational firms in an industry in which producers need specialized components and potential suppliers need to make a relationship-specific investment in order to serve each prospective customer. They find out that such investments are governed by imperfect contracts. A final-good producer can manufacture components for himself but its per-unit cost is higher than for specialized suppliers. Therefore, there are a number of factors that cause firms to outsource the production of components relative to those that produce their own components in foreign subsidiaries and determine how production in a globalized world is organized.

Starting from a position of industry equilibrium, the first is the difference in productivity between specialized and integrated producers of inputs. An increase in the productivity advantage of firms that specialize in producing components raises the fraction of firms that engage in outsourcing. The second is size. An expansion of the market size also raises the fraction of firms that outsource. An increase in the industry size favors outsourcing as well because it increases the spending on final products relative to prices and costs and generates more demand for specialized manufacturers of components. The third is contracts. The more complete the contracts that can be written to govern the relationship-specific investments, the larger the fraction of firms engaged in outsourcing. The fourth is the relative wage. An increase in the relative wage in the developing country reduces the fraction of firms that outsource. A fall in the relative wage in the developed country tends to reduce world income to the cost of entry by intermediate produces and increases the relative cost of product design, which tends to reduce the production of final goods and, therefore, the profitability and number of component producers.

Another important contribution to this issue is made by Swenson (2004). He looks at the pattern of US overseas assembly activities between 1980 and 2000 and examines how outsourcing decisions are affected by changes in country and competitor costs. A number of interesting regularities emerge. When a country's assembly costs rise, the share of US overseas assembly activities fall in that location. Conversely, a country's share of US overseas assembly activities grows when a competitor country's costs increase. While own and competitor country costs affect overseas assembly in all countries, the magnitude of these effects is larger for developing countries than it is for developed countries. If more developed countries produce goods that are more highly differentiated than those originating from developing countries, cost changes may exert a greater influence on decisions about more homogeneous products assembled in developing countries. Further, higher skill levels in developed countries may also provide better insulation from cost- based production shifts. To the extent that lower-skilled workers are more interchangeable, there may be fewer frictions that prevent the movement of simple assembly operations from a low-wage developing country to the next, such as the search costs that are highlighted in Grossman and Helpman (2004). Therefore, developing countries are more adversely affected by increases on their own costs or declines in competitor costs than are developed countries. It also depends on the industry characteristics. The allocation of outsourcing activities in less capital-intensive industries responds more vigourously to costs changes than outsourcing activities in more capital intensive industries.

Why multinationals are subject to critique?

Their large size and their rapid growth have made multinationals the object of widespread criticism: First, by governments. As they are responsible for the vast majority of foreign direct investment, countries compete to attract them at whatever cost, because they rightly consider them of enormous importance for their growth and development. This means that governments feel a loss of sovereignty, especially in the case of small countries, when they have to accede to the demands of a private company. The criticism is even stronger when a multinational decides to move to another country because it considers that the labor, environmental, or tax legislation is too restrictive. But that does not happen very often because companies try to negotiate better conditions with the government of the day before they move. On other occasions the complaints are more justifiable, especially when multinationals evade taxes in some countries by moving their profits to offshore tax havens, through transfer pricing, inflated loans or other internal mechanisms. It is understandable that many small countries feel at a disadvantage compared to large multinationals.

In a small country such as Ireland, multinationals represent 50 percent of total employment and 66 percent of production. Most European regions or small countries would want to be in a similar situation because, thanks to this multinational investment, Ireland has increased its productivity and its per capita income more quickly than any other country in the European Union.

A second set of criticisms comes from trade unions, especially in the developed countries, where they put increases in unemployment down to the transfer of production to low-wage countries. However this delocalization only takes place in the production of labor-intensive goods such as clothing, shoes, toys, etc., not in the majority of products. It should not be forgotten that, on average, labor costs represent 10 percent of the cost of production in OECD countries, so this form of delocalization cannot be of very great importance. Another union criticism is that investment abroad replaces exports and therefore reduces employment in a multinational's home country while increasing it abroad.

Despite these criticisms, all developing and many developed countries try to attract as much foreign direct investment as they can and know the way to do so is by attracting investment from multinationals. In recent years about 60 percent of foreign direct investment by multinationals has been in developed countries, especially the United States, but also in Europe, and 40 percent in developing countries, above all in emerging markets with the greatest growth potential: Asia and Latin America. China, Brazil, and Mexico have been the recipients of most FDI, mainly thanks to the size of their domestic markets.

Almost 50 percent of all FDI is accounted for by cross-border mergers and acquisitions, designed to achieve economies of scale, increased market shares and to develop global networks. Most of these mergers and acquisitions take place between companies in developed countries, which are the ones who are really competing for regional or world leadership, with US companies playing an especially important role. Of the 500 largest companies in the world, 222 are from the United States, 130 from the European Union, 71 from Japan, 28 from the rest of Asia, 8 from Latin America, 8 from Africa and 33 from the rest of the world (Canada, 13; Australia, 8; Switzerland 9; and Russia, 3). With a few exceptions – Switzerland, which has 9, Holland with 13, Sweden with 8, and, above all, the United Kingdom with 51 – there is a discernible relationship between the size of a country's GDP at current prices and the number of large companies based there. Spain, which has 2 percent of world GDP, has 6 of the top 500, i.e., 1.2 percent, and so has fewer than could be expected. Germany and France, with 8 percent and 5.5 percent of world GDP, respectively, only have 4.2 percent and 3.8 percent of these companies (*Financial Times*, 2004). The clear bias in favor of Anglo-Saxon countries (United States, United Kingdom, Holland, etc.) is probably due to their more advanced capital markets. This allows their firms to grow and to finance their mergers and acquisitions more easily. Kumar *et al.* (1999) confirm that firms tend to be bigger in countries with more developed financial systems.

Globalization and the size of firms

We can expect that as the globalization process advances, firms will grow in size, and the number and volume of mergers and acquisitions will increase. Global M&As in 1990 were less than $500 billions in value and they have been increasing to 1 trillion in 1995 reaching $3.1 trillion in 2000. After the bursting of the "financial bubble" they came down to $1.6 trillion in 2001, to $1.2 trillion in 2002 and they have started to recover in 2003 with $1.3 trillion. There is a large concentration of M&A activity in the US and in Europe, where they account for 77 percent of the total value (Thomson Financial, 2004). In 2003, hostile M&A activity has increased as well, driven by overcapacity in some key sectors of production, which pushes industry leaders to consider consolidation.

How big can firms grow? Theorists disagree about this. As ever, Adam Smith was the first to suggest that firm size is related to the size of the market. Lucas (1978) uses a neoclassical model to explain size in relation to the amount of management ability available, which increases with per capita income. Rosen (1982) shows that size is limited by management's control and supervision capacity because it shows decreasing returns as the firms grow in size. Kremer (1993) identifies the availability if human capital is the key variable: the more a country has, the bigger its firms will be. Other economists (Grossman and Hart, 1986) suggest that size depends on the number of available physical assets that can be owned. Others (Caves, 1998; Sutton, 1997) suggest that size depends on national anti-monopoly regulations and legislation on barriers to entry. Finally, others relate the size of firms to the development of financial systems and to the factors that contribute to it (Pagano, Panetta, and Zingales, 1998).

Is it possible that the spectacular growth in the size of firms will undermine competition and create global monopolies? This obviously will not happen because national authorities exist in every country to ensure that competition is not infringed. However, in a globalized world, national authorities will not be enough. The European Union has the Directorate General for Competition and a Commissioner to oversee the whole union competition issue. There will, therefore, have to be close collaboration between all national authorities or global regulation of competition. It seems logical that the country where a monopolistic company is based will not be the first to take action because it benefits from the company's position, though this has not been the case with Microsoft in the United States, perhaps because it damages the interests of other domestic firms. Edward Graham and David Richardson (1997) have analyzed this problem in detail. They identify three alternatives: the present situation, which is inefficient because national competition authorities take unilateral action without coordinating this with other institutions; the alternative of unilateral action coordinated bilaterally with other countries, within integrated regions or through international organization and, finally, the alternative of a supranational mechanism.

It is the third of these alternatives that has shown the best results so far, since the European Union has followed this route successfully over a number of years through its Directorate General IV. The problem is that it will be very difficult to apply this model at international level, at least in the next few years. So the second alternative is likely to have more of a future. Graham and Richardson, therefore, suggest two possibilities: the first is that the WTO uses its settlement of disputes procedure and consultation system to coordinate unilateral action of different countries; the second is that an agreement on trade-related anti-monopoly measures (TRAMS), equivalent to those for trade-related investment measures (TRIMS) and trade-related intellectual property rights (TRIPS), is signed by WTO members. This would provide a mechanism for dealing with situations of monopoly, cartelization, discrimination, unfair trade agreements, etc. that go beyond national markets.

Finally, the size and multinational nature of some companies raises the question of their problematic relations with governments. Economists are divided on this issue. For some, such as Vernon (1971), multinationals may be able to dominate governments, both in their home and host countries, but he sees this as beneficial because these countries are more than compensated by the enormous gains in welfare and other benefits to their economies. The opposite position is taken by Barnett and Muller (1974) and Tolchin and Tolchin (1998, 1992), who see these companies as a threat to society against which governments are impotent, that have perverse effects especially on host countries. Others such as Gilpin (1975) think they are the imperialist or mercantilist instruments of their home governments. Finally, others such as Bergsten, Horst, and Moran (1978) believe that they have virtually no effects on their home countries and usually come to mutually beneficial agreements with host governments to maximize profits, taxation, employment, and exports for both sides. It is difficult to say who is right in this debate because there have in fact been examples of behavior by multinationals that support each position. However the latter position seems the most reasonable. Multinationals and governments need each other and usually come to an agreed solution that avoids either side losing out. They agree on a situation in which the company maximizes a reasonable level of profit and the government maximizes its fiscal revenue and the firm's contribution to generating economic activity and employment. Game theory is very useful for finding this sort of solution.

The best solution, however, as Graham (1996) suggests, is for governments to cooperate in finding a constructive way of regulating these companies, through the relevant international organization (WTO, OECD) or through regional integration authorities (European Union, NAFTA, Mercosur, APEC, etc.).

In conclusion we can see that by widening markets and increasing competition, globalization creates huge opportunities for the development of companies and the countries in which they are located, as well as huge challenges of adjustment and transformation, for them to be able cope with a much more competitive world.

Only those companies and countries able to meet these challenges will be the winners in this new situation and will be able to exploit the tremendous opportunities that globalization is offering. This will be the great challenge to business in the twenty-first century. The internationalization and globalization of firms will help the countries where they originate and those they move to, bringing investment, knowledge, and technology.

In this process there are undoubtedly dangers concerning size, the formation of oligopolies and monopolies, difficulties in controlling the behavior of large multinational companies, and, finally, in safeguarding competition. These problems will have to be resolved through greater coordination and cooperation between governments, and through supranational institutions, to minimize the possibility of abuses of power and the infringement of competition, and ensure that the positive aspects that the internationalization or globalization of firms undoubtedly has for all countries, are enjoyed.

We have to get used to the fact that, thanks to the globalization process, companies rather than states will be the leading actors in the world economy. However, states still have the regulatory power to ensure that this process is a success and minimize its possible adverse effects on competition.

Globalization, State, and Government

Economic globalization is having, and will increasingly have in the future, a significant impact on the way the state is understood, in terms of its functions, policies, size, and number, which will inevitably lead to a radical redefinition and restructuring. The world of politics and its institutions is undergoing profound change that cannot be ignored, and will be analyzed in this chapter.

Globalization and the number and size of states

If we compare the number of countries existing in 1946, after the Second World War, with those today, we see that the number has multiplied two and half times. In 1946 there were 74 countries and today there are almost 200, with more appearing every year.

The most important factors behind this increase are the decolonization process, in its widest sense, and the rise of nationalism, but globalization and the opening of markets are enabling these new countries to survive once they have separated from their colonial or dominating power. The decolonization of Africa gave rise to 48 new states; the dismemberment of the Soviet empire to 15; Yugoslavia having split into 5 states. These and many others would find it very difficult to survive if an increasingly open, globalized economy did not exist in the world.

In other words small countries have, by definition, got to live from trade because they lack the minimum resources necessary for self-sufficiency, and they are therefore the greatest beneficiaries from globalization (Alesina and Spolaore, 1997).

There are 85 countries in the world today with fewer than 5 million inhabitants, including 40 with fewer than 2.5 million, 35 of which have fewer than half a million (*Economist*, 1997a).

These small countries not only survive, they also tend to be more prosperous than bigger ones. Of the 10 biggest countries in the world, with more than 100 million inhabitants, only the United States and Japan are really prosperous; six (China, India, Indonesia, Pakistan, Bangladesh and Nigeria) have per capita incomes below 1,000 dollars a year; the rest, Brazil and Russia, have incomes of just above 5,000 and 2,000 dollars respectively. Of the ten smallest, with fewer than 100,000 inhabitants, only two (Kiribati and Tuvalu) are poor, having per capita incomes of below 1,000 dollars a year, while the rest (St. Vincent, Tonga, Grenada, Seychelles, Dominica, Antigua and Barbuda, St Kitts and Nevis, and Nauru) have per capita incomes between 1,600 and 8,000 dollars a year. There are also very small wealthy countries, such as Luxembourg and Monaco in Europe or Brunei, Singapore, and Hong Kong in Asia.

How can these small countries be viable entities? The reasons are: First, because they tend to be more globalized than the big countries and, therefore, more dependent on trade and international finance. Their average trade to GDP ratio is 80 percent, three times higher than that for developed countries. Second, they are viable because they have been able to exploit better the enormous development of transport and communications technology and from the general growth in services, which provide them with the resources they lack: from natural resources to finance or information. Third, many small countries have been able to increase their efficiency through specializing in the production of services, either in finance or in tourism, which have a higher rate of productivity than agricultural production. Fourth, the poorest of them have easier access to foreign aid, given that the sums they receive are very small in absolute terms, but they represent an important part of their GDP. Finally, they can overcome the political disadvantages of being small, i.e., the lack of negotiating power internationally, by joining regional defense or economic organizations, where they normally have greater voting power than their populations would warrant.

What kind of implications does this have for the future? Three are particularly important. Firstly, the fact that there are a large number of small independent states, which can only survive in an open globalized economic world, is a guarantee that the globalization process will continue. The growing number of small countries will insist that markets stay open. They will lobby for multilateral trade negotiations, through the WTO, to take precedence over the regionalization of trade dominated by large blocs. A reversal in the process would be fatal for their survival. Second, the more open they are, the harder it is for them to avoid democracy. Countries that are closed to trade and international investment can maintain dictatorships or authoritarian regimes. Once they have been opened up, the markets bring these regimes to an end. One of the positive aspects of the Asian crisis is that it has brought down, or is undermining, a whole series of corrupt, closed, and non-democratic regimes. The cases of Korea or Indonesia are clear examples.

Finally, there is another implication that is of enormous political importance for many countries. An increasingly open and globalized world makes the disintegration of existing political entities more likely (Alesina, Spolaore, and Wacziarg, 1997). Globalization tends to favor separatist politics. Many small regions that are homogeneous from a cultural, linguistic, or ethnic point of view may attempt to democratically negotiate their independence from the countries in which they are integrated. In an increasingly democratic and open world, minorities will be able to freely choose greater autonomy or even independence. The voluntary separation of Slovakia, which was the poorest part of the old Czechoslovakia, from the Czech Republic would not have been possible in a more closed and less globalized world.

Globalization and the erosion of the nation-state

Some of the economic and political foundations of the nation-state are being undermined by economic globalization. The liberalization of trade and international investment, together with the falling cost of transport and the increased speed with which goods, services, and ideas reach all countries from anywhere in the world, have demolished one of these foundations: the idea of national self-sufficiency. Since the Second World War, an increasing proportion of the goods and services for domestic consumption have been supplied by imports, at low or moderate prices. The idea of national self-sufficiency has been reduced to the maintenance of strategic stocks of petroleum, gas, and grain. Even the European common agricultural policy, which is based on this antiquated idea, has proved itself to be expensive and unviable in the medium term, if the WTO Millennium Round finally goes ahead.

The development of communications, transport, and information technologies has allowed the citizens of different countries to know each other better, and this makes it increasingly difficult for nationalism to be used as the cohesive force in nation-states. It is very difficult in the present situation to try to demonstrate that the citizens of another country are different or worse than one's own, because the barriers to mutual understanding that can prevent people discovering the opposite, no longer exist. Traditional nationalist arguments now only have an impact in very underdeveloped or isolated countries.

Another foundation of the nation-state to be washed away is that of national security. Very few countries in the world can defend themselves, unaided, from a nuclear attack or from chemical or bacteriological warfare. National security is so important that countries safeguard it by integrating themselves into supranational or international organizations such as the European Conference for Security and Cooperation or NATO. Almost no country can now guarantee its own security. The same is true of terrorism, drugs trafficking, and environmental problems, each of which have a global dimension and can only be confronted through international cooperation or supranational organizations.

This growing lack of national independence in the face of economic, political or security problems means that the nation-state is slowly giving ground to regional integration or supranational institutions.

At the same time, citizens are becoming more demanding of their politicians as countries democratize. This means they have to be closer to the citizens and therefore that public administration is gradually being improved. Globalization is also bringing with it an increase in defensive nationalist, regional, or localist sentiment. Many citizens are beginning to feel more Basque or Catalan than Spanish or European. The same is true of the Scots, Bretons, Corsicans, Lombards, or Padanos, and this is leading to the decentralization of the state. The principle of subsidiarity inscribed in the Treaty on European Union is becoming more and more central to the way public administration works. It means that an issue is only dealt with at a higher administrative level if it has been shown that it cannot be effectively dealt with at a lower level. Anything that can be dealt with efficiently at a local level should not be raised to the provincial or regional level; anything that can be dealt with at a regional level should not be dealt with at the national level, and the same applies to the national with respect to the supranational levels.

These two trends mean that the nation-state as it was conceived after the French revolution is gradually being left behind. On the one hand it is losing sovereignty to supranational political institutions, at a regional, continental, or world level, and on the other hand it is losing power to regional, provincial, or local governments. As Daniel Bell (1987) has observed, "the nation-state is too small to deal with the big problems in the world today and too small to deal with the small day to day problems of its citizens."

This does not mean that the nation-state is going to disappear in the near future, but it does mean that the process of disintegration described above will lead to important changes in the way it functions and is understood. For the moment it defends itself by becoming part of more powerful areas, but at the cost of losing sovereignty, i.e., of transforming itself into part of a more extensive future federal or confederal state, of the sort that will inevitably appear in Europe in the not too distant future.

Globalization and the limits to the growth of the state

Despite everything that has been said so far the state has grown spectacularly in size throughout this century, at least in the developed countries.

In the OECD countries, public spending increased from 9 percent of GDP at the beginning of the century, to 48 percent in 1999. Only in the United States, Japan, Australia, New Zealand, Korea, and Switzerland is it below 40 percent.

The underlying reason for this permanent growth contradicts the expectations of political and economic theory. The state has tended to grow in periods of uncertainty, such as recessions and wars, to compensate for the difficulties faced by some or all of its citizens. In principle, this is correct. But it has also grown in times of prosperity with the justification that more needs to be done to ensure high long-term growth.

Why has the presence of the state in the economy continued to grow even in times of globalization? This has occurred because paradoxically greater economic openness has tended to stimulate the growth of government. Various authors, especially David Cameron (1978) and Dani Rodrik

(1996), have shown that of all the factors that could explain the increase in the size of the state, the clearest correlation is with economic openness.

For Cameron, the reason is that those OECD countries most open to trade and international investment also have larger firms, which means that the level of union membership is higher and collective demands for higher transfer payments from the state are therefore growing. Unions fear the impact of external risk and competition on their members and demand higher transfer payments for unemployment, training, and pensions, so the social security budget increases as the economy opens up.

Rodrik, whose analysis also covers the developing world, finds that the correlation for these countries is greater with government consumption than with social security payments. This is because, in general, developing countries have a much more rudimentary system of transfer payments, since they lack the administrative capacity to implement them. Therefore, in an effort to reduce the risks of greater openness to family incomes, they increase the size of the civil service, because this represents secure employment shielded from external competition. Meanwhile countries with a higher level of development try to reduce this risk by increasing transfer payments to families in the form of unemployment benefit and pensions.

In all cases opening the economy has come first and the response of the state second, demonstrating that it is the state that is trying to protect its citizens and stabilize their incomes in the face of the increased competition and greater external risks that come with increased openness.

However, this argument linking the existence of a larger state to increasing openness has been criticized by Alesina and Wacziarg (1997). They differentiate between government consumption and transfer payments, and introduce country size as a factor.

According to these authors, the size of a country is negatively correlated with the size of the state and at the same time negatively correlated with its openness to trade. Given that public goods have very high fixed costs and economies of scale that are related to the indivisible nature of many of these goods, the state tends to be larger as a proportion of GPD in small countries. Some public goods and institutions cost the same whether a country is small or large, such as a parliament, a central bank, a system for assessing and collecting taxes a diplomatic service, etc. In other cases, the costs of certain public goods have economies of scale and grow less than proportionally with the size of the population, as in the case of parks, libraries, roads, telecommunications, etc. For all these reasons, the cost of public goods is relatively smaller in comparison to GDP or the tax base in a large country than a small one.

Equally, as small countries tend to be, of necessity, more open to international trade and have a larger state as a proportion of GDP, because of the fixed costs, indivisibility and economies of scale of public goods, Rodrik's argument only holds for transfer payments to families and not for state expenditure on consumption as a means of stabilizing incomes in the face of greater external risk. In this case, the size of the country plays an equal or greater role than openness to trade as a determining factor in the size of the state.

The end result of this rapid growth of the state has, in most cases, been a fiscal crisis and the accumulation of an enormous public debt in relation to the country's production of goods and services. In the OECD countries the average for public debt as a proportion of the GDP has reached 70 percent and if we add to this future commitments in the form of pension payments that have not yet been capitalized (because of the intergenerational nature of the pension system being used), the debt could reach 140 percent in many industrialized countries (OECD, 1996b and 1998a).

This fiscal crisis is creating a serious problem of hostility to the state by current taxpayers, which will become more acute if future taxpayers inherit a situation in which expenditures on pensions and debt servicing can only be sustained through increases in taxation.

The result of this greater public awareness of the crisis has been a wave of privatization and deregulation in all countries. Governments of whatever political color are unanimously opposed to the big, expensive state and for a small efficient one. Important center-left leaders such as Clinton, Blair, Schroeder, and Prodi are clearly converging with the center-right in what they see as a desirable size for the state in the future, although not in their understanding of the functions that the state should carry out.

Economic globalization also has a lot to do with this change in the way the state is perceived. The reasons are clear. In a globalized world companies compete, but so do regions and states. A large state with excessive expenditure in relation to GDP reduces the competitiveness of its companies because it has to raise taxes and therefore their costs of production. In the end this may cause them to lose market share and have to close or move to another country where the burden of taxation and social costs are not as great. It should not be forgotten that public deficits caused by high spending can only be financed by raising taxes now or by allowing public debt and raising them later. Debt today always means a future tax increase, especially when its value cannot be reduced by inflation, i.e., by making citizens pay through its decreasing value.

A state that indulges in excessive spending and has to offer its growing debt at higher and higher interest rates, crowds out private investment, which finds it safer and more profitable to invest in government securities than increase production or restructure to make itself more competitive.

Highly indebted states also reduce their ability to carry out one of their principal functions: to deal with economic crises by raising public spending in times of recession to avoid the excessive suffering of its citizens, and reducing it or collecting more revenue in periods of expansion, in order to avoid excessive growth that may lead to inflation and lost competitiveness. In other words, the automatic budget stabilizers, which are so important for reducing cyclical fluctuations in the economy, have ceased to function in most OECD countries because they are obliged to spend increasing amounts in interest payments on their growing debt at whatever stage of the cycle.

Finally, in a globalized world with free capital movements and increasing freedom of movement for individuals and corporations, tax systems compete with each other. Therefore countries with high rates tend to lose their tax base and employment to other countries when capital, wealthy individuals, and companies move their place of residence to take advantage of lower rates.

Since the 1990s we have seen how tax rates on capital, wealthy individuals, and companies have fallen considerably. In the OECD countries company tax rates have fallen on average from 43 percent to 33 percent and personal tax rates from 59 percent to 42 percent. This has been compensated for by an increase in the rates of indirect taxes from, on average, 34 percent to 38 percent, to maintain public spending and debt servicing. But this will be increasingly hard to do because indirect taxes, especially VAT, also have a direct impact on inflation through an increase in the price of consumer goods and services, and, in the last instance, on the competitiveness of the country (*Economist*, 1997a).

Globalization and the markets control of governments

Economic globalization has introduced a further element of great importance; it has brought into existence a new supervisory power over states that did not exist before: international capital markets. In addition to national electorates, parliaments, political oppositions, and some international organizations, a new and extremely important watcher or auditor of a government's economic policies has appeared.

These markets impose a strict discipline on states and governments, reacting immediately to any economic policy decision that is unsound or is seen as detrimental to the future of the economy in question (Fischer, 1997; Stiglitz, 2000). Tom Friedman (1999) calls this phenomenon the "electronic herd," which is ready to stampede at the first sign of economic or political weakness. When governments take an economic policy decision, they have to think not only about the reaction of the opposition and public opinion, but also that of national and international investors, economic analysts, and ratings agencies who observe and scrutinize every important move they make.

Governments that achieve international credibility benefit from larger and cheaper, flows of capital and investment, and in the long run from higher growth, than those who take what the financial markets consider unsound, capricious, or unorthodox decisions.

This new supervisory power presents governments with various problems. The first is that it reacts extremely quickly and can severely punish anything it sees as a negative economic policy measure by withdrawing its confidence, and therefore its capital, thus creating an immediate economic crisis in the country concerned. In other words the reaction of the markets is asymmetrical in time. Market confidence or credibility takes a long time to build up but can be lost in a matter of days. This is not like national politics where citizens have to wait to punish bad economic management until an election is called or the opposition wins a no-confidence vote. The withdrawal of capital from a country can provoke the immediate fall of a government, as happened recently in the Asian crisis. In fact, the asymmetry in national politics is completely the other way round. In a few months a politician with an attractive or sometimes populist programme can persuade the electorate to vote for him or her and stay in power for years without doing a good job, while the voters have to wait until the next election to throw him out. While it is easy to gain the confidence of the electorate, their ability to react is much slower once a politician is in power. In contrast, the reaction of the markets to bad policy is immediate, but it takes many years to gain their confidence.

The second problem is that of sovereignty. As far as they can, governments try to reduce their dependence on global financial markets and attempt to introduce measures that limit capital flows and therefore avoid the economic crises these can cause. However, this is extremely difficult to do because the very act of trying can provoke a crisis of confidence, which leads to an economic crisis. The sovereignty argument is based on the idea that governments are accountable to those who have elected them and their citizens in general, and not to other world citizens who control international capital flows. Nevertheless, the loss of relative sovereignty is a fact and, unless there is some sort of catastrophic event or a coordinated reaction on the part of all governments, this situation will be continue to grow in importance. No country can escape this new supervisory power. We have even seen how a world power such as Japan, with one of the highest savings rates in the world and a net exporter of capital, can suffer a crisis of confidence in its policies and see it currency fall like any other smaller country. However, empirical evidence shows that the disciplinary effects of capital markets on government policies is larger on monetary than on fiscal policy (Tytell and Wei, 2004).

What role does the state have after globalization?

Faced with this globalizing revolution in international markets, states have no alternative but to rethink their functions, their role, and their size. Undoubtedly, globalization has placed serious limits on the ambition and power of states, fundamentally because it sets them in competition with each other and because investors can now compare them before deciding where to freely invest their capital. However this does not mean that states or governments have ceased to play an important role.

The reduced effectiveness of macroeconomic policy, both monetary and fiscal, in a globalized economy, means that governments have to put more effort into institutional and microeconomic policy. This is undoubtedly a good thing since they have to continuously reform and increase the flexibility of their economies so that they remain competitive, through improvements in the performance of their human capital, their physical capital, their markets, and their companies.

A good education system, high-quality training, good infrastructure, an efficient health service, a solvent and well supervised financial system, a quick and impartial judicial system, public safety, etc.; these are some of the decisive factors that a country needs to benefit from economic globalization, build up greater credibility and access to stable sources of finance as reasonable prices (Chibber, 1997). The combination of corruption, crime, and political and judicial insecurity that many developing (and some developed) countries suffer is an enormous disincentive for international investment.

The best way for the state to fulfil its role, and therefore contribute to the correct functioning of the markets, is to first establish a completely open and transparent framework of rules. The ideal way to do this is through a clear collaboration between the public and the private sectors (without this leading to corruption which damages the public interest) so that each side knows the rules of the game and the limits to their spheres of action, and both act with transparency and honesty (Stern and Stiglitz, 1998).

There are several aspects to this sort of cooperation. Firstly, it requires that the state, in the last instance, ensure that rules are adhered to and sanction infringements, while allowing the private sector to regulate itself at lower levels and so facilitate the state's overall supervisory and disciplinary role.

Secondly, there should be cooperation to ensure that these rules adhere to international standards. Here international organizations can provide general guidelines that are applied in each country according to local conditions.

Thirdly, those problems that exceed the reach of nation-states, such as terrorism, environmental degradation, drugs, and even excessive short-term volatility in capital markets, must be dealt with by global cooperation in representative supranational bodies.

Fourthly, this collaboration between the public and the private sector should include the provision of certain public services where the market is taking a greater role. I am referring here to areas such as education, health, social security, pensions, etc. In these sectors the state and the private sector must operate together, with the former supervising the latter. To avoid market failures there has to be a balance between the two, clear boundaries, and rules for the public and private provision of education, health services, and social security, regulated by the state or independent public bodies.

The state also has to continue to supply social services for all those who, for reasons of ill health, age or poverty, cannot take advantage of the services provided by the private sector. And it should intervene in those areas where, because of economies of scale or indivisibility of some public goods, it can reduce the cost of services or the transaction costs between economic actors or in the case of blatant market failures.

A mixture of public and private provision, within a strictly applied framework of rules, can improve the quality and the cost of that provision, with the result that all citizens gain.

In sum, the reform of the state in response to globalization requires a greater emphasis on microeconomic policies and, at the same time, greater collaboration between the state and civil society. This will mean that rules are more objective, transparent, and better complied with, and this will in turn give states greater credibility and mean that citizens and the markets will have more confidence in their policies and politicians than they do now; this is the only way to benefiting from the globalization process.

Even though it is smaller, and its jurisdiction more limited, the state has not become less important. It will have fewer functions, but these will remain essential in determining whether a country benefits or loses out from economic globalization.

Globalization and Economic Policy

An important contradiction within the globalization process concerning governments and economic policy can be expressed as follows: while everyone is fully aware of the beneficial impact of globalization on global growth and overall income levels, it is also recognized as having a number of costs, in the form of marginalization for some developing countries that may be left behind in the process, and unemployment or lower wages for some in the developed countries, especially those who already find themselves in a disadvantaged position because of their low level of training and qualifications.

Fiscal policy and social protection

In considering how to deal with these costs we immediately think of the state. Through taxation and public spending, governments can use part of the additional income generated by globalization to help those groups who lose out by it. I outlined a number of such proposals in the chapter on employment and wages.

However, as discussed in the previous chapter, globalization imposes strict limits on government economic policies that make it difficult to compensate those who lose out with transfer payments. If a country raises taxes on skilled workers and income from capital to compensate unskilled workers who lose their jobs or are forced to accept low pay, the reaction of companies and those who earn income from capital may be to relocate in another country with lower tax levels. This would make such a policy difficult to introduce. As globalization proceeds, and the mobility of capital, firms, and skilled workers increases, it will be increasingly difficult to carry out state-led redistributive policies. The possible, in fact more than probable, winners from globalization are, by definition, the higher skilled, the more mobile, those working in a more competitive environment. Therefore, to avoid higher costs and stay competitive, they may choose to relocate to another country that imposes fewer tax or other restrictions.

In other words, mobility becomes a determining factor in the efficiency and competitiveness of both firms and wealthy or higher skilled individuals, who, thanks to globalization, can relocate their production where costs are lower, place their capital wherever after-tax returns are greatest, and sell their labor where after-tax salaries are highest. However, the majority of voters are in favor of an increase in taxes to compensate the losers of globalization, the "market," i.e. firms and financial institutions, can avoid this through their mobility.

Given that governments' ability to spend on investment, consumption, and transfer payment depends on their ability to levy taxes, the mobility of factors of production, which are the source of most public revenue, will make it increasingly difficult to maintain the spending power of states.

As we saw in the previous chapter, this has not happened up to now; in fact, the opposite has occurred. Public spending is still growing as a proportion of GDP in the overwhelming majority of countries. In the OECD countries it has grown steadily from 10 percent of GDP in 1913, at the end of the first wave of economic globalization, to 48 percent in 1997. The increase was especially sharp during the two world wars and between 1960 and 1980. Since then the growth in public spending and been slower.

How has it been possible for public spending to increase while the process of integration and globalization was being consolidated?

The answer is that although globalization has advanced quickly, it is still far from complete, so taxpayers are not as mobile as they might appear at first sight. Financial capital moves easily from one country to another, but once it has been invested in physical capital rather than financial instruments, i.e., in assets such as buildings, factories, or machinery, it is very difficult to move from one place to another. It is not easy for multinationals to leave a country where they are located, especially if they have set up important production plants there. Before this occurs, governments are always willing to offer them concessions in the areas of tax, labor, and direct transfers.

Labor, especially wage-labor, is the least mobile factor of production, because of its familial, cultural, and linguistic roots, and it is, therefore, easier to tax.

Another factor that will make it increasingly difficult for governments to collect taxes is the Internet and electronic commerce. Firstly, money will be able to move extremely quickly across the net and accumulate in tax havens without the fiscal authorities being able to regulate it. Secondly, it will be very difficult to regulate payments made in electronic commerce. And finally, it will be possible to create money in the Internet that will never leave it, and, therefore, will be enormously difficult to regulate (*Economist*, 2000).

For these reasons, governments have been able to continue increasing public spending, but have moved the burden of taxation from income from capital to income from labor. In 1980, the average effective tax rate on capital in the OECD countries was 40 percent and it has now fallen to 22 percent. The average effective tax rate on labor has increased in the same period from 23 percent to 30 percent. Today, average effective taxes on capital in the EU are 23.6 percent, in the US 22.7 percent, and in Japan, 18.7 percent. Average effective taxes on labor (taxes on gross wages plus social security contributions) are 37.9 in the EU, 23.9 percent in the US, and 20.3 percent in Japan (Albi, 2003). In other words, the fall in taxation on capital has been more than compensated for by the increase on revenue from labor, thus, demonstrating the shift in taxation that has taken place as a result of the differential mobility of the factors of production.

Another consequence of increasing mobility as a result of globalization is that direct taxation on incomes and profits has tended to fall compared to indirect taxation on spending (Vito Tanzi, 1996). Effective tax rates on consumption are today 20.8 percent in the EU, 0.3 percent in the US, and 13.6 percent in Japan (Albi, 2003). In the OECD countries, since the 1990s, tax rates on incomes and company profits have fallen by 6 percentage points and 10 percentage points respectively, while indirect tax rates have increased by 4 percentage points. Vito Tanzi also highlights the problem that taxation is based on the principle of "territoriality," since taxation systems were developed for closed economies, i.e., the right to levy taxes on earnings and activities within a national territory. Nevertheless, that principle is losing effectiveness, in the context of a globalized world, because it is undermined by the international mobility of taxable economic agents.

It is likely that both trends will increase, so the burden of taxation will shift increasingly to income from the least mobile factors of production and economic activities (semi- and unskilled work, real estate, small and medium-sized businesses) and to spending rather than income, until there is either greater tax harmonization in the world or a significant reduction in taxation that will reduce the ability of states to formulate economic and social policy. But this shift will take a long time to come about, given that in Europe, the region where integration and free movement of goods, services, people and capital are most advanced, there are still significant differences between countries in income tax rates and slightly smaller differences in rates on capital and companies.

On the other hand, the demand for social protection, sometimes provided by the state, sometimes by the private sector and sometimes in a mixed form, is increasing in all developed countries. Since the range of health and pensions needs that the state will be able to provide for is set to decrease because of the fall in public revenue, the next few decades will probably see a clear tendency toward those citizens with sufficient means of paying for themselves, while state provision is confined to those who cannot afford private healthcare and pensions. Public welfare provision will probably, therefore, be limited to a minimum safety net for those with fewest resources while other provision will be privatized.

This brings us back to the contradiction mentioned earlier, between the need for greater social protection for the "losers" from the globalization process and the difficulties that states will face in obtaining the resources to provide for this protection. The arguments put forward by Dani Rodrik (1997) are important in this context. For Rodrik, greater economic openness is accompanied by greater uncertainty about consumption, especially on the part of lower-paid workers who lack the resources to underwrite their incomes in the financial markets. Up to now in the globalization process that began in the 1960s, states have been able to provide the necessary level of security against this perceived risk. However, in the future, if the recent fall in tax revenue from capital continues, they will have to increase the tax burden on wages to politically unacceptable levels if they are to maintain this level of security, or alternatively, make cuts in the social protection programs that have enabled governments to gradually reduce barriers to trade and capital movements, and, therefore, have made the present process of globalization possible. The result may be a popular backlash against this process that may be strong enough to end it altogether.

A similar result is reached by Scheve and Slaughter (2002) who signal to FDI by multinationals in developing countries as the main factor generating worker insecurity through the increase of firms' elasticity to labor demand. More elastic labor demands, in turn, raise the volatility of wages and unemployment, all of which tends to make workers more insecure, even in the case in which aggregate volatility is fixed. It is not only true that individuals more exposed to FDI activity are more likely to report greater insecurity but also the case that changes in exposure for a single individual, controlling for previous levels of insecurity, are correlated with changes in worker insecurity.

In an interesting historical essay, Jeffrey Williamson (1998) examines the reasons why the previous wave of globalization at the start of the twentieth century came to an end. In his opinion this was due to the fact that high levels of migration into the countries with labor shortages (the United States) led to a fall in wages and an increase in wage inequality, while countries with labor surpluses (the European periphery) experienced a rise in wage levels. The correct functioning of the market led to a convergence in the price of factors of production and meant there were more winners than losers from the globalization process. But it was the losers – workers in the United States and landowners in Europe – who made their voices heard and who were best able to defend their interests. This led to a marked slowdown in globalization, which was halted completely in 1914 by the First World War.

It is difficult to predict the political future of the present wave of globalization because the circumstances, which Williamson describes, are not in existence today. On the one hand, although it is highly protected, agriculture only accounts for a very small share of European employment and GDP, but when this excessive protection disappears (and it will have to disappear since it is one of the factors blocking the Millennium Round at the WTO), this will probably cause serious political problems. As electoral laws and the distribution of constituencies remain unreformed, despite widespread rural–urban migration, one rural vote today equals between 3 and 10 urban votes in Europe, and rural populations continue to play an important part in elections. On the other hand, there is much less migration than at the start of the twentieth century, and this is the "Achilles heel" of the present wave of globalization, because many poor countries are failing to benefit from a convergence in per capita incomes because they are not able to export enough and their workers find barriers to emigrate to the rich countries. However, despite the low level of migration, in those countries where it has reached some importance, such as Germany, France, and Austria, there is a growing reaction among unskilled workers, who are voting in greater number for emerging ultra-protectionist, far-right parties. Since mass migration will inevitably take place in the twenty-first century, an extremist or conservative reaction may lead to a growing rejection of globalization.

However, Rodrik's position has been criticized by other economists. Maurice Obstfeld (1998) believes that the supposed competition between taxation systems in different countries is not leading to a decline in social protection. Nor is it leading to an equalization of tax rates, even in Europe, which is more globalized than other regions.

For example, Germany has had a completely open capital account in its balance of payments for many years, but 21.8 percent of its GDP goes to social spending, compared to 14.7 percent in the United States, 15 percent in the United Kingdom, and 19.2 percent in Spain. Marginal income tax rates in Germany and France are close to 55 percent and over 65 percent in Japan, while they are only 40 percent in the United Kingdom and 50 percent in the United States.

Sorensen (1993) finds that fiscal revenue from company tax has not diminished as a proportion of GDP to the same extent as total fiscal revenue, despite the fact that rates have been reduced throughout the OECD countries because the tax base has grown.

In the United States, where integration has gone further and taken place over a longer period, the variation in tax rates between states was 40 percent less than that between members of the European Union in the 1980s. This suggests to Maurice Obstfeld (1998) that fiscal competition in Europe will not lead to a greater equalization of rates than that which has already taken place in the United States, and Rodrik's fears will therefore prove groundless. In addition, the solution to the progressive decline in fiscal revenue from capital lies in increased taxation on consumption, not on labor (King, 1996). This would be equitable because it can be assumed that the wealthy will consume and spend more than the poor in absolute terms.

In many European countries social provision is not determined by income levels and its objective is to act as a long-term supplement to income rather than a true insurance system (Siebert, 1997). This means that its inefficiencies, and therefore the total cost, can be reduced without endangering payments.

Finally, if fiscal competition does become a direct threat to social cohesion, and indirectly to globalization, the logical solution would be to seek a formula for international tax coordination that avoids the possibility of a few small tax havens accumulating a significant part of the tax base of the large countries.

There is one aspect of globalization that may allow governments to have greater room for manoeuvre in fiscal policy. That is, the possibility they have to place debt in the international capital markets. These are increasingly globalized and competitive, and therefore ever more liquid, plentiful, and attractively priced because, as Stulz (1999) argues, the globalization of capital markets substantially reduces the cost of capital. In times of recession, the ability to borrow in international markets may allow government expenditure to exceed its revenue for long enough to respond to the demand or supply shocks by temporarily increasing spending. This would reduce the traumatic effects of these shocks by financing unemployment payments and other social costs, and also financing a greater investment spending to compensate for the reduction in economic activity. The debt can be repaid in times of growth when fiscal revenue increases. This allows fiscal policy to play a stabilizing role in both the downswings and upswings of the business cycle, without taking an excessive share of GDP.

Monetary policy

In a globalized world it is much more difficult to follow an independent monetary policy. The existence of open capital markets places limits on monetary and exchange-rate policy in the form of what is known as the "inconsistent trinity," or as Obstfeld, Shambaugh and Taylor (2004) have termed it "the open economy trilema." This refers to the fact that no country can simultaneously stabilize its exchange rate, enjoy free international capital mobility and, at the same time, try to pursue a monetary policy aimed at national economic objectives. Governments can only choose two of the three. If they follow a monetary policy aimed at national objectives such as inflation and macroeconomic stability, open capital markets or the fixed exchange rate must be abandoned. If a fixed exchange rate and open capital markets are to be maintained, the independent monetary policy must be subordinated to these two objectives. If they wish to maintain a fixed exchange rate and an independent monetary policy, they have to introduce controls on capital movements, or as James Tobin (1978) has put it "throw sand in the wheels" of open financial markets, by means of a tax that discourages undesirable or destabilising short-term capital inflows, but does not affect long-term investment based on an evaluation of economic fundamentals.

The problem with the Tobin tax is that not all short-term capital movements are undesirable and there is no clear formula for distinguishing between financial transactions that are desirable and undesirable from a social point of view, or stabilising and destabilising from an economic point of view. Nor is there any data to show a relationship between lower transaction costs and greater instability in the price of financial assets (Anderson and Breedon, 1997). Moreover, unless a tax is effectively applied throughout the world, and across a wide range of financial instruments, its effect will simply be to relocate trading in those instruments from one country to another. As Michael Dooley (1996) has argued, the experience of capital controls and the Tobin tax have not been the success that could be expected.

How does this "inconsistent trinity" work? Let us look at two countries, Germany and Holland, which have fixed their exchange rates for at least ten years and are completely open to international capital movements. Since the financial markets are aware that the exchange rate between the two will remain fixed, the nominal interest rates in Holland and Germany tend to be almost identical. Given that both offer the same country risk, the markets ensure their interest rates stay in line because otherwise arbitrageurs would detect that the interest rates in one country are lower than in the other, and borrow in the country where rates are lower and lend in the country where they are higher, making a profit without incurring a risk. But the fact that they have the same interest rates means the Holland cannot pursue a monetary policy independent of Germany; its interest and exchange rates are therefore determined exogenously, the only possible option for monetary policy is to maintain a fixed exchange rate with its dominant partner, Germany.

Holland can try to pursue a monetary policy independent of Germany in two ways. It can try to reduce its interest rate to below that of Germany's while maintaining the fixed exchange rate, but it will only succeed in this if it prohibits arbitrageurs from moving funds from Holland to Germany to take advantage of the differential in interest rates, i.e. if it introduces capital controls. Alternatively it can continue to allow free capital movements but allow its currency, the guilder, to float freely. This will mean that it can reduce its interest rates and let the guilder depreciate against the German mark, since it will experience a substantial outflow of capital to Germany.

However, as Smithin (1999) argues, international capital markets can help to compensate somewhat for capital outflows because by definition they improve a country's current account balance and its debt rating. Reducing a current account deficit entails less indebtedness to the rest of the world and, therefore, a better international credit position. This will allow a country access to new capital a few basis points cheaper.

In fact, as Maurice Obstfeld (1998) points out, it is flexible exchange rates that have led to the explosion in international capital markets. They have allowed national markets to be opened to capital from throughout the world, without giving up an independent economic policy, directed at national economic objectives. In other words, in his opinion, globalization implies a trend toward flexible exchange rates and independent monetary policies. However, as I will explain in the following chapter, things are a lot more complicated than they seem.

The depoliticization of macroeconomic policy

The last important point to make about the relationship between globalization and economic policy is the growing "depoliticization" of economic policy.

The negative experience that, firstly, citizens and then the international financial markets have had of government monetary and fiscal policies, especially in developing countries, but also in many developed countries, has provoked a growing tendency (now being accelerated by the markets' increased supervision of national policy, discussed in the previous chapter) toward the depoliticization of economic policy.

Citizens and markets alike have begun to lose confidence in the way in which politicians formulate economic policy. Sometimes this is because of their short-termism and continual changes of direction, derived from the, usually four-year, political timeframe in which they operate. This provokes enormous uncertainly among economic actors who often have to take decisions over the long term. At other times it is because of problems caused by the so-called "political business cycle," that is, the tendency of politicians to try to guarantee their re-election by introducing expansionary fiscal and monetary policies in the year or several months before an election. These policies provoke inflationary tensions, high indebtedness and a subsequent recession when attempts are made to throw them into reverse once the election is over (Tufte, 1978). Finally, it is because of problems derived from what Finn Kydland and Edward Prescott (1977) calls the "temporal inconsistency of optimal plans" in the area of monetary policy. These problems occur, for example, when the monetary authorities have committed themselves to maintain inflation at zero and, believing this to be credible, economic actors tend to negotiate wages agreements without indexation clauses. From that moment on, the authorities have a great incentive to change their stated objective because by raising it to just 1 percent, for example, they can also achieve a reduction in unemployment. If economic actors then believe in this new objective, the authorities have a further incentive to increase it to 2 percent. Finally, when economic actors have lost all confidence in government monetary policy, the result is higher inflation and an unchanged unemployment rate.

Similar problems have been found, in relation to fiscal policy, by other economists, such as, Alberto Alesina and Roberto Perotti (1995). They show that excessive public spending is always the result of political competition in democratic countries.

This has given rise to an increasingly important school of economic thought, derived from public choice theories (Buchanan and Tullock, 1962; Buchanan and Wagner, 1977) and theories of rational expectations (Lucas and Sargent, 1978). It calls for clear, transparent rules to be established in both areas of policy, and that these are adhered to over the long term, to avoid repeated, destabilising interventions by politicians (De la Dehesa, 1999b).

The initial victory for these ideas is the fact that central banks are now gaining their independence from government and are being run by individuals with no ties to political power and a deep knowledge of monetary policy. The result of this development has been that economies with independent central banks have greater macroeconomic stability and lower inflation (Alesina and Summers, 1993; De la Dehesa, 1998b). As the late Rudi Dornbusch (2000) has said: "Amateur management of the national currency is too costly, especially for poor countries that aspire to international credibility and prosperity."

Their next victory, which would be an independent fiscal policy, is still a long way away, although the European Monetary Union has already taken an intermediate step, with its Stability and Growth Pact, which places a strict corset on the fiscal authorities of the member countries, who are obliged to observe maximum limits on the public deficits.

It is not out of the question to think that, in the not too distant future, we will also see a depoliticization of fiscal policy aimed at achieving increased "credibility," a reduction in "temporal inconsistency" and therefore less uncertainty for economic actors who have to take long-term investment decisions. Certain economists are pressing hard for this to happen as soon as possible. Some, such as Niskanen (1992), have proposed a new fiscal constitution for the United States through the introduction of an amendment that obliges the federal government to maintain a balanced budget, as is already the case in the majority of the states of the Union. However, many economists, above all neo-Keynesians, take the opposite position (Schultze, 1992 and Blanchard, 1997) because they consider that control of fiscal policy can have very positive effects, at least in the short term.

Naturally the idea that governments will no longer be able to formulate macroeconomic policy, which has been one of their fundamental policy instruments, up to now, is a very radical one. However, that is the way in which things are going and globalization is propelling that process toward it ultimate conclusion, especially for states that have little international credibility because of previous excesses.

CHAPTER

8

Globalization and Exchange Rates

The eternal debate as to whether exchange rates should be fixed or flexible has returned with a vengeance in recent years after a series of crises in emerging economies. One group of economists urges the return to flexible rates (Obstfeld and Rogoff, 1996; Edwards, 1996; Collins, 1996; Eichengreen, 1999b) while others support currency boards or monetary unions (Dornbusch, 1997; McKinnon, 1996, 1998). However, financial globalization, in the form of short-term capital flows liberalization and financial market integration, has radically transformed the terms of the debate.

The present situation can be summed up as follows. Most emerging economies and several developed countries have used fixed exchange rate systems in the past to impose on to themselves greater internal discipline and stability thus signaling to financial markets that they are prepared to adopt a rigorous budgetary stance and sacrifice independent internal monetary policy in the interest of eliminating inflation and gaining credibility.

While many of these experiences of stabilization policy using an exchange rate anchor have been temporarily positive, most of them have ended in tears, either because the exchange rate has not been perceived as permanently fixed or because fiscal policy has not been as credible as the authorities had hoped (Frankel, 1995). In other cases fixed exchange rate systems have come under fierce speculative attacks (Obstfeld, 1996) or been subject to financial contagion effects originating in other emerging economies undergoing crises (Masson, 1998). Whatever the reason, fixed exchange rates have not turned out to be the stabilizing panacea that people had hoped. Most have imploded in recent years, providing rich pickings for speculators, who had discounted devaluation, at the expense of central banks, who stubbornly tried to defend their currencies at whatever price. (Cooper, 1999; Kamin, 1998; Edwards and Savastano, 1999)

A pegged or quasi-fixed rate needs a very large volume of foreign currency reserves available to fight speculative attacks and if they are not able to repel it the exit, through a devaluation, is always quite dramatic and costly. Empirical evidence shows that inflation has been higher and more volatile the more fixed or dollarized the exchange rate (Reinhart, Rogoff, and Savastano, 2003).

Meanwhile, countries, and especially emerging economies, which have chosen flexible exchange rates, either voluntarily or through *force majeure*, after suffering a forced devaluation, have seen how their apparent theoretical advantages have proved just as elusive. Barring a few exceptional cases, they have neither insulated economies from the effects of external shocks or shifts in international interest rates, nor enabled more competitive real domestic exchange rates to be introduced, nor have they created the conditions for lower real interest rates. The theoretical disadvantages of flexible rates, however, have been borne out in practice. Some of those countries, particularly smaller open economies, which have gone for a free flotation of the exchange rate, have generally been subject to greater volatility and destabilization (Hausmann, Gavin, Pages, Serra, and Stein, 1999). For example, a central bank has to take into account that if the local banks have made a large volume of dollar denominated loans a strong depreciation could turn them into insolvency, this is the main reason for what Calvo and Reinhart (2002) have called "fear of floating," which is very clear today in the case of China, Japan and other Asian countries. The great benefit of floating is that the central bank can have an autonomous monetary policy, but in reality, they have strong limitations in developing their own monetary policy. Interest rates as set worldwide by the central banks of the dominant reserve currencies and if the national central bank has not achieved enough credibility, it cannot implement a counter-cyclical monetary policy, because if it increases money and liquidity in a recession its interest rates or its rate of inflation will increase.

In truth, neither of the systems has lived up to its name. Fixed exchange rates have not been fixed and flexible regimes have been less than flexible. Most fixed systems were given flexibility via fluctuation bands or crawling pegs that gave some room for depreciation. Meanwhile, free-floating regimes have generally been limited by continual interventions from central banks and have therefore became known "as dirty floating" (Obsfeldt, 1998).

The empirical studies made about the efficiency of the different exchange rate systems show diverging conclusions: Williamson and Rogoff (2000) find that the countries with intermediate systems have grown fastest and those with free floating the slowest. Levy-Yeyati and Sturzenegger (2001) by contrast find that flexible exchange rates have produced the highest growth and intermediate systems the lowest. Ghosh, Gulde and Wolf (2000) show that currency board countries have grown more than floaters and the latter more than intermediates: Three studies, three different results. As Jeffrey Frankel (2003) says, all the variables chosen as nominal anchors are not exempted from problems of fluctuation and volatility: The quantity of money anchor produces money velocity shocks; the inflation targeting produces money supply shocks; the gold standard produces high price volatility in international markets; the commodity basket produces terms of trade shocks and fixed exchange rates depend on the fluctuations of the currency to which they are pegged. Frankel proposes to try the price of exports as the best nominal anchor.

Few countries have been able to maintain policies compatible with the exchange rate regime of their choice. Nor have they been able to generate enough credibility in the markets to sustain the system. In the end, they have suffered the inevitable consequences: a loss of confidence and the sudden withdrawal of short-term capital, with the inevitable destabilizing impact on their economies.

Financial markets have aggravated these problems. Convinced, at the beginning of the cycle, of the credibility of stabilization programmes, investors have sent large capital flows to these countries, which, in many cases, have been unable to absorb them. The result has been overheating and the emergence of financial bubbles. Subsequently, perceptions of the economy have shifted, setting off massive disinvestment and abrupt capital withdrawals that have brought down fixed-rate regimes or caused heavy depreciation in flexible rates. In the process, the solvency of already fragile financial systems in most of these countries has been called into question (Calvo and Talvi, 2004).

Exchange rate extremes

The end result is that financial globalization appears to have eliminated the viability of a halfway house solution for exchange rates. Neither fixed rates that are really semi-fixed nor floating rates that are, in fact, dirty floaters seem to be viable. Therefore globalization is pushing countries to one of two extremes: totally fixed regimes, on one hand, such as currency boards, monetary unions or dollarization or free floating, on the other.

Of these two options, most countries have chosen free flotation, but a growing number are toying seriously with the idea of creating an irreversible link with other currencies. The reason is clear. In such an open, liberalized world economy, maintaining a flexible exchange rate requires an extremely strong and stable currency that is in great demand throughout the world, to the extent that it is considered a reserve currency. Of course, most currencies do not meet these conditions. They cannot float freely for long because their international credibility has not been proved. They are, therefore, subject to excessive volatility both in the exchange rate and in commercial and financial transactions. This is because free-floating regimes do not impose sufficient discipline upon monetary policy. If previous monetary policy has not gained credibility, either because of fiscal indiscipline or because the central bank is not sufficiently independent, volatility will be very high and the country in question will need to intervene repeatedly in exchange markets as if it were defending a fixed regime (Fidler, 1999).

For this reason, the other extreme option, that of an irrevocably fixed exchange rate, has also gained ground in other countries and regions. There are three different versions. The first is a single currency, as in the European Monetary Union. The second is the sort of currency board chosen by Argentina, Hong Kong, and several Eastern European countries. The third is the unilateral adoption of the currency of another country, an option exercised by Panama, Ecuador, and other Central American countries with the US dollar, and some Central and Eastern European countries, with their eye firmly set on their entry into the European Union, have also linked up with the euro via a currency board.

The long-term trend here is that, as financial globalization advances, those countries which do not have a high-quality currency that is in demand internationally, will increasingly be forced to create a single currency, like the single European currency (created in the image of the German mark, one of the then three basic reserve currencies), or adopt one of the reserve currencies, the dollar, the yen, or the euro.

The driving force behind this trend is a global financial system where the currencies of different countries compete and where economic agents are increasingly able to choose between different currencies. Logically, they prefer more stable liquid currencies that protect the value and purchasing power of their savings. In other words, they prefer the "higher-quality" currencies (Cavallo, 1999). Presently, citizens of emerging countries who have access to dollars, immediately hoard them and, where possible, abandon their own currencies (in which their savings tend to lose relative value) either by buying goods and services or, if it is freely convertible, by acquiring other more stable currencies. If the world's citizens could choose their own currency via a referendum, most, especially those in emerging economies, would adopt the dollar and reject their own national currency. In the words of the late Rudi Dornbusch (2000):

> Democratic money is not good money. Nobody believes that devaluation is a step towards prosperity or that inflation creates jobs. Nobody can believe that printing money is an intelligent way to finance government. The stability of a currency is more important for gaining prosperity. For that reason unconditional surrender is the only way: close the central bank and renounce the bad currency.

The example of Argentina is extremely relevant. In 1991 the Argentine government fixed its currency at a rate of one peso to the dollar and guaranteed the rate by legally preventing the central bank from issuing pesos unless they were covered by dollar reserves, at the central bank, a system known as a currency board. While the currency board has functioned in exemplary fashion since the 1990s, imposing strict stabilizing discipline, sharp fiscal adjustments and large real productivity gains, which have helped Argentina survive the Mexican, Asian, and Russian crises, it did still not won complete credibility. As a result, domestic interest rates in Argentina were far higher than those theoretically associated with a currency board, system and the unemployment rate increased.

The Brazilian crisis intensified the uncertainty surrounding the Argentine currency board and increased spreads between domestic and dollar interest rates. The final devaluation of the Brazilian real raised serious doubts about the ability of Argentina to compete with Brazilian goods and services, given the high levels of trade integration between the two countries. This, in turn, heightened uncertainty about the sustainability of the currency board.

The logical reaction of the Argentine authorities, adamant that they will not abandon the currency board, and at the same time, worried to check the widening gap between domestic and international interest rates, should have been to propose, if necessary, all out dollarization. The adoption of the US currency would bring permanent credibility and, by finally eliminating speculative attacks, would enable the authorities to bring down interest rates and avoid recession (Hildebrand and Reggling, 1999; Hanke and Walters, 1992). Meanwhile, thanks to the still closed nature of much of the Argentine economy, it could negotiate temporary tariffs on Brazilian imports in order to balance the two economies' relative competitiveness, and so avoid too much damage being done to the tradable goods sector and come out of the recession. Nevertheless, Argentina ended abandoning its currency board, defaulting on its debts and being forced into asymmetric devaluation, without the supervision of the IMF, which produced the largest recession in the history of the country.

In sum, there seem to be only three options for foreign exchange regimes in the long term. The first is to try to create single currencies in areas where economic integration is taking place, as some economists (Cavallo, 1999) and countries (Brazil) have proposed for Mercosur, following the example of the euro. The drawback with this proposal is that, unlike the European Union, no Latin American currency has had the quality or stability of the German mark. When the single currency was introduced in Europe, the most rational and economically logical solution would simply have been to adopt the German mark. This was not done for political reasons to avoid one currency being imposed on the other countries. Nevertheless, the design of the euro and of the European Central Bank is a near carbon copy of the deutschmark and the Bundesbank, the currency and the central bank with the highest credibility.

To grasp the logic of this, imagine if Europe were to decide to adopt a lingua franca. The logical choice would be English since it is the most widely spoken language throughout the continent. But the adoption of English would have posed serious political problems and the European might have finally chosen Esperanto. The euro, in this sense, is the Esperanto of the European currencies but it is more deeply rooted in the German mark than any of the other currencies.

The second option is the dollarization of a group of some national currencies and the euroization of others. In Latin America, the most logical procedure would be to adopt the dollar as the regional currency, not just because it is the world's largest reserve currency but also because it circulates widely in the region and enjoys a high degree of acceptance among Latin Americans. In principle, it certainly does not appear rational to invent a new currency (a new Esperanto money) for each common market in the region, one for Mercosur another for the Andean Pact countries and another for Central America, given that the dollar already is widely used in these economies and the dollar area is its leading trading partner (Barro, 1999). Meanwhile, there is little doubt that euroization should be the choice of many Eastern European countries, while they remain outside the European Union, and for most African countries, which were closely linked to the French franc, the pound sterling, or the deutschmark. The main problem with dollarization and euroization is the fact that many countries which adopt them as a national currency do not fulfil the requisites of an Optimun Currency Area, as explained by Robert Mundell (1961) and can provoke serious cyclical problems and a high interest rate and growth volatility.

The third option is a totally free flotation of national currencies, which today is a feasible choice only for certain OECD countries with long traditions of macroeconomic stability such as Canada, Australia, and New Zealand. The latter has been able to maintain a free-floating currency regime with minimal foreign reserves to show the financial markets that it is never going to intervene in the exchange market. This system of free or semi-free floating, after the failure of the currency board in Argentina and the problems with dollarization in Ecuador, is gaining full support at the moment, from most academics and politicians, as well as the IMF and the World Bank, but it is not exempted either from exchange rate volatility problems.

But if we follow the previous reasoning, unless there is a *volte face* in the process of financial globalization, in the long term, the world seems eventually to be condemned to make do with a handful of currencies: mainly the dollar for the American continent and other Pacific regions, the euro for the European and the African continents and the yen or the yuan or both for Asia. Each of these currencies, except temporarily the yuan or remminbi, is widely accepted and with a proven and consolidated credibility. These few future currencies will float freely as the dollar, the yen, and the euro, do at present (De la Dehesa, 1999c).

Dollarization and euroization

In the short term, the relative strength of, or greater demand for, one currency over another depends on the level and expectations of interest rates. If dollar interest rates are higher than euro rates along the whole of the yield curve, the demand for the dollar in the short term will be greater.

In the medium term, it is the evolution and expectations of economic growth and the economy's position in the economic cycle that determine the strength or weakness of the currency. An economy that is in an expansionary phase with higher growth will tend to have a stronger currency than that of a slower-growing economy. This is because expectations of returns on investments in the stock market or in unlisted companies are greater, given expected higher earnings as well as on currency appreciation, and on shorter-term investment, given the perceived likelihood of interest rate hikes by the central bank (Pastor, 1999).

However, in the long term, the relative strength of the euro and the dollar will depend on the overall competitiveness or relative productivity trends of the European economy versus the United States. Up to now, the US economy has adapted more rapidly and thoroughly than Europe to the demands of globalization and the rise in international competition. US companies were the first to invest in new technologies and they have directed more capital towards innovation. The US has also carried out more radical structural reforms than Europe and has gone further in corporate restructuring both in terms of organization and productive capacity. This process has been helped by the existence of more flexible internal markets. Proof of this superiority is its second ten-year period with high growth rates, low inflation, and near full employment.

As long as Europe is unable to advance along the road of structural reform and while European companies are unwilling to take larger strides in innovation towards greater competitiveness, especially in services and non-tradable goods, it is highly unlikely that demand for the euro will rise significantly in the medium term or that the single currency will be able to start challenging the dollar as a reserve currency (Cooper, 1999; McKinnon, 1999; De la Dehesa, 2003). In the final analysis, the success of the euro depends on in increasing global demand from businesses and households seeking stability. It will also have to be used more in trade and capital transactions and perceived as a reserve currency by investors assured of its stability and confident that it will not lose value in the long run (Portes and Rey, 1998).

If the European Union manages all this, euroization will be intense and could compete with the growing trend towards dollarization, at least in the rest of Europe, in Africa, and even in Latin America. Logically the euro should very soon become the common currency of the whole of Europe, including most of the transition countries, although Russia is still highly dollarized, and Africa and parts of Latin America, which are far more closely integrated with Europe than the US.

Dollarization, after all, is proving enormously advantageous to the US but no so much for the few developing countries, which have adopted the dollar. In the first place, the fact that half of the dollar bills issued by the Federal Reserve Board end up in circulation abroad offers the US the opportunity for obtaining financing at zero interest, since the creation of dollar notes is the equivalent of issuing perpetual bonds that citizens of other countries are prepared to buy and save without receiving any interest. Estimates put savings on interest payments by the US at $20 billion per annum thanks to this phenomenon, known as "seniorage."

The second advantage is that the US no longer needs to post current and capital account surpluses in order to obtain foreign exchange to pay back and service its debt. This means that the US can maintain high current account deficits for a longer time than any other country in the world and its debt levels can be much higher. For the US there is no difference between domestic and external debt. It is all denominated in dollars. This means that it can repay external debt simply by issuing more domestic debt. Meanwhile, there is virtually limitless demand for all US debt despite having the lowest interest rates in the world given its top rating. The present situation where Asian Central Banks finance, with their reserves in dollars, a large percentage of the US current account deficit is clear evidence of such a wide demand for US financial instruments, even if their return is lower than in other currencies.

In the third place, US importers and exporters, as well as its borrowers and creditors, can carry out international transactions without exposing themselves to exchange rate risk. This makes operations far more straightforward and saves billions of dollars in hedging costs.

Finally, US monetary policy is ultimately imposed upon all those countries that accept the US currency as legal tender. This, obviously, further augments the economic and political power of the already almost omnipotent US.

All these advantages could be shared by Europe in the long term through an intensified process of euroization provided, of course, that European governments and companies implement the appropriate macro and microeconomic policies and increase their competitiveness in the future.

As Alan Greenspan (2001) has pointed out, no international currency can become truly monopolistic. Those currencies which become widely used in the international markets tend to become natural monopolies through the centripetal forces of scale economies and agglomeration.

Those economic agents which are engaged in international transactions have the problem of coordinating the purchases and sales of currencies to avoid higher costs. When the sale of a currency by an agent cannot be matched by the simultaneous purchase of the same currency by another, the currency intermediaries must carry very expensive inventories, but when the volume of transactions in a currency is very high, the waiting time is short and the needed stocks very low. Therefore, to channel international transactions in the most used currency brings a strong cost reduction. The more utilized a currency the more its liquidity increases, and the lower are its purchase-sale price spreads, making it more attractive to be used, generating lower costs until it can become a natural monopoly. Nevertheless, there are also centrifugal forces that can counteract its scale and agglomeration benefits. These are based in the need of investors to diversify their porftfolios of assets, reducing their risk exposure to one currency and distributing them to other currencies as well. Currency diversification is a better option than any other, such as diversifying through equities and bonds, given that the average price of all currencies, by definition, has no trend: When one appreciates another depreciates, reducing the covariance and the risk of the portfolio. These centrifugal forces made possible, at each moment in time, the existence of at least two currencies which are widely used, even if one is dominant.

This important fact makes it possible for the euro to gain a higher world market share and to become an increasingly more utilized world currency.

Globalization and Financial Crises

For several reasons, trade and financial globalization via the integration of product and financial markets, should bring the economic cycles in different countries more closely into line. On the one hand, intensified world trade, as we have already seen, tends to equalize the prices of homogenous products and, indirectly, of the factors of production. At the same time, movements of capital and labor, tend to lead to a convergence of interest rates (excluding country risk) and wages for similar jobs and qualifications (after tax). Meanwhile, greater trade and financial integration means that economic shocks in one country are transmitted to others. Therefore, integration also increases the frequency of shocks that affect all economies (Masson, 1998).

As the level of synchronization increases between economic cycles in different countries, the world cycle should, in theory, become more volatile as a result of the greater correlation of economic growth across a range of countries. However, if we observe the economic cycle of the three economic giants, the USA, the EU, and Japan, since the 1970s, this hypothesis is not borne out. Far from becoming more pronounced, world cycle volatility has fallen substantially in recent years and is now at its lowest level since the 1970s. If we factor developing countries into the analysis, volatility does rise in this period but even then to relatively subdued levels (Prassad, 1999). Meanwhile, synchronization of economic cycles during the same period is low both between the three major economic blocks and within the world economy as a whole. This is one of the paradoxes of globalization.

How can we explain the discrepancy between theory and empirical evidence? The first point to make is that asymmetric country shocks are still as important as collective shocks, if not more so. This was evident in the recent round of financial crises (Fabricio and López, 1996; Lumsdaine and Prasad, 1996). Secondly, the fact that trade integration has generally been through regional blocs, such as the European Union, NAFTA or Mercosur, has meant that international trade has not transmitted shocks to the extent that globalization theory would predict. Intra-regional trade has increased far more than inter-regional trade so there has been a greater volatility in cycles within regional blocks but lower volatility on a world scale (Kumar and Prassad, 1997).

Globalization also tends to intensify specialization in the world economy. As trade barriers disappear, each economy specializes in those products and services in which it has greater comparative advantage (Krugman, 1991b). This increasing specialization trend tends to increase country-specific or asymmetric shocks. These might occur, for example, where there is a fall in demand, or an excess supply, for a good in which a country specializes. Collective (or symmetric) shocks, such as an increase in the price of oil, can also affect some countries or regions more than others.

Part of the explanation for low world cycle volatility and synchronization concerns the nature of financial globalization. This is more advanced than trade globalization having developed more rapidly in recent years, although it is still far from complete. Financial globalization tends to transmit negative shocks very rapidly from one country to another, especially where emerging economies are concerned. Conversely, positive shocks are transmitted slowly. Emerging economies' cycles have been highly correlated because exchange rate and other financial crises are often transmitted via the so-called "contagion effect." This is why the volatility of the world cycle does rise over the past 30 years, once emerging economies are included in the equation. Positive shocks, however, emanating from the large economies, such as the long US expansion during the 1990s, have not been fully transmitted yet to other countries or regions except Canada and Mexico. There is a significant asymmetry between the transmission of positive and negative shocks. Positive shocks from the US have not been transmitted to Europe or to the rest of the world whilst negative shocks *are* transmitted with great speed, such as the effects of the shock emanating from Japan within Asia. This phenomenon begs the question: Could financial globalization actually be the cause of this asymmetric transmission of shocks and, if so, why?

Globalization and recurrent crises

Financial globalization has been held responsible for the increasing frequency of financial crises. Yet theory would suggest, as we have shown in chapter 2, that financial liberalization and innovation, combined with free capital movements, are fundamental factors in economic growth, together with high savings rates, budgetary discipline, low inflation, quality institutions, and high levels of human capital and technological development. Why should such an apparently positive process tend to increase the likelihood of crises?

In theory, in countries with more developed financial markets, capital is allocated more efficiently and therefore more profitably (giving households a higher rate of return on their savings). Capital is also far more widely diversified with lower portfolio risk. Financial globalization allows even greater development of these markets as capital becomes more mobile and foreign financial entities bring competition and innovation to national financial sectors. This brings down the cost of capital (interest rates), reduces risk and increases profitability, all of which raises potential growth rates in these countries.

However, there is a serious drawback. As Federal Reserve chairman Alan Greenspan observed after the Asian crisis (1998a): "Efficient global financial markets expose and punish underlying economic difficulties but they also facilitate the transmission of financial distortions with greater speed and more efficiently than ever." This means that shocks affect other countries and crises are propagated far more easily.

Recent experience shows how market liberalization, free capital flows, and financial innovation are not devoid of problems. Where these conditions prevail, financial crises tend to be more frequent. We have seen a crisis in Wall Street in 1987, another in the European Monetary System in 1992, others in Latin America, both in 1982, and after the tequila crisis in Mexico in 1994, which affected the whole region, and another in southeast Asia in 1997, which began in Thailand and whose contagion spread through most of Asia, Russia, Eastern Europe, and, once again, to Latin America. Capital inflows do seem to generate financial bubbles and contagion between countries.

This pessimistic view of financial globalization is confirmed by Martin and Rey (2002), who show that the potential benefit of financial globalization for emerging economies, in terms of lower cost of capital, higher investment and income, and their corresponding higher vulnerability to a financial crash come from the same and unique factor that differentiates emerging economies from developed ones. Their lower productivity and income level, and, therefore, all the policies that try to address the information and institutional credit market imperfections and to improve the emerging country institutions by enhancing transparency, better information, and better banking regulation, may not be sufficient to prevent crises in emerging economies.

Nevertheless, not al crises are the same. Cohen and Portes (2003) introduce a simple taxonomy of the origin of crises into three components: a crisis of confidence, which promotes higher spreads and currency devaluation; a crisis of fundamentals, which is due to a low growth rate; and a crisis of economic policy, which is the result of big budget deficits. According to them, the confidence crisis is the one which the IMF can best resolve, through liquidity support and ex-ante incentives.

As Bloomenstein (1999) points out: "Financial innovation has spectacularly increased the variety and complexity of financial products and markets during globalization." From the traditional trio of loans, bonds, and shares, we have progressed to instruments that are hybrids of fixed income and equity, and of loans and bonds; from derivatives such as options, futures, and swaps, to financial instruments linked to the securitization of loans, mortgages, credit cards, to insurance. These new instruments have allowed financial entities greater leverage capacity through repo repurchase agreements, options, futures, swaps, and other tailored products. All this has increased the risk of their positions. Finally, competition for capital has increased dramatically, giving rise to a sort of beauty contest for countries and markets. Those perceived to be virtuous and well managed attract more capital flows than ever, only to lose them suddenly at the slightest sign of weakness or imbalances. Technological development allows investors to enter a market and leave in a matter of seconds, volatility soars and investment in stocks or debt tends to be more and more short term.

The volatility and speed of reaction of financial markets has also increased with globalization, giving rise to recurrent financial crises. These do, nevertheless, appear to have been less profound than previous crises since both markets and economic authorities have been quick to respond to consolidate recovery.

In this chapter, I will review the debate on feedback and contagion in financial crisis caused by globalized financial markets and problems inherent to their structure and development or the behavior of their participants.

What is contagion?

Today's contagion theory draws heavily on early work on banking crises. The history of banks, after all, is something of an epic with a salient central theme: How to avoid crises. Yet crises continue to occur despite the lessons of the past. According to Honohan (1996) the frequency and depth of the banking crises, since the last 1980s, is unprecedented bringing more serious consequences than any other crisis before 1950. Banking crises have occurred more often in emerging economies in the1990s and on occasions their cost has been as high as 25 percent of GDP (Caprio and Klingebiel, 1996).

When a crisis occurs in a bank with solvency problems it generally spreads to other banks via so-called banking panic or contagion (Calomiris and Gorton, 1991). When depositors perceive that a bank is in trouble, a massive withdrawal can take place, which may then trigger runs at other apparently healthy banks. These then have to sell assets and try to recover credit and loans. But many debtors cannot pay back their loans and so they too have to sell their own assets. The result is a collapse in asset prices which then feeds back into the cycle of panic and contagion, not only in the country where the crisis originated but also in foreign banks, all of which are closely linked across the inter-bank market and through joint holdings.

Traditionally, economists have considered bank runs and panics to be manifestations of irrationality. Modern theory, however, tries to explain the phenomenon in two different ways. Information asymmetry theory argues that depositors who lack information about the credit portfolio of a given bank are in fact behaving perfectly logically by withdrawing their savings at the slightest sign of weakness. Other economists try to explain bank runs as a problem inherent in the business of banking. For this school of thought, the dilemma lies in the fact that the first customer to solicit the withdrawal of his or her funds is the first to receive the money. As these are liquid assets, the bank will be unable to meet the demand for liquidity by all depositors and those who are last to solicit withdrawal will not receive their money back. This means that the banking system is inevitably and permanently unstable and subject to panics (Diamond and Dybvig, 1983).

To prevent these outbreaks of panic, most countries have introduced systems of deposit insurance to protect depositors if their banks collapse. Unfortunately, this insurance gives rise to other problems, most notably what is called "moral hazard," by giving banks perverse incentives to make risky loans in the knowledge that they will ultimately be bailed out in the event of bankruptcy. This means that crises continue to occur with an increasingly high cost for the taxpayer who, ultimately, finances the deposit insurance system. Financial globalization has definitely worsened the problem of contagion from one country to another. Paul Krugman (1998d) made a very clear comparison between traditional bank panics and contagion effects in the 1998 Asian crisis. Edward Kane (1998), however, notes that while financial crises are more frequent than ever, they are less intense if a foreign bank is involved since the presence of foreign entities in the national system forces local authorities to improve supervision and insurance, in order to compete with the regulatory regime in the bank's country of origin, and so improves the efficiency of the banking system.

Does contagion exist?

The financial crisis that began in Thailand in September 1997 spread rapidly throughout Asia, from there to Russia and Latin America, and a year later, after the bankruptcy of Long Term Capital Management, was on the verge of sparking off a genuine world financial crisis. Economies, which had previously seemed quite healthy, suddenly ceased to appear so despite the absence of any apparent internal problems or shocks. The culprit was an external shock that triggered a sudden withdrawal of capital inflows and a massive disinvestment in these countries' markets. The existence or absence of contagion, then, has crucial consequences for the world financial and monetary system.

On the one hand, the fear that relatively sound economies may become victims of contagion raises serious doubts about whether a country should open totally its capital account, a basic aspect of financial globalization and of the recent development of international capital markets in a large number of developing countries. In theory, if the risk of contagion is greater than the benefits of cross-border capital flows, there is no clear incentive for the process of financial globalization to continue. On the other hand, if contagion does exist, it would seem worthwhile to offer support to those countries first affected by a crisis, in order to avoid it spreading and deepening, even if they are considered to deserve their fate because of poor policies. Helping sick economies may prevent other healthier ones being contaminated. For this reason, measures taken to try to reduce contagion might be considered as a international public good, with wider interests at stake than the simple rescue of a crisis-stricken economy or the investors who ran the risk of investing there in the first place. As we will see, if contagion is not tackled, a crisis may end up generating systemic risk. In this sense, the moral hazard implied by rescue operations, which have been so fiercely criticized in the recent crisis, is far less important if one considers the benefits that are obtained in the long run. For this reason, contagion is one of the key aspects in the debate around financial global-ization and liberalization, and has been the subject of profound analysis in recent years. Economists have opened up a new mine of research, which has produced an extensive literature.

Starting with the most radical contribution to the debate, Michael Bordo and Murshid (1999) deny that financial contagion exists or has ever existed. He has studied a series of crisis throughout history and fails to prove the existence of contagion in any of them. For Bordo, on every occasion that investors have withdrawn their capital from a country they have had a good reason to do so based on the domestic conditions of the country concerned. In this analysis, capital has never been withdrawn *en masse* from any sound economy except when there have been spillover effects from other countries with problems.

According to Bordo and Murshid's theory, the fact that most financial crises develop in the form of clusters is not a proof of contagion but of the so called "demonstration effect." Up to that moment investors have not perceived that certain economies are in a difficult situation. When an economy of similar characteristics or a neighboring country enters a crisis, investors become more cautious and examine more closely the credentials of the economy in question. If they discover that problems are more serious than they had originally been aware of and that they are similar to those of the crisis-hit economy, they may decide to withdraw their capital, setting off a crisis in this and other economies. But Bordo does not consider this to be contagion because the new victims were not innocent bystanders. Their economies, when placed under close examina-tion, were found to be unsound. So the spread of he Thai crisis of 1997 to other Asian economies with similar weaknesses and then on to Russia and Brazil was a natural development, and this is proved by the fact that both Russia and Brazil ultimately devalued their currencies and adopted IMF adjustment programs. For Bordo, the demonstration effect is a more accurate description of the mechanism whereby a crisis spreads than con-tagion because the change in perception is a result of new information about the liquidity and solvency risk in other countries and this leads to a change in investor confidence.

Arguably it is simply a question of semantics, but the Asian crisis shows that contagion does exist, as we will see, and furthermore, that it moves from less sound to more sound economies before finally coming to rest. It is logical that, at some moment, the effect peters out because flight capital has to be invested somewhere, in accordance with the return–risk ratio, and some healthy economies will always remain where lower returns on the investment are justified by higher solvency. Or alternatively, because the large lenders of last resort have managed to halt the contagion when there is serious danger of systemic risk to the whole world economy. This occurred in October 1998 when the Federal Reserve Board decided to inject massive amounts of liquidity into the system and organized the forced rescue of Long Term Capital Management by a series of investment banks.

Contagion usually spreads from crisis economies with poor fundamentals to others whose fundamentals are sounder but which are vulnerable to external shocks. The sequence is not entirely haphazard but nor is it linear and predictable. In the second line of contagion the process affects countries that are far healthier but are affected by the general deterioration of an ever-larger group of countries (Tornell, 1999). The basis of the contagion is sometimes, as Bordo argues, new information, but on other occasions, shifts in perceptions lead investors to change their mind quite suddenly about the solvency and liquidity of certain economies.

The question is how justified these changes in perception are. Why did Mexico metamorphose in the space of a day from being an industrial economy and member of the OECD situated just to the south of the USA, into a developing country located just north of Guatemala? If Russia is a relatively small economy which barely trades with Latin America nor competes with the region in other markets, nor even has missiles with nuclear warheads pointed in her direction, why did the rouble devaluation and debt default in the summer of 1998 have worse effects on Latin America than the Brazilian crisis? Argentina then had some of the healthiest macroeconomic balances in the developing world, after having adopted a bolder structural reform programme than most of the European Union countries. Why, then, was it paying a risk premium of 250 basis points above US Treasury bonds while less virtuous European countries pay only 40 basis points and China which had not even completed its economic and political transition, and where uncertainty about its future was still high, paid a spread of 100 basis points?

Why does contagion only seem to affect the most promising emerging economies? Why does it tend to occur to a greater extent in those countries which, responding to OECD and IMF pressure, have opened their economies to international trade and liberalized their capital transactions, than in other economies with worse fundamentals that protect their economies with tariffs and capital controls?

These are the questions we must try to answer in an economically coherent and satisfactory fashion. In the following overview of the different factors that gave rise to contagion in the recent exchange rate and financial crisis, I hope to make some preliminary and modest attempts at an answer. This is not, I should add, a question of finding a scapegoat. The blame is shared by all, from investors to the countries receiving capital flows, and from creditors to debtors. The important thing is to analyze the causes of contagion and try to find formulae and policy measures that can help minimize the impact of the next crisis.

Is contagion irrational?

One of the most controversial areas of the debate around the abrupt changes of direction of capital flows in emerging economies, the rapid rise and fall of stock markets and their immediate repercussions, as well as the phenomenon of contagion, concerns rationality and irrationality. Is this all a result of irrational behavior by financial markets or, alternatively, can it be explained by economic fundamentals and therefore be consistent with theories of the rationality and efficiency of these markets? By definition, rationality only exists if the present price of financial assets truly reflects the present discounted value of future cash flows.

Irrational behavior by financial markets in situations of uncertainty is at the origin of many of the financial crises that have occurred time after time in the long history of the world economy. These extracts from John Maynard Keynes's seminal work *The General Theory* (1936) have an eloquent testimony:

> As the organisation of investment markets improves, the risk of the predominance of speculation does, however, increase. Speculators may do no harm as bubbles on a steady stream of enterprise. But the position is serious when enterprise becomes the bubble on a whirlpool of speculation. (pp. 158 and 159)

When the capital development of a country becomes a by-product of the activities of a casino, the job is likely to be ill-done it is usually agreed that casinos should, in the public interest, be inaccessible and expensive. (p. 159)

Worldly wisdom teaches that it is better to fail conventionally than succeed unconventionally. (p. 157)

Speculators are more concerned with forecasting the next shift of market sentiment than with a reasonable estimate of the future yield of capital assets. (p. 316)

These quotes perfectly encapsulate many of the problems concerning financial crises, feedback, and contagion to be discussed in the following section.

Risk and uncertainty

Before continuing, we should make some preliminary observations. First, there is the distinction between risk and uncertainty. Pure uncertainty is a situation in which we know nothing about the probability of a particular event occurring. Pure risk, on the other hand, is the situation in which we know that the probability varies between zero and one. Pure certainty is the situation in which we know that the probability is either zero or one.

Obviously, in most circumstances our knowledge varies between pure uncertainty and pure risk but recent crisis have often occurred in a situation closer to pure uncertainty (Mishkin, 1991). As Hans Bloomenstein (1999) has pointed out, recent financial crises seem to be different from those of the past in the sense that they not only involve an increase of risk but also greater uncertainty. Neither politicians nor market agents are capable of evaluating the type of risk that new technologies are creating, nor its complexity. This is generating increasing uncertainty in the world financial system.

Robert Lucas (1977) observed some time ago that the rational expectations and efficient markets hypotheses do not hold in situations of uncertainty. Instead, uncertainty tends to produce "herd behavior" and, eventually, panic. Herd behavior, a crucial concept to understanding financial contagion was first described by Keynes and has been developed in the work by Gwynne (1986), Banerjee (1992), and Scharfstein and Stein (1990), who have applied the theory specifically to financial markets. These economists distinguish between smart and foolish investors. The smart group, receives information signals about the value of an investment, the foolish receives only noise. At first, it is impossible to tell one type of investor from the other. However, once the investment has been made, markets can try to distinguish between the two on the basis of two facts: whether the investment has been profitable or not, and whether the behavior of the investor in question differed from that of the other investors. The first test will be of no use where parts of the investment are systematically unpredictable since it is possible that the smart investor will have received misleading signals. For that reason, the second test assumes greater importance. If the return on the investment is considered to be fixed, investors will be more highly regarded if they follow the decisions of others than if they behave differently. This guarantees that even an unprofitable investment will not tarnish their reputation since everybody will have committed the same mistake. In the event of an unpredictable shock, they can share the blame. This blame sharing occurs when smart investors receive correlated signals (since they are observing a part of the same truth) while foolish investors do not (because they receive only uncorrelated noise). Consequently, if an investor copies the behavior of others he suggests to the market that he has received a signal that is correlated with his own, and for that reason it is highly likely that he is smart. If, alternatively, he takes a dissident position he will probably be perceived as foolish. For that reason, even if an investor's private information sources suggest that an investment will have a negative future value, he may still proceed, if others have invested before him.

Asymmetric information

Work on asymmetric information has also played a central role in the contagion debate. Sanford Grossman and Joseph Stiglitz (1980) were the first two economists to argue that efficient markets are not possible, from the point of view of information, because efficiency would prevent equilibrium. The efficient market hypothesis that prices reflect all available information and that information has a cost would actually lead to the collapse of competitive markets, according to them.

Under this hypothesis, every informed investor in a competitive market feels he can stop paying for information and be as efficient as another investor who is paying for it. But all informed investors feel the same need. The complete lack of informed investors is not an equilibrium situation since each investor by taking the price as given, feels he can gain greater profits by being better informed. The efficient markets hypothesis states correctly that costless information is a sufficient condition for prices to reflect all necessary information, but it does not state too that it is also a necessary condition. Nevertheless, this is a *reductio ad absurdum* since price systems and competitive markets are important only when information has a cost (Hayek, 1945).

Under the efficient market hypothesis, then, equilibrium is only attained when information has a very low cost or when informed investors obtain very precise information. But since this information has a cost, prices cannot reflect all the information that is available because, if they did so, those who pay for the information would receive no reward. There is, consequently, a fundamental conflict between the efficiency with which markets distribute information and the incentives that exist to acquire it.

How does asymmetric information affect financial crises? There are two opposing views of financial crises in economic literature (Mishkin, 1991). The first is the monetarist thesis developed by Friedman and Schwartz (1963) that associates financial crises with bank panics. Bank runs lead to the contraction of the monetary supply and this, in turn, causes a severe contraction of economic activity. This is why the monetarists propose that central banks assume the role of lender of last resort as a means to prevent crises. Situations where there is a rapid fall in wealth which, nevertheless, does not trigger either bank panic or a contraction of the money supply, do not give rise to genuine financial crises. These are so-called *false crises* where the intervention of the central bank is not only unnecessary but may also be counter- productive.

The second thesis is that of Kindleberger (1978) and Minsky (1986) who argue that financial crises lead to sudden falls in asset prices, bankruptcy of financial and non-financial institutions, deflation or disinflation, and devaluations or a combination of these effects. Given that these shocks will have serious effects on the economy, these economists assert a far greater role for state intervention during a crisis than the monetarists. The problem with Kindelberger and Minsky's argument is that, unlike the monetarists, they do not provide a rigorous explanation of exactly what they consider to be a financial crisis. Recent literature on asymmetric information fills this gap by offering an alternative theory of financial crises although they do not automatically justify state intervention when there is an abrupt fall in wealth.

This asymmetric information literature is centered upon the impact that financial structures have on economic activity through differences in the access to information of those who subscribe to a financial contract. Borrowers have an information advantage over lenders, since they know more about the projects that they intend to finance. Asymmetrical information gives rise to two phenomena: moral hazard and adverse selection. If the first is absent, the second will inevitably occur.

Adverse selection

Borrowers' information advantage leads to adverse selection and the classic "lemon" problem described by Akerlof (1970). The lemon problem occurs in debt markets when lenders have difficulty determining whether a potential borrower is a good risk, that is, who intends to finance a promising low-risk project, or a bad risk, where his project is of low quality and high risk. If the lender cannot distinguish between good and bad or "lemon" in the example of Akerlof, he or she will lend at an interest rate that reflects the average between the bad and the good borrower. The result is that top-quality borrowers pay a higher interest rate than they ought to and poor-quality borrowers pay less. Because of this, quality borrowers may end up leaving the market and the best projects may be left without finance.

Another effect of asymmetrical information is that demonstrated by Stiglitz and Weiss (1981) who suggest that it can give rise to a type of credit rationing in which some borrowers are denied loans for arbitrary reasons. This happens because the higher the interest rate the more adverse the selection. Borrowers with the highest-risk projects are those most disposed to accept high-cost loans. If the lender is unable to identify high risk borrowers, he or she may decide to reduce the number of loans as interest rates rise which means that the supply of credit falls instead of rising as interest rates go up and, as a corollary, that the price does not clear the market. George Mankiw (1986) has shown how a small increase in interest rate without risk can lead to a reduction in the number of loans and even to a market collapse. Bruce Greenwald (1999) has developed another model of adverse selection to explain the Mexican and Asian crises and shows how imperfections in financial markets can create negative externalities that intensify, rather than counter, initial imbalances. If the interest rate increases because of an excessive rise in the demand for credit or a fall in the money supply, the problem of adverse selection can worsen and cause investment to plunge and economic activity to contract.

One way in which borrowers can try to minimize the problem of adverse selection in loan and debt markets is by providing collateral to guarantee the loan which the lender can then sell in the event of default and so compensate his loss. The problem with collateral guarantees is that financial crises tend to cause a fall in the price of the assets, which are used as collateral. This, obviously, aggravates the problem of adverse selection as a lender stands to lose even more in the event of default (Calomiris and Hubbard, 1989; Greenwald and Stiglitz, 1988).

Asymmetrical information between borrowers and lenders also causes problems of moral hazard, which negatively affect the efficiency of financial markets. If lenders have difficulty discerning the quality of the borrower's projects, there is an incentive for borrowers to engage in activities which will personally benefit them but which increase the likelihood of default and of greater losses for the lender. The borrower can, for example, divert funds for his own personal use or take on high-risk projects which offer him the chance to make more money if the investment works out, but which jeopardize the solvency of the lender in the event that they do not (Bernanke and Gertler, 1989).

This so-called "agency problem" and adverse selection increase the likelihood of a financial crisis wreaking serious damage on the real economy. Unforeseen disinflation or deflation redistributes wealth from debtors to creditors by augmenting the real value of debt and by reducing the net worth of debtors. This can intensify the problems of adverse selection and its impact on the economy as Fisher (1933) showed in his analysis of the Great Depression and, specifically, the effect of deflation on debt.

The problems of adverse selection get worse if we consider not just the present value of the debtors' assets but also the discounted value of his future profits. In a stock market collapse, the best companies suffer a relatively greater fall in their net worth, measured by discounted future profits, than the worst companies. This aggravates the problem of adverse selection for the best companies.

Finally, shocks in financial markets as well as reducing the volume of loans or debt issues for those investors with the best projects, causing a greater contraction of economic activity, can also set off a wave of panic amongst depositors who may withdraw their savings without distinguishing between solvent and less solvent banks. The more solvent banks will seek protection from a bank run by increasing reserves, which means they will be able to lend even less. The total volume of credit will fall, further increasing the cost of intermediation and causing a further contraction of investment and economic activity.

As Frederick Mishkin (1996) has shown convincingly, problems of asymmetrical information and adverse selection are especially important in emerging economies. On one hand, banks generally play a greater role than in developed economies because capital markets are underdeveloped and have little weight in the financial sector. On the other hand, it is much more difficult for banks to obtain reliable information about borrowers in emerging economies where transparency is lower and information generally more scarce. The problem of adverse selection due to asymmetric information is, therefore, much more serious in these countries and the impact on economic activity can be much greater than in the developed economies. Moreover, property rights are less clearly defined in most emerging economies, the judicial system is generally weaker, and bank supervision is rudimentary in many cases with few resources to improve it.

As we will see, this has been one of the differential factors in the Asian crisis and its contagion in Russia and Latin America. The quality of bank loans in many Asian countries was poor and even fraudulent due to a lack of control and a network of collusion between bankers and businesspeople and politicians (Krugman, 1998a). All of this has meant that the use of external capital flows was inefficient and short-termist, intensifying liquidity and solvency problems and worsening the final impact on economic activity. Many banks went to the wall.

Irrationality

There are three different types of analysis on rationality and irrationality in financial markets. The first is Robert Shiller's work (1981) from the early 1980s on the relationship between efficient markets and excess volatility. This sparked off a lively debate. Shiller has provided abundant evidence that stock markets in the US have been excessively volatile when compared with long-term economic fundamentals. The outcome of the debate was a consensus around the idea that markets can be inefficient because they are unable to rationally discount future cash flows. Financial asset prices are often subject to influences, behavior and perceptions, which distract them from economic fundamentals for a period of time. De Bondt and Thaler (1985) and Lakonishok, Shleifer, and Vishny (1992) reached the same conclusions as Shiller. Since then, research has continued using models which aim to improve understanding of investor behavior.

One of these models develops the concept of rational speculative bubbles as an explanation for the excess volatility revealed by Shiller. The idea that buying stocks or other financial assets that appear overvalued to everybody during a speculative bubble can, nevertheless, be defined as a rational behavior was first discussed by Blanchard and Watson (1982). Their model explains that it is possible for the price of such assets to rise even further, and that the likelihood of the bubble bursting is small in the short run. For that reason, a decision to continue buying in expectation of greater returns can indeed be perfectly rational. Almost everybody believes, for example, that Internet companies' stock is overvalued in relation to expected income flows but, since at least a few stocks may continue to rise for some time into the future, many investors prefer to keep buying in the expectation that the bubble continues to inflate. Despite warnings expressed in 1996 by Federal Reserve chairman Alan Greenspan about irrational exuberance in the US stock market, the markets continued to rise until early 2000.

Other theoretical developments in recent years are the latest models of "irrationality" and irrational investor behavior. One of the most persistent paradoxes of financial economics, for example, is the size of risk premia on shares, or the excess profitability of stocks versus Treasury bonds (Mehra and Prescott, 1985). Between 1962 and 1992 the premium was 6.1 percent in the US (Siegel and Thaler, 1997). Standard economic models of rational behavior predict a far lower premium. The greater risk of equity over bond investments cannot justify such a premium if investors make long-term investments. Yet shares tend always to outperform bonds. There is no 30-year period since 1871 in which the returns on a diversified portfolio of stock investments have not been superior to bonds or Treasury bills. This begs the question of why investors have not bought more stock, increasing their price and reducing the risk premium (in fact, in recent years, they have done so in the US during the equity technological bubble).

One reason for such a high-risk premium is that suggested by Bernatzi and Thaler (1995) who polled investors as to how they would allocate their contributions to a pension scheme between shares and bonds on the basis of data showing their relative profitability. The answers varied depending on the information provided about returns on the respective investments. When participants were shown 30 annual returns they allocated 40 percent to shares and 60 percent to bonds. But when they were provided with information on returns for a 30-year period, they allocated 90 percent to shares. This investor behavior is known as "myopic aversion to loss." Investors were reluctant to take a sequence of small bets but they are, nevertheless, prepared to accept the sum of the same bets taken as a whole.

Economic historians have provided the third area of research into the financial markets. They have analyzed the classic speculative bubbles of the past such as the eighteenth-century South Sea bubble, tulip mania in seventeenth-century Holland, and the stock market crashes on Wall Street in 1929 and 1987.

These economists have fiercely criticized quantitative models as a means to analyze market rationality or efficiency and prefer qualitative descriptive methodology centering on hysterical investment behavior and panic as an expression of extreme irrationality amongst investors. Charles Kindleberger (1978) rejects all rational bubble models as an attempt to impose technical criteria on common sense. Even Alan Greenspan has observed that any credible or rational scenario cannot explain the 20 percent collapse of the US stock markets on October 27, 1987.

This skeptical position is backed by a series of analyses, which attempt to explain or rationalize investor behavior. Literature on individual decision-making (Kahneman, Slovik, and Tversky, 1982) suggests that individuals are heavily influenced by the most recent information and this tends to amplify price movements. Work on investor behavior also outlines the possibility of errors of judgment in investment decisions as investors identify good companies or countries with good investments, whatever the price. (Shefrin and Stataman, 1984, 1985). Noise traders such as central banks that intervene to support a currency or companies that buy their own stock, can also undermine rational behavior since they do not seek expected returns. These "noise" activities move markets away form economic fundamentals without there necessarily being loss-inducing arbitrage (De Long, Shleifer, Summers, and Waldman, 1990).

What is beyond doubt is that even in what are considered to be the most efficient markets such as the US stock exchange, rational models of efficiency in financial markets cannot explain the existence of sudden huge price variations. If this is the case in the best markets, investor behavior in emerging markets where information is sketchy, opaque, and almost always asymmetric will inevitably give rise to more errors of judgment and irrationality in the form of fashions, perceptions and intuition. Therefore, panics and waves of euphoria will be more and more frequent and contagion far more likely in emerging markets.

There are, nevertheless, cases of contagion, which are rational or at least can be subject to rational analysis. These are related to the interdependence of trade flows, the effects of devaluation on competitiveness and financial interdependence all of which will be discussed forthwith.

Why do crises affect the most promising emerging economies?

Going back to basics, we should remember that only those emerging economies, whose macroeconomic policies are considered credible, with a reasonable potential rate of growth, gain access to international capital markets. The benefits of direct access to these markets are that a country can compensate inadequate levels of internal savings with foreign savings. This means it can invest more and, consequently, grow faster and so increase welfare.

That said, by definition, a country, which invests more than it saves runs up a current account deficit. The greater the volume of capital inflows, the greater the current account deficit. A large deficit is an external imbalance that can make a country vulnerable to crisis and so be considered a cause for concern both by analysts and investors. At the same time, the more capital inflows a country attracts the more overvalued its exchange rate will be, as a logical result of these inflows. This can also be considered to be a factor of vulnerability by investors and analysts since it can slow export growth and, of course, foreign sales for goods and services are essential to generate the foreign exchange necessary to meet interest and dividend payments on foreign capital inflows. To counter this exchange rate appreciation, the central bank often has to intervene in forex markets, selling its own currency and building foreign exchange reserves. This accumulation of reserves is analytically equivalent to a capital outflow from the public sector that compensates private-sector capital inflows. But this is a very expensive way to manage currency appreciation because by compensating the inflow with an outflow it pays an additional price since the cost of private capital is always higher than the returns on public investment in foreign exchange reserves (Wolf, 1999).

All this means that if a country wishes to diminish the risk of a crisis it has to accumulate foreign exchange reserves to slow exchange rate appreciation and reduce liquidity risk in foreign currency since the greater the ratio of reserves to foreign currency denominated short-term debt, the lower the risk. But paradoxically, in order to diminish this risk of crisis, the country is forced to minimize the benefits of the capital inflow. If, on the other hand, the country wishes to maximize the benefit of its access to foreign capital it inevitably increases its vulnerability to crisis. As a third option, trying to steer a middle course can be interpreted as a sign of weakness and so trigger a crisis. This dilemma is illustrated in the so-called models of self-fulfilling crises (Obstfeld, 1996; Krugman, 1996b), which show that crises can occur where weaknesses are really very slight. This is not perceived by markets to be a sign of bad fundamentals until the country becomes the object of speculative attacks. The crisis is possible but not inevitable. It is only when the attacks are mounted that weaknesses become serious and there is an ex-post justification of the crisis (Wyplosz, 1998; Artus, 1997).

To sum up, a promising emerging economy that has won the credibility and the interest of international investors is, bizarrely, more likely to suffer a crisis than other more poorly considered countries. These countries do not even have to develop serious imbalances to find themselves in trouble. It is enough to show vulnerability for different reasons: the build-up of short-term foreign currency debt (Mexican crisis 1994), weakness in financial systems where regulation and supervision deficiencies interfere with the efficient use of capital inflows (Asian crisis 1997) or high current account deficits, budget deficits or unemployment that prevents the country resisting speculative attacks (Spain in the ERM crisis of 1992).

Why are financial crises self-fulfilling?

Before analyzing the different channels by which crises spread we should analyze why they feed upon themselves and end up becoming so profound that contagion results (de la Dehesa 1998c). Greenspan (1998b) has suggested that "global markets facilitate the transmission of financial distortion more efficiently than ever" and that "periods of euphoria and depression tend to feed upon themselves."

Paul Krugman (1998d) says pretty much the same thing when he states that the propagation of recent crises may be a result of a dangerous efficiency of financial markets or that the combination of global financial markets and national monetary policy is like "walking a tightrope without a safety net." In these phrases, he sums up, succinctly and objectively, the possibility of feedback in financial crisis.

Intuitively, we can imagine several factors inherent to the running of financial markets, which could explain the existence of feedback in crises. The first is a result of central banks' response to attacks on their currencies, when markets perceive them to be overvalued, and which usually end up with a devaluation of their currency. Speculators attack a currency by short-selling it generally to a bank for periods of a month, a week, or a day. The bank then sells the currency for dollars at the spot rate, and hedges the position by means of a currency swap delivered at spot prices in exchange for the national currency and the national currency in exchange for dollars at 30 days, a week or even a day. The central bank of the country under attack has several means of defence. It can intervene in the market by buying the national currency in the spot market and selling dollars. If it then sterilizes this intervention the central bank is implicitly and directly extending credit in the national currency to the speculator who needs to finance his short position in the currency. By doing so the central bank also provides dollars to the non-resident or resident who wants to sell a national currency asset and change the proceeds into dollars in order to invest them outside of the country in question. These facts mean, ironically, that, if it sterilizes and sells dollars, the central bank is actually encouraging speculation and the sale of the national currency.

Alternatively, the central bank can intervene in the futures market. If its forward position in the national currency against dollars coincides with a forward sale of the national currency by another market participant, the bank's intervention in the forward market will absorb the sale in the spot market which relieves the bank of the need to intervene in that market. Speculators who sell short will not need credit in local currency.

The bank can also increase the cost of speculation by hiking interest rates and forcing the speculators' financing costs above the capital gains they expect to make in the event of a devaluation, which would oblige them to undo their short positions. But this final option is extremely costly. By way of example, 10 percent devaluation in one day would need interest rates of 3,600 percent in order to wipe out possible gains for the spectator. Why have banks not used this last option to fend off speculators instead of directly or indirectly financing speculation via spot or future purchases of the currency?

There are several answers. The first is that by raising interest rates to such stratospheric levels they inevitably hurt those who have taken short positions for importing and exporting reasons in order to hedge against devaluation. This means there is a direct impact on economic activity. The second reason is that in many of the emerging economies that are most vulnerable to speculative attacks the banking system tends to be weak and such a drastic increase in interest rates can create huge problems of bad debts and threaten the solvency of the whole financial system (this was the case in the Asian crisis of 1997–8. Finally, the country under attack might easily be in a recession with high levels of unemployment a situation aggravated by interest rate hikes (this was the background to the ERM crisis in 1992) (Ozkan and Sutherland, 1993).

Finally, the central bank can try to introduce exchange controls or controls on capital flows, which increase the cost of currency transactions, or limit the amounts exchanged. Imposing controls at a moment of crisis, however, can be dangerous and have the opposite effect. This has happened recently in Russia as the loss of credibility led to a complete drought of external capital inflows for a sustained period even after the crisis was over.

The experience of the Mexican crisis of 1994 and the Asian crisis of 1997–8 have shown that central banks, as a rule, tend to choose intervention, and only when their reserves of foreign exchange are exhausted do they resort to interest rate hikes or accept a devaluation, which, after all, is the most likely final outcome.

The self-fulfilling effect in all these speculative attacks is apparent. As the central bank uses up its forex reserves there is a greater incentive for investors to join the ranks of the speculators since devaluation is increasingly likely and, ultimately, inevitable. The second factor in producing feedback effects is a result of the way capital inflows are managed. For many years investors have been, principally, wealthy individuals or companies acting on their own behalf or through bank intermediaries. These investors gave directions directly to banks after seeking advice from experts and so directly assumed responsibility for their investment decisions. Nowadays, however, investment is primarily institutional. Individual investors, companies, and investment agents in general deposit their savings or surpluses in investment or pension funds, which are managed by professionals. This process of concentration has been propelled by the advantages that the funds offer in terms of portfolio diversification and economies of scale. Professional managers, however, cannot have perfect knowledge of the situation in all of the countries and companies in which their funds invest. Fund analysts, inevitably, are more familiar with some countries than others. In other words, managers' information is asymmetrical, although to a lesser extent than individual investors. The fact that these are professional managers is also significant since their compensation is closely linked to the returns they obtain. They are under periodic scrutiny from the owners or participants in the funds.

These three parameters give rise to clear incentives to follow the crowd and therefore, intensify the herd effect. When a fund manager observes other managers or analysts scale down or withdraw their investments from a country with which they are purportedly well acquainted, he or she will tend to imitate them, with the end result that everybody withdraws capital from that country. The logic of the herd effect is quite obvious (Scharfstein and Stein, 1990). If a manager decides to buck the trend by increasing or maintaining his positions in a jilted economy, aside from the danger of losses as capital leaves *en masse*, he is also running the risk of losing his job as investors accuse him of recklessly going against the market. If, alternatively, he sticks with the crowd he may still lose money but will at least keep his job provided at least he is not the last out. Of course, this also means that there is an incentive to get out as soon as possible when the stampede begins so as to lose less than others (Krugman, 1998a). Often, the first to warn of danger in a particular country are the managers of national funds and those who lead the stampede are often nationals. The Asian crisis was a clear example of this sequence, proof of the error committed by those politicians who made xenophobic complaints and blamed international capital markets for their woes.

The third factor in the self-fulfilling effect is caused by creditor behavior and failures in bank regulation. The Asian crisis was intensified by the short-term nature of so much bank lending to the countries affected. Two-thirds of the loans extended to Asian companies were redeemable in less than a year and many in less than a month. This was a direct result of the regulatory framework set out in the Basle accord, which sets out banks' solvency ratios, i.e., the capital requirements needed to cover credit risk. Under these ratios bank loans cannot exceed 12.5 times the total capital of the bank. The problem is that the system of quantification and weighting of loans to capital assigned to maintain an average solvency ratio of at least 8 percent allows the bank to grant a volume of short-term loans which is four times greater than long-term loans with the same ratio. This has meant that banks have multiplied their short-term and cut long-term credits to maximize margins on the same volume of capital. This regulation makes sense for each bank taken as a separate entity. Short-term inter-bank loans do seem much less risky than long-term ones. But when there are too many short-term foreign loans in the international financial system as a whole, the solvency and liquidity risk of debtors who have to refinance debt at regular intervals is greatly increased. If creditors refuse to roll over debt, countries have only one short-term option: draw on the central bank's currency reserves to pay back their debts in foreign tender.

So what appears to be an eminently sensible measure for the prudent regulation of a single bank becomes a liquidity risk for the system as a whole by increasing the vulnerability of borrowers in the short run. To quote Jeffrey Sachs (1999), "the international banking system had created a house of cards in which thousands of short term interbank loans could return rapidly to where they came from causing economic collapse."

Another aspect of the Basle accord, which has proved to be a serious weakness, is the smaller capital weighting granted to those loans, which are guaranteed. In many Asian countries, loans were covered by real estate guarantees at clearly inflated prices. As a consequence, banks were lending more than 100 percent of the real value of these assets in spite of the fact that nominally they were lending at 60 or 70 percent. This meant that in the event of default they stood to lose money not just because of the difference between value and price, but also because these guarantees were impossible to realize. All of this increases the probability of panic and financial collapse.

What are the causes of contagion and how does it spread?

While macroeconomic fundamentals may help to explain why countries suffer exchange rate and financial crises, it is a lot more difficult to explain the causes of contagion despite the fact that there is a growing correlation (still insufficiently documented) which tends to prove that crises can be contagious.

Recent literature on financial contagion include a "taxonomy" of the different factors and channels which seem to facilitate the spread of crises from one country to another either across regional clusters or along far more dispersed, and less obvious, contagion paths. Masson (1998) classifies them in the following way:

1 Crises can arise from a common cause, which is usually an external shock that simultaneously affects a group of countries. This is what Paul Masson and Michael Mussa (1995) call *monsoon effect*. These common external shocks are of different types: an increase in world interest rates; a contraction of aggregate demand in a large group of countries, or in one of the G7 economies; a fall in the price of raw materials, or significant shifts in exchange rates between the leading currencies. The Latin American debt crisis of the early 1980s was sparked off by a huge increase in interest rates in the US. In 1997–8, the fall in raw materials prices after the Asian crisis, and the deep recession experienced by several Asian economies, has had a direct impact on Latin America which is highly dependent on exports of wheat, meat, minerals, metal and oil. This worsened the external weakness of many Latin American economies through deteriorating real terms of trade. In the crisis that affected the European exchange rate mechanism in 1992, a key factor was the interest rate hikes by the German Bundesbank, needed to counter the fiscal expansion created by German reunification. Rising interest rates in the US were also responsible for intensifying pressure upon the Mexican peso, which led to devaluation and the tequila crisis. Finally, the depreciation of the yen, the devaluation of the Chinese yuan, and the stagnation of the Japanese economy (one of the biggest trading partners of the Asian economies) all added to exchange rate pressure on the Asian currencies, and were key factors in triggering the Asian crisis.

2 The second category of factors influencing contagion is trade relations. A country in crisis tends to devalue its currency and therefore becomes more competitive at least in the short term vis-a-vis its main trading partners. At the same time, it enters into recession and this leads to a fall in imports (Glick and Rose, 1998). The joint effect is a reduction in exports from the affected country's trading partners. This trade contraction, which also affects third party markets where the crisis-stricken economy competes with its trading partners, can intensify pressure on the exchange rate of these partners and finally force them, too, to devalue. As these countries devalue, their trading partners, in turn, are subject to exchange rate pressure and a domino effect can occur. This effect was seen throughout Asia during the 1997–8 crises. The devaluation of the Brazilian real and its impact on Mercosur is another example of this trade effect on neighboring countries. Diwan and Hoekman (1999) underline the role played by competition from below

(China and India) and from above (Japan) in the Asian crisis and point out that complementary relations between Asian economies did not play a stabilizing role due to the demand effects arising from the crisis.

3   The third channel by which contagion is transmitted is financial. The globalization of financial markets can augment the contagion effect spreading the crisis to countries outside of the region of origin. Markets are increasingly interconnected through interbank operations, loans, futures contracts, options swaps, or through portfolio diversification by the big institutional investors. Interest rates also play an essential role as mechanisms of transmission the shocks (Edwards, 1998). When a crisis breaks out and the price of its financial assets collapses, investors try to reduce their exposure to the risk, now greater than previously. For this reason, they sell assets whose returns are variable and positively correlated with the assets of the crisis-stricken country. This is the so-called risk effect. But so-called liquidity and profitability effects can also set off contagion. The managers of highly diversified investment funds need to keep a part of their portfolios liquid in order to meet the demands of clients who wish to withdraw their funds, a common occurrence during crises. In many cases, the managers guarantee a minimum return on the investment. This means that when a crisis breaks out and losses mount, managers are forced to sell assets or investments in other countries which are still not affected, either to maintain a minimum amount of liquidity in their portfolios or to guarantee minimum returns as required by the contracts with investors. Often both imperatives occur at the same time. Investors too can choose to sell their most liquid assets in other countries, apparently unrelated to the crisis, because, as the value of their assets in the crisis-hit economy falls, they are confronted suddenly with an immediate need for cash in order to meet margin calls. This is especially acute when their investments are highly leveraged. Asset sales in third countries may also occur because they are considered to be of greater risk, or, conversely, because they are liquid and profitable and can therefore be cashed in quickly. Investors may also opt to sell them because their relative weight in the portfolio is perceived to be excessive during the crisis (Goldfajn and Valdés, 1997).

There is a further effect known as spillover, which is also rooted in financial interdependence but this time on the asset rather than liability side of the balance sheet. Positions held abroad by investors based in crisis-hit countries can also be subject to contagion. Korean banks, for example, which found themselves in an extremely delicate situation as their margins fell in the run-up to the crisis, had accumulated high-yield financial assets issued by Russia and Brazil. Brazilian banks had done the same and held notes and bonds issued by the Russian Treasury. When the Korean crisis broke out in December 1998, Korean banks encountered serious liquidity problems and wound up their positions in Russian and Brazilian debt causing a collapse in prices with severely negative effects for these countries. At the same time, Brazilian investors pulled out of their Russian investments, intensifying contagion. Its impact on prices was all the more dramatic because markets in Russia and Brazil are shallow and lack liquidity.

Another channel for contagion is what Morris Goldstein (1998) calls the "wake-up call effect." This describes the way that the Thai crisis acted as an alarm call for international investors who immediately reassessed the solvency of other Asian borrowers. The reassessment revealed that other economies in the region showed similar weaknesses to Thailand: weak financial sectors, poor supervision, current account deficits, overvalued real exchange rates, deteriorating investment quality, declining exports and excess capacity in many industries. Once this reality was brought home to them, investors reacted rapidly, and exited other Asian economies. Sachs, Tornell, and Velasco (1996) reached similar conclusions in their analysis of the tequila crisis in 1994 and Corsetti, Pesenti, and Roubini (1998) made similar findings on the Asian crisis.

Of course, it is hard to guess why investors had not perceived these weaknesses *before* the Thai crisis broke. How could international investors, analysts, lenders and ratings agencies have slept so soundly before Thailand's wake-up call? Interest spreads on Asian investments vis-a-vis US treasury bonds gave absolutely no hint of the danger. Nor did any of the rating agencies express any concern about imbalances (Radelet and Sachs, 1998). Many investors shared the optimistic view of the World Bank's celebrated report *The East Asian Miracle* that Krugman (1994) had rightly questioned.

There are three ways of explaining this mistery. The first is that investors and lenders did not possess the right information on the solvency of these countries. External debt was far higher and the level of foreign exchange reserves far lower than the official data led them to believe. The second explanation is based on the concept of *moral hazard*, the idea that investors were indeed aware that the reality if these countries was much worse than official statistics showed but did not "wake up" because of expectations that, in the event of a crisis occurring, governments or the IMF would come to the rescue as they did during the tequila crisis in Mexico in 1994. The third explanation holds crony capitalism (Krugman, 1998b) to blame, arguing that investors believed that their investments were safe thanks to a network of implicit guarantees and other instances of collusion between private and public sectors in Asia. The real story is probably some kind of combination of the three explanations.

Guillermo Calvo and Enrique Mendoza (1999) rationalize the herd effect and contagion as a product of poor information. One cause of instability, volatile capital flows and contagion, they argue, is that financial market globalization actually *discourages* the search for reliable information on emerging countries and so intensifies the herd effect as we would expect when expectations are formed in a context of imperfect and asymmetric information. As globalization extends the range of markets available for investment and reduces the percentage of assets from a specific country in an investment portfolio, the advantage of gathering information on any particular small or marginal market is less apparent, and fund managers who are assessed via a system of benchmarking tend to follow the crowd rather than engage in their own research.

Globalization, then, exacerbates the problem of contagion because the range of multiple equilibria becomes ever more indeterminate as the financial market grows. If the cost of gathering and processing information on a country is fixed, the utility gain tends to diminish as the number of countries where the fund invests increases. Even if the information process is considered a variable cost or a benefit but is dependent on the average profitability of their portfolios versus other portfolios, managers will simply decide to copy the benchmark portfolio. When a rumor favors another portfolio, managers follow the herd.

The changes in attitude by investors that set off contagion can also be self-fulfilling in that they cause the crisis to develop just as they had feared (Obstfeld, 1996; Artus, 1997). If an exchange rate crisis in one country generates fear of speculative attacks in others, investors may try to obtain profits by speculating against other currencies that they consider will be sold by other investors as contagion advances. In this sense expectations of crisis are self-fulfilling. The countries that offer the best perspectives to speculators will be those whose monetary authorities are expected to defend their exchange rates with interventions in foreign exchange markets but which have limited currency reserves with which to do so. This combination makes devaluation more likely and improves the odds of making speculative gains. Indeed, during the Asian crisis, contagion was rife and several countries were forced to throw in the towel and devalue after defiant attempts to defend their currencies. Only the currency boards in Argentina and Hong Kong withstood the charge of the speculators and they paid the price of a severe recession.

Both crises and contagion have been blamed on foreign investment funds, especially offshore and hedge funds who are generally criticized for being the first to abandon a country when things turn sour, so exacerbating the crisis. This is known in the trade as "positive feedback" trading. The funds are accused of diving in to make money when the market is expanding and then selling when it begins to fall, paying little attention to fundamentals and generally following the herd (De Long, Shleifer, Summers, and Waldman, 1990). Hedge funds are criticized as well for their aggressive investment style and for operating from tax havens where regulation is difficult.

Woochan Kim and Shang-Jim Wei (1999) analyze this behavior and reach the conclusion that offshore funds do indeed change positions more rapidly than the rest but that there is no evidence to suggest that they engage in pro-cyclical trading. US and British funds, in fact, carry out a far greater volume of positive feedback trading and are more likely to follow the herd than the offshore funds.

Eduardo Levy-Yeyati and Angel Ubide (1998) show that the prices of closed-end funds in one country do not tend to converge with changes in market value of their underlying portfolio. This contradicts the efficient market hypothesis and is known as the "closed-end fund enigma." The reason, argue Leuy-Yeyati and Ubide, is that international investors are less sensitive to changes in global conditions than domestic investors. This means that the relationship between the price of these closed funds and the underlying value of the instruments in which they invest tends to increase sharply in times of crisis.

This asymmetry of investor sensitiveness means that foreign investors tend to amplify the contagion effect on other countries and reduce the effects of the crisis in the country where the crisis has originated. The reason for this is that national investors are much more exposed to risk in the local market than foreigners, and the contraction of liquidity associated with the crisis causes the immediate sale of national assets by domestic investors. This means that countries that restrict portfolio investment by international investors to protect themselves from speculation, are actually exacerbating the impact of the crisis on national assets.

Experience shows that the first to react to a crisis are national investors who tend to have more direct sources of information and a greater concentration of risk. They are generally the first ones to sell national assets. However, contagion really begins to occur when international investors decide to leave the country in question, as well as other countries in a similar situation, which are considered to be likely candidates for the next crisis. In these cases, there is generally a substantial herd effect because, as Froot, O'Connell, and Seasholes (1998) have shown, these international investors' concerns are based on global factors and they are more likely to consider the behavior of other investors than economic fundamentals in the countries where they have invested.

Finally, Allan Drazen (1999) has drawn up a model of political contagion from exchange rate crises in an analysis based on the political decisions to devalue or not to devalue in the European Union and the extent to which, once devaluation has taken place, speculative pressure makes further devaluations inevitable in other members of the integrated region. The case in point was the devaluation of the British pound in 2002, which triggered other devaluations in other EU countries like Spain, Portugal, and Italy.

One of the most important attempts to verify the hypothesis of financial contagion is that of Taimur Baig and Ilan Goldfajn (1999). These authors argue that the best way to measure contagion is by observing financial market correlation between previously uncorrelated countries. If correlation increases abruptly it is a clear sign of contagion, but if there is not a substantial rise in correlation, markets in these countries are simply reacting to the movements of the rest. They enrich the analysis by comparing correlations with reference group European countries. These economists do not, however, distinguish between wake-up call and herd effects or other factors that might create or augment correlation. Their conclusion, though, is unequivocal: in moments of crisis there is a considerable increase in the degree of correlation between different countries both in foreign exchange and stock markets. During periods of instability and crisis in markets, investors tend to move together across a whole range of countries. There is clear proof of substantial levels of contagion and financial panic during the Asian crisis since correlation increases much more within the region than in the European reference countries. Roberto Rigobon (1999) holds that the opposite occurs. The speed of propagation of shocks and financial contagion is similar in times of crisis and times of stability. Rigobon argues that contagion is transmitted via trade, and the aggregate effect of shocks together with a learning effect, rather than through liquidity, multiple equilibria, and political contagion.

How contagion may lead to systemic risk?

Contagion, as we have mentioned, can develop into a much more serious phenomenon, known as systemic risk. Indeed, contagion from the recent Asian crisis at one point threatened the world financial system. Systemic risk occurs when socially inefficient equilibria arise in which rational individual behavior does not generate a spontaneous market adjustment to allow the financial system to emerge from difficulties (Aglietta, 1998) There are two general hypotheses concerning the circumstances in which financial systems tend to generate systemic risk. The first is asymmetric information in credit markets (Mishkin, 1996), which can generate an underestimation of risk, and, therefore, a tendency toward excessive indebtedness, which, in turn, worsens financial fragility. This causes a rapid increase in the costs of intermediation and/or the strangulation of credit. The second hypothesis concerns the valuation of assets in a situation of restricted liquidity (Minsky, 1986). The key here is a series of alternate states of euphoria and disillusionment in markets caused by subjective interactions between market agents, which tend to generate contagion and panic.

These hypotheses are based upon failures in coordination in the interaction between individuals. In this situation, mutual improvements in overall welfare, which, in other circumstances would be feasible, are unattainable because none of the market agents has incentives to shift from the existing malign equilibrium. This lack of incentives occurs because of the strategic interaction between individuals who are seeking knowledge in circumstances of endogenous uncertainty. Endogenous uncertainty arises when there is a crisis of confidence or a failure in implicit collective coordination between economic agents or where uncertainty results from difficulties in predicting the future by means of information accumulated in the past. Both hypotheses are based on theories of cognitive processes. The first is a variation on the theory of complementary strategies (Cooper and John, 1993). Here, the strategic actions of economic agents are mutually self-reinforcing which gives rise to the contagion effect, to multiple equilibria, and to herd effects. The second hypothesis arises when agents respond to a potential danger whose likelihood of occurring is impossible to calculate following estimated probabilities of similar past events. There is, therefore, an abrupt discontinuity in individual behavior because, up to a so-called *heuristic threshold*, the probability of the feared event occurring is zero but once the threshold is crossed the probability is high. This acute short sightedness is compounded by the fact that the awareness of systemic risk tends to fade with time (Kahneman, Slovic, and Tversky 1982).

Both hypotheses concur in holding that systemic risk is not the result of an exogenous shock on a fundamental variable (although this may indeed be a catalyst), but rather of endogenous failures of coordination. The example of the recent Asian crisis is representative of many of these failures, which are self-reinforced by contagion. In less than a year, a relatively insignificant crisis in Thailand led to contagion throughout the Asian region, then Russia, from Russia to Brazil, and from Brazil to the whole of Latin America. Finally, systemic risk was generated with the collapse of the hedge fund Long Term Capital Management. Investors' perceptions moved from concern about the situation in Thailand to a wholesale rejection of the region's debt, to a so-called flight to quality after the Russian debt moratorium in August 1998. Finally there was a flight to liquidity after the bankruptcy of LTCM. This flight to liquidity is what usually triggers a systemic risk. Liquidity is a central component of systemic risk in financial markets and is the key to coordination failures. A financial market is liquid when participants believe in liquidity. If this belief wavers, however, huge selling pressure is generated in a cascade effect, which can quite easily lead to panic. Participants rush to sell assets because they are unable to predict where the floor of the market may prove to be. This endogenous uncertainly then generates the failure of implicit coordination that leads to systemic risk.

In these situations the double-edged role of the banks becomes obvious. They are both units of production of private profits and suppliers of liquidity (which is a collective public good) to the economy as a whole. Liquidity enables the development of financial markets and allows entities to meet debt repayments. Processes of systemic risk tend always to bring the bank onto the central stage during financial crises because they are responsible for reducing or eliminating liquidity in times of growing uncertainty. The enormous development of financial markets in the 1980s, embracing both derivatives and underlying assets, is the mechanism by which markets have responded to this problem. Instruments for the management of liquidity and risk have grown spectacularly creating a whole range of new opportunities for arbitrage, diversification, and insurance of risk and liquidity.

However, this development has also meant that financial markets, when in situations of uncertainly, have been subject to recurring shocks with huge increases in volatility and of liquidity problems. Derivative markets play an ambiguous role, acting as risk-assuring instruments but also as transmitters of liquidity problems to other markets. The added problem of derivatives is that there is no limit to their creation and no way of knowing how many are in existence since each derivative is a private bilateral contract between banks (Mayer, 1999). This, obviously, heightens uncertainty.

A liquidity problem, for example, in one segment of the wholesale market, can force intermediaries, acting as a counterpart to the hedge, to transfer the liquidity deficit to other market segments. But if the counterparts then perceive that they are going to run up important losses on their capital, or consider that their credit conditions are too onerous or risk-laden for them to finance their growing exposure to depreciating assets, they may be forced to renounce to the role of price support at a particular level which inevitably leads to an increase in volatility and a reduction in liquidity. The concentration of option contracts which follows sets off an upward spiral of hedging as long as the future price remains above the option's strike price. This hedging process generates excess demand in the market for underlying assets, which increases with the price, and this heightens price movements in the underlying market and disturbs liquidity in the cash market. (Aglietta, 1998). More pressure on liquidity in the underlying asset market is caused by margin calls from lenders who have to cover the deficit of collateral on their derivatives and cover margins. In all markets in conditions of temporary disequilibrium, self-generating multiple equilibrium and asymmetric information can generate liquidity problems and systemic risk if a large number of intermediaries acting as counterparts try to escape simultaneously from involuntary, high-risk exposure. Institutional investors who play a fundamental role in debt, equity, and derivative markets and participate in highly competitive markets can respond in the same way to common signals and enact the same strategies to protect their portfolios. This sets off the herd effect, which is aggravated by a structure of incentives that, as we have seen, tends to encourage mimetic behavior as a result of asymmetric information in fund management.

Finally, fund management creates a serious agency problem. Savers want high returns on their investments which leads them to evaluate profits and the fund managers' remuneration at ever more frequent intervals. Managers' contracts are increasingly short-term. In a situation of uncertainty and instability, measures adopted to reduce conflicts of interest between principal (the investor) and agent (the fund manager) tend to generate herd behavior. When economic fundamentals are so uncertain that short-term profitability cannot be assured, managers follow the sentiments of the crowd either because they receive common signals or because they simply copy each other, generating uni-directional buying and selling (Scharfstein and Stein, 1990).

The "original sin"

The practical impossibility of developing countries to issue debt in international capital markets in their own currency or even in the long term in their own national capital markets has been named by Barry Eichengreen and Ricardo Hausmann the "original sin," which has generated a strong debate among international financial economists. For Eichengreen and Hausmann (1999, 2003) and later for Eichengreen, Hausmann, and Panizza (2003) the origin of this sin is to be found in the behavior of international capital markets, while for Reinhart, Rogoff, and Savastano (2003), Jeanne (2003), and Goldstein and Turner (2003) it is due to the failures of the economic policies of the same developing countries.

The question that both sides address is the same: Why are developing countries not able to attract more foreign capital when all will gain by doing so? Developing countries could gain by using foreign savings to compensate for their low saving rates and enhance domestic development, reduce their macroeconomic volatility and stabilize their economy against severe shocks. Developed countries could gain by getting a higher return for their savings and a greater diversification of their investment portfolios; therefore the world's welfare would improve.

The problem with the original sin is that if the debt of these countries can only be denominated in foreign currency, a real depreciation of their exchange rate will reduce the purchasing power of their GDP, in terms of the foreign currency, it will make it very difficult to serve their debt and the lenders will not be willing to buy their debt. The options left to these countries are all suboptimal. They can try to reduce their external debt but they will be left without any protection against shocks. They can try to accumulate foreign currency reserves to mitigate, through intervention in the exchange markets, the volatility of their exchange rate and to have a cushion to pay their external debt, but matching their assets and liabilities in foreign currency means that there are no net inflows of foreign capital, besides being very costly, given that the return of the investment in foreign currency is much lower than in their own currency.

For some economists, mentioned above, this is a normal outcome of their own track record of bad economic policies, such as their history of uncontrolled inflation, of excessive debt accumulation and of recurrent defaults. These economists called this situation: "external debt intolerance." Eichengreen and Hausmann do not reject fully this critique because they recognize that these countries need a policy of structural reforms in their institutions and more credible policies, but they think that it is not a sufficient condition. They reckon that some countries have been able to meet these conditions and continue to suffer from the "original sin." The clearest case is that of Chile, which has been a very stable country, with a good institutional framework, but which was not able not only to ameliorate the adverse terms of trade, in 1998, when the price of copper plummeted, but which also suffered a "sudden stop" to its capital inflows, which obliged it to reduce imports by 22 percent, that is, 6 percent of its GDP, and to fall into recession (−0.8 percent) when it was growing at 6.8 percent.

Other economists, such as Morris Goldstein and Philip Turner (2003), think that the "original sin" is the same as a currency mismatch balance sheet of their assets and liabilities in foreign currency, giving rise to a net positive debt in foreign currency, which makes it difficult to attract more foreign debt from foreign investors. Eichengreen and Hausmann reject this thesis, because they think that a country can suffer from the "original sin" without having such a mismatch. That is, the mismatch is a necessary condition for the "original sin" but not a sufficient one, because some countries have suffered the "original sin" even when they have increased their foreign currency reserves to be able to make their foreign debt payments or when they have a currency board with the dollar.

Olivier Jeanne (2003) thinks that the root of the "original sin" is the lack of credibility of the domestic monetary policy of many developing countries, which is determined by the weakness of their fiscal policies. An uncertain monetary policy causes lenders to become unsure about the future real value of their debt in the domestic currency in dollar terms. The dilemma of the borrower is whether to issue an excessive volume of debt in local currency and then default if the exchange rate is fixed, because the domestic interest rates are much higher than in foreign currency or to issue an excessive volume of debt in foreign currency and default if there is a depreciation in their exchange rate. If the probability of the first option is lower than the second it will issue debt in foreign currency. Only gaining a higher credibility in its monetary policy will allow the country to issue debt in local currency ex-ante, which increases the autonomy of its monetary policy ex-post.

The basic solution to the "original sin" proposed by Eichengreen and Hausmann is the creation of a synthetic unit of account, based on a selected basket of developing country currencies, in which all their debts can be issued. Then, to develop a large market for these debts, liquid enough to be able to be quoted daily in the international capital markets. To achieve such a large market, the IFIs should start issuing part of their debts in such a basket, then the G10 countries and finally, the developing countries themselves. This idea is not totally new. The World Bank, in 1999, made a proposal to develop insurance markets for the risk produced by the terms of trade variations of developing countries. Robert Shiller (2003) has proposed that governments issue derivatives to allow a swap market of risks from different countries with different levels of development to diversify the macroeconomic risks of a given country, since there is a high correlation between GDP per capita and real exchange rate and Ricardo Caballero (2003) has proposed developing financial instruments indexed to the export price of commoditties of the developing countries, and Borensztein and Mauro (2002) have proposed that the developing countries issue "growth bonds" indexed to the rate of growth to their GDP, where annual coupons fluctuate with their real GDP evolution.

Another proposal by Hausmann and Rigobon (2003) is to ask the IDA, the Development Agency of the World Bank for the poorest countries, which is not financed through the markets in dollars, but directly through the budgets transfer of its member countries if it could lend to those countries, to avoid provoking to them into a "currency mismatch," in its own inflation indexed currency or in a basket of IDA currencies.

Whatever the solution chosen for the "original sin," there is another major problem that needs to be solved: the excessive debt levels of most developing countries.

"Excessive debt," "debt intolerance," and "sudden stops"

In almost every major financial crisis of developing countries in recent times there has been a common denominator: an excessive level of government debt, as in the case of Russia, Brazil, or Argentina, or even of private debt, as in the case of the Asian crises. The problem is not the issuing of government debt, in the sense that it is necessary for a developing country in order to invest in education, health, or infrastructures, to cope with the reconstruction after natural disasters or to smooth economic cycles, but to issue an excessive level of debt, which always ends up in higher taxes, higher real interest rates, and, therefore, a crowding out of private investment and less growth.

Moreover, once the level is excessive, the major problem is to try to get out of it. If the government tries to reduce it, it has to cut down expenditure, usually public investment, which is easier politically, or to increase taxes when growth is already slowing down, so fiscal policy becomes procyclical and ends up in a recession. If there is no effort to reduce it, then the only way out is through an explicit default or an implicit one: reducing the real value of the debt with high inflation.

How did these countries reach such a situation? There are three basic explanations: the first is structural. Most developing countries which have achieved an excessive level of debt have a low level of tax revenue as a percentage of GDP. The average is 27 percent versus 44 percent in developed countries. Their effective tax on income is even lower with an average of 10 percent versus 35 percent for developed countries (Reinhart, Rogoff, and Savastano, 2003) and both the rates and the revenue are very volatile due to their cycles being sharper (Kose, Prassad, and Terrones, 2003). Their debt service payments represent a very high percentage of the total budget expenditure: 17 percent versus 10 percent of the developed countries, and, finally, their saving rates as a percentage of their GDP are very low, mainly in Latin America, being an average 17 percent.

The second is exogenous. The increase in interest rates by the Central Banks of developed countries, notably the US Fed, can be a major cause of this excessive debt accumulation. The huge raise of the fed-funds rate in 1980 was decisive in unchaining the 1982 crises in Latin America, and it also happened in 1994 which gave way to the Mexican crises. The same effects have caused excessive increases in the oil price and the strong appreciation of the dollar.

The third is endogenous and related to their economic policies themselves. The unrealistic fixed, pegged, or indexed exchange rates to the dollar which have eventually produced major devaluations which have increased the value of their debts in local currency is one issue. The large increases in domestic interest rates due to the amount of debt outstanding is another. The recapitalization of their domestic domestic banks which reached insolvency because of a very lax risk control is a third issue. The recognition of large contingent liabilities or hidden debt accumulated by their federal, regional or provincial governments is a fourth (Burnside,

Eichenbaum, and Rebello, 2001); fifth, there are many situations which belong to the political economy of public debt, in the sense that many governments and politicians increase the debt levels or even reduce taxes, in order to be re-elected, the election year.

Finally, one of the most serious problems today in developing countries is the issue of "pro-cyclicality." Capital markets tend to be procyclical because they always lend to developing countries when they are growing faster and they stop receiving capital flows when they are in recession. But, at the same time, their governments do not save and reduce their deficit and debts when they are growing above potential by generating fiscal primary surpluses, that is, excluding debt service payments, and they logically spend even more when they are in a recessive situation, getting an excessive level of debt. Pro-cyclicality is an area where economists are trying to devise instruments or markets which would allow for more efficient risk-sharing among countries. One of these is the proposal made by Eichengreen and Hausmann to alleviate the "original sin" problem, but it should be complemented by better economic policy behavior by developing countries.

When does a level of debt becomes excessive and intolerable? The most recent studies about defaults show that, on average, the level of public debt as a percentage of their GDP was 50 percent, a year before the default, a not very high level for a developed country, but very high when compared with the average level of their tax revenue in the case of domestic debt or with the level of export revenue in foreign currency in the case of external debt. The empirical work made by Reinhart, Rogoff, and Savastano tries to find out when the debt level becomes "intolerable" or where the debt threshold reaches a stage that should not be surpassed. They find out that this threshold can be as low as 15 percent of GDP or as high as 100 percent; it all depends on the history of each country in terms of their number of debt default or restructuring, or episodes of hyperinflation, or the weakness of their political and legal institutions, or of their fiscal and financial systems and the relationship between domestic and external debt. Hemming, Kell, and Schimmelphennig (2003) have elaborated advanced fiscal indicators to try to predict and prevent debt crisis after analyzing most of them. They have found out that budget deficits are a good indicator because it tends to be very high two years before the debt crises. On the contrary, total debt is a poor indicator because it does not show large variations before the crises or in their absence. Their debt composition seems to be more useful, since short-term debt piles up on the way to the crises.

Once the debt level of a country is perceived by the markets to have surpassed a reasonable threshold of intolerance, their capital inflows stop abruptly, provoking a default. This is what it has been called by Calvo and Mishkin (2003) and Calvo and Talvi (2004) "sudden stops."

They argue that the "sudden stops" are the result of a combination of external shocks and domestic vulnerabilities. The poor growth performance and the new crop of crises in Latin American economies after 1998 were not an accident waiting to happen as a result of the reforms in the early 1990s; rather, they had a lot to do with the disruption in the international financial markets after the Russian crisis in August 1998, which brought about an unprecedented, across-the-board increase in interest rates for emerging economies and a systemic collapse of capital flows to the region which brought it to a strong recession, given the high correlation between capital flows and growth. This systemic collapse in capital flows combined with "domestic financial vulnerabilities" that acted as amplifiers of the external shock, explain how individual countries in Latin America were badly hit, experiencing a major financial crisis and economic collapse, which spread even to countries with exemplary economic policies and institutions, such as Chile.

The lesson to learn from this terrible episode is not to throw overboard the reform efforts of the 1990s but to increase the focus in identifying the key points of vulnerability of these countries and try to consolidate a concrete set of policies to solidify the financial position of governments, the private sector, and the financial system. Nevertheless, the interruption of capital flows was so sudden, synchronized, and widespread that it appears implausible to argue that it was caused by a sudden and coordinated reassessment of the economic fundamentals of each individual country in the region. Rather, the "sudden stop" of capital flows was the result of a disruption in international capital markets in the aftermath of the Russian default that resulted in a systemic external financial shock to Latin America and other emerging economies (Calvo and Talvi, 2004) Therefore, on the one side, emerging economies should continue their reform process and reduce their domestic vulnerabilities; in the case of the 1998 crisis the major one was their "liability dollarization." Taking the example of Argentina, its private debt – domestic bank credit plus foreign lending to the non-financial domestic private sector – was highly dollarized. Before the "sudden stop" 80 percent of the Argentinian debt was denominated in US dollars compared to 38 percent in Chile. The high dollarization of private debt implied large financial mismatches in the balance sheets of Argentinian households and firms since only 25 percent of productive activities were in the tradable sector (the share of tradable goods as a percentage of GDP) and potentially capable of generating earnings in hard currency. In contrast, Chile's tradable sector was 35 percent of GDP, a similar share to the dollar liabilities of the private sector.

But, on the other hand, something has to be reformed in the international capital markets to avoid countries such as Chile, which have sound finances and economic policies, also suffering a sudden stop in capital flows. The behavior of international capital markets after the Russian default shows that they have sometimes lower efficiency and rationality than they are supposed to have, and they can even produce a systemic risk crisis in which everybody ends up being a loser.

What can be done to reduce or avoid the recurrence of crises?

On the one side, feedback and contagion in financial crises is caused, to some extent, by economic and financial globalization. This seems to be unavoidable not only because it derives from economic and political liberalization and technological development but also because it is a result of the structure of financial markets and the behavior of their participants. The conjunction of financial globalization, national monetary policy, and structure of markets tends to amplify the failures of coordination between financial agents and generates a spillover effect into other economies. This gives rise to contagion effects that can generate systemic risk.

These problems are inherent in globalizing markets, and if they are not faced, crises and contagion could become more frequent and more serious, a trend that could lead to the questioning of the very process of globalization. This outcome would be extremely damaging to the development of the world economy in the twenty-first century. This is the reason why a more organized and coordinated effort should be made to avoid these inherent failures of international financial markets when they find themselves surprised by unexpected outcomes.

But, on the other hand, emerging economies have to continue to reform their fiscal, monetary, and financial institutions and policies and to increase their trade openness, to improve their political and legal institutions to gain more credibility, and to avoid the dramatic economic collapses such as those suffered by some Latin American and Asian countries.

I have simply outlined the problems and paradoxes of the process in this chapter and I am loath to propose solutions. But what does appear clear is the need for a global regulator and a lender of last resort, together with more thorough self-regulation by market participants. These are necessary conditions for reducing the frequency of crises, limiting contagion, and avoiding systemic risk that could endanger the whole of the world economy, as happened in 1929.

The main lines of action for an improvement of the so-called "International Financial Architecture" should be as Stanley Fischer (2002) proposes, first crisis prevention, and, second, adequate response to crises.

In crisis prevention, the role of emerging countries' economic policies is crucial. The first one is to find the right system of exchange rate for every country, which is not easy. Some countries, mainly from Asia, have been successful using a managed float, with recurrent interventions to limit excessive exchange rate fluctuations. Other countries are now doing better with free floating, together with inflation targeting, such as Brazil and South Africa. Others combined flexible exchange rates with capital controls, like some Asian countries. Others still, have pegged exchange rates with heavy intervention, such as China. Yet others, have dollarized or eurized their economies, with mixed results. Only a process of "learning by doing" could eventually accommodate the most beneficial exchange rate system for each economy. Nevertheless, the shift to more flexible exchange rates since 1994 has proved to be a good isolator from crises, and now is the preferred system for many emerging countries.

The second is to have an anti-cyclical fiscal policy, which produces surpluses during booms and deficits during recessions, but always with the target of reducing permanently, albeit slowly, their debt to GDP ratio to avoid reaching an intolerable level in terms of fiscal revenue and of foreign currency revenue, through exports and further trade opening. Another way to prevent dangerous surprises is to try to avoid at any time an accumulation of too much short-term debt, both domestic and external. Finally, it is important to avoid currency balance-sheet mismatching by trying to balance, as much as possible, foreign debt liabilities with assets.

The third is capital account liberalization and capital controls. Past experience shows that the capital account liberalization should be slow until the domestic financial system is well organized, well supervised and has the proper risk controls. It should also be done in the right sequencing, first, FDI inflows and later portfolio inflows and, finally, only when the country is ready, the rest of inflows and outflows. In the meantime, capital controls can play a positive role to avoid sudden fluctuations of capital inflows and outflows. Even the IMF has acknowledged that its initial push for rapid liberalization was a mistake after having learned more from the Asian crisis (Eichengreen and Mussa, 1998).

Capital controls can indeed be effective if they are introduced temporarily while the banking system is reformed or while the external situation is improved. But unfortunately, experience shows that controls tend to be used over much longer periods of time. They can also lead to corruption. It is also increasingly difficult to enforce them, given the increasing technological capacity and financial market innovation (Hufbauer and Wada, 1999; Edwards, 1999).

The fourth is to increase economic information transparency meeting the standards set by the IMF. A better and standardized knowledge about the country's debt both internal and external, reserves, banking and insurance supervision, securities regulation, payment systems, corporate governance, accounting systems, insolvency, bankrupcy and creditor rights, can help considerably in crisis avoidance.

The role of the IMF is also important in crises prevention by improving the quality and frequency of country surveillance and reporting. On the contrary, IMF public concerns about or warnings to countries, when it believes that they may be heading for a crisis, can be sometimes wrong, or self-fulfilling and, therefore, counter-productive. But it should strengthen its internal research on crisis vulnerability indicators and try to encourage member countries to publish their Article IV reports to improve the efficiency of international capital markets. The same can be said about the setting up of the Capital Markets Consultative Group, to discuss general issues with market participants, without giving any details of individual member countries, which is helping the markets to understand better some of the issues affecting indebted countries. The introduction of the CCL, Contingency Credit Line facility, has also been a major step toward crisis prevention. The rationale of this facility is to offer a precautionary line of credit to countries which have developed sound economic policies but could be vulnerable to a contagion from crises elsewhere. It allows those countries to increase, at low cost, their foreign exchange reserves by drawing from this facility to avoid a speculative attack (Fischer, 2001). Unfortunately, the countries which are eligible for this facility have not yet made use of it; thus it may be necessary to engage in a dialogue with member countries to try to make it more effective.

The other important role in crises prevention should be the international capital markets participants, because they also contribute to the excessive volatility and pro-cyclicality of international capital flows and to contagion. In this area very little has been accomplished yet (Dobson and Hufbauer, 2001). Implementing the new Basel capital accord, improving the present financial markets regulation, reviewing the rules, behavior and pecuniary incentives of large portfolio investors, tightening the frameworks governing the G10 deposit insurance and private-sector involvement in financial crises resolution are the main issues to be addressed. Only the Financial Stability Forum set up in 1999 to bring financial supervisors from the G7 together with their ministers of finance and representatives of the major international regulatory agencies and IFIs, and the creation of the G20 adding the larger emerging economies, today absent from the most important international economic discussions, to the G10 are going to be helpful.

The second important issue is how to respond better and quicker to crises and how to resolve them with as little damage as possible. In this area, the main discussion has been around private-sector involvement (PSI) in financial crises resolution. (Fischer, 2002). This has many meanings. On the one hand, it means the contribution of the private sector to meeting a country's financial needs, given that the official sources are limited, and help the IMF and other IFIs to offset its wild swings in capital flows. On the other, it means persuading the private sector to reduce the level and speed of net capital outflows from a country facing a capital account crisis and it also means for the private sector to suffer pain and losses as well during a crisis. Until now there is only one agreement, signed in Prague in 2000, by market participants and the IMF, about PSI. The agreement is based on market-oriented and voluntary solutions, not imposing anything upon the private sector. The starting point is that official financing is limited, that creditors and debtors should take responsibility for their decisions to lend and borrow and that contracts should be honored, except in extreme cases. Finally, the IMF would provide the assessment of a member's underlying payment capacity and the prospects for regaining market access, trying to categorize crises as of liquidity or insolvency.

Another major issue in the case of crises resolution has been the debate between the Anne Krueger proposal (2002), under the name SDRM, (sovereign debt restructuring mechanism), that is, creating a legal procedure for sovereign bankruptcy, finding legal mechanisms for the approving payments standstills by sovereigns and for the restructuring, and, if necessary, writing down sovereign debts, and the G10 deputies' proposal of introducing collective action clauses (CACs) in bond contracts in order to reduce the costs of restructuring when debt crises appear. Debt contracts are incomplete and CACs can promote orderly workouts of international debt to avoid chaotic situations such as that of Argentina in 2003 and 2004. In the end the CACs option has been the one supported by the member countries' issuers as well as for the private market participants, mainly because these clauses had already existed in the UK, for many years, in the British trust-deed bonds, and have proved to be effective. The SDRM option, which, in a similar way had been already proposed by Eichengreen and Portes (1995) proved to be politically too ambitious, because of the large transfer of sovereignty to an international court with authority for suspending legal procedures against a country, but at least it gave some impetus to the adoption of CACs (Cohen and Portes, 2003).

Finally, there is the important issue of the problems derived from the operation of intenational capital markets, which have been perceived to be too powerful, too volatile, and not very able to discriminate countries by their economic soundness. These charges are not so true today, where markets discriminate better, and sounder countries have lower credit spreads but there is still a question mark about what will happen if, in the future, a large increase in dollar interest rates reappears.

In any case, from the point of view of creating a true "international financial archtecture" it is clear that the ultimate goal to avoid future crises and contagion should be to have an "international lender of last resort" (ILLR) which can create liquidity (the IMF cannot do so today), by giving such a role to the IMF and allowing it to create liquidity and improving its present governance (Fischer, 1999a).

Experience of banking crises show that the best answer to financial contagion is always the same: a "lender of last resort." Walter Bagehot's famous maxim (1873) is probably still relevant: "It is necessary to lend freely and temporarily to banks with liquidity problems, provided they are solvent, at an interest rate higher than that of the market and in exchange for good collateral."

Yet this advice is difficult to apply even for the regulators of national banking. In the international sphere the problems are even more complex (Giannini 1999). National bank authorities have discovered that the suitability of "lending freely" is countered by the need to avoid any explosive increase in monetary aggregates. Distinguishing between "illiquid and insolvent" banks is extremely difficult during a crisis. Meanwhile, demanding "interest rates above those of the market" can actually intensify the problems of the stricken institution and "good collateral" is extremely hard to come by in times of crisis.

In the case of international financial crises, there is no lender of last resort, money is never freely lent and it generally arrives late. The distinction between illiquid and insolvent countries is all the more difficult and the need to establish good collateral collide with the principle of sovereignty, which prohibits the execution of state property. Moreover, as Krugman (1998c) points out, those Indonesians who tried to recover their deposits during the 1997 crisis did not want local currency. They were after US dollars and neither the Bank of Indonesia nor the IMF could ever give them that.

The IMF would seem to be the best candidate, given its experience as an international financial institution. But in the present situation, the fund cannot fulfil that role since it has no mandate to issue money (Fischer, 1999a). This is an issue of some urgency, since a lender of last resort should be in place before the next crisis. That would give emerging economies time to reform their financial systems and improve corporate governance and accountancy, and introduce greater transparency of information. Tackling liquidity problems is the key factor in avoiding or reducing financial contagion and of preventing systemic risk. Jeanne and Wyplosz (2001) arrive at similar conclusions and show immense skepticism regarding the size of the injections of liquidity that the lender has to allocate in the case of a "twin crisis" (banking and currency) and how big the lender has to be. They think that if lender resources have to be injected into the marked this has to be done by the issuer of the international currency, the US Fed, and not by a limited fund. The only way that a limited fund can become a lender of last resort is if its resources are used to back domestic banking safety nets, then the international lender resources do not need to be larger than the liquidity gap in the domestic banking sector. However, this second approach, being more practical, has agency problems that seem difficult to address under the current international financial architecture, without introducing major reforms.

A different approach is developed by Corsetti et al. (2004) who refute the two main arguments against international liquidity provisions. First, they assert that "corner solutions" in the form of exceptionally large and potentially unlimited liquidity provisions are not necessary to reduce the incidence of liquidity runs. The presence of limited contingent liquidity support can be effective in inducing a fraction of private investors to decide to roll over their exposure to the country. Second, the idea that liquidity support always induces "moral hazard" distortions is considered incorrect, because contingent liquidity funds may tilt the incentives of a government toward implementing desirable but politically difficult policies and reforms, whereas the same government would have found them too costly and risky to implement if the outcome of its efforts were highly exposed to disruptive speculative runs. Eichengreen et al. (2005) use another similar argument to the previous economists when analyzing the role of the IMF in attempting to stabilize capital flows to emerging economies by providing public monitoring and emergency finance. They contrast cases where banks and bondholders do the lending. Banks have a natural advantage in creditor monitoring and coordination, while bonds have superior risk sharing characteristics. Consistent with this assumption, banks reduce spreads as they obtain more information through repeat transactions with borrowers. By comparison, repeat borrowing has little influence in bond markets where publicly available information predominates. But spreads on bonds are lower when they are issued in conjunction with IMF-supported programs, as if the existence of a program conveyed positive information to bondholders, helping the countries with vulnerability crises to overcome them.

A very interesting proposal has been made by Daniel Cohen and Richard Portes (2004) through the idea of a "lender of first resort." They reckon that the idea of an "international lender of last resort" (ILLR) to be performed by the IMF, as proposed by Fischer, have proved to be very ambitious in constituting a realistic agenda for reform. An ILLR must have at its disposal either the resources to inject an indeterminate quantity of fresh liquidity or perfect information regarding solvent and insolvent financial intermediaries. As the latter assumption is virtually ruled out by the very nature of financial crises, the former needs to give the IMF the means of creating liquidity ex nihilo. Such a transfer of sovereignty, which was extremely difficult to implement in the European case, seems to both authors totally unrealistic on a world scale, therefore the ILLR should be naturally conformed around the FED, the ECB and the Bank of Japan. Moreover, there are two main issues: The first is that it is not always possible to distinguish between the "good" debtors which have been unlucky from the "bad" debtors which have continued to implement unsustainable policies; therefore, intervention by the IMF has tended to swing between too much and too little, which has produced accusations of "moral hazard" by the Meltzer Commission. The second is that crises tend to be self-fulfilling in the sense that when the countries start to lose credibility all the creditors end up lending at punitive rates or exiting from that risk altogether and provoking a crisis. In some cases, confidence can only be restored by a bailout; in others, the country may be willing to act to restore its confidence, but the markets do not give it the time to do so and start raising rates and spreads, leading to a self-fulfilling crisis.

The proposal made by Cohen and Portes is based on three complementary measures. The first is that IMF member countries should commit themselves ex-ante not to borrow at punitive rates of interest, say above a spread of 400 basis points, even if their situation deteriorates because of an internal or external shock and investors start to lose confidence, but are still willing to lend them at higher spreads. The second is that, immediately the IMF works with the country to analyze the problem and find the remedies that could solve it and designs a program, which, if agreed upon, gives the country access to IMF money, at below market rates and at the limit rates that the country can afford, on the condition of taking the agreed measures. The country acts and the IMF responds, when spreads reach the "trigger" level, regardless of fundamentals, which will be assessed later. Therefore, the IMF acts as a "lender of first resort" to prevent the crisis and helps the country to regain its lost confidence. This mechanism could replace the non-used and by now defunct CCl (contingent credit line) facility. The third is that it is necessary to solve the ex-post problem and have an efficient debt resolution in the case that debt restructuring would be necessary. They propose both including CACs in all bond contracts and creating a third negotiating "club," which will be the club for bonds restructurings: besides the Paris club, which deals with debt to governments, the London club, which deals with debt to banks, it will be necessary to create the New York club to oversee the negotiations with bondholders. Finally, they propose a mediation agency with an administratively "light" structure that will coordinate the three clubs, to ensure the timely exchange of information and comparison of assumptions, verify claims and bondholder voting, and endorse or not a standstill.

Presently, as a result of the hangover from the last crises, some emerging economies still have great difficulty in attracting international capital at anything but highly prohibitive interest rates. This means that they are still in an illiquid situation and so are extremely vulnerable if another crisis should break out. In the meantime, a pragmatic measure would be for developed countries to allow institutional investors to include lower than investment grade assets in their portfolios even if only at the margin since this would allow greater risk diversification and marginally raise their average rate of return (Fernandez Arias and Hausmann, 1999). Until an international lender of first or last resort is in place, however, emerging countries have no alternative but to arm themselves with *liquidity self-protection*, as Martin Feldstein (1999) puts it. It requires more than simply sound economic policies to avoid exchange rate crises. After all, as we have seen, even virtuous countries can be vulnerable to contagion. Only those countries with high levels of currency reserves and foreign currency-denominated contingency credit lines available at short notice, can feel confident that they will head off a crisis.

As Tom Friedman (1999) argues "the most basic truth about globalization is that nobody is in charge and when something goes wrong there is nobody to call." "Globalization," says Friedman, "is Americanization. But the US monetary authorities seem unwilling to accept that responsibility."

Globalization and Culture

Globalization is changing world culture in two fundamental ways. First, as Friedman pointed out at the end of the last chapter, globalization is, in many respects, a synonym for Americanization. US media, and especially TV, has ever-greater influence throughout the world, through Hollywood-produced movies, news channels such as CNN, NBC, CBS, and Fox, TV serials, music channels and advertisements for big US brands. Then there is also the development of the Internet, dominated by the English language, with a massive predominance of US portals and browsers. In short, the industries producing content and the key means of communication are generally US owned, from AOL to Time Warner to Disney, from Microsoft and Viacom to Yahoo and Google.

Two basic forces have driven this process of media globalization: First, technology, which has improved audiovisual production and distribution systems to an extraordinary extent, bringing entertainment to the global market at ever more reasonable prices. Technology has also enabled a huge increase in frequency spectrum capacity through digital compression, which has transformed communication by creating room for 12 or 24 channels where previously only one existed. Second, media privatisation and deregulation polices by governments have accelerated globalization.

Deregulation and privatization, together with technological change, have led to a dramatic rise in the number of media companies on a world scale, just as they did within the United States. US homes are years ahead of their European and Asian counterparts in the availability of cable and satellite channels, but the rest of the world is catching up fast. European and other governments, however, have often adopted restrictive policies in a bid to maintain control over TV and radio, an attitude that has placed their countries at a disadvantage by blocking the creation of big conglomerates that could compete with the American ones (*Economist,* 1997b).

In the early 1980s, multichannel TV began to extend to other countries thanks to technological advances, which drastically cut the cost of transmission and broadcasting. At first, only cable companies were able to assume the costs of erecting and maintaining the huge antennas needed to receive satellite signals. Satellite development was also exclusive to the US and the ex USSR which had used them for espionage throughout the cold war. Later, miniaturization of electronic components made possible that transmission via satellite could be picked up by small dishes placed on the roof or the balcony of the potential users. Unfortunately for many countries, content production remained in US hands radically diminishing the potential for production. The US majors continued to dominate content production and sold it from an oligopoly position at prices well above marginal cost, which fell constantly.

Though it is technology that has made such rapid content development possible on a world scale, it is this content that will dominate in the future. As Peter Drucker (1999) points out:

> Technologist companies will soon fall back to another level as printers did in the Middle Ages, when having been the princes of the Gutenberg revolution between the fifteenth and sixteenth centuries, they became the servants of publishers. The publishers were then the Church and Universities. They are now Bertelsman and Murdoch.

Because of the high fixed costs of producing a film or a TV series, only companies with extensive distribution capacity are able to maintain reasonable profit margins. If markets are national, the necessary scale of production is just not available for profitable production unless the market is of the size of the US or EU. But, of course, the main difference between these two single markets is that languages segment the EU market, while the English-speaking US can exploit much greater economies of scale.

Globalization is hastening the process by which English is becoming the world's primary language of communication. More than 800 million people now use English as first or second language and its use is spreading at a faster pace than any other language, propelled by Internet where Anglo-dominance is even more pronounced. Spanish also has an advantage over other languages being the second most spoken language in the world (excluding Mandarin) with 450 million speakers of Spanish as their first or second language. Mexico, with 100 million inhabitants, is the biggest Spanish-speaking country in the world. Brazil's decision to recognize Spanish as its second language will eventually bring 170 million more into contact with the language in coming years. Japanese, German, and French will face far greater problems obtaining the economies of scale necessary for profitable content provision. US corporations can cover the fixed costs of film and TV production in the US market and then export finished products to the rest of the world at marginal cost. This is a critical advantage. Every year Europe purchases 2 billion dollars worth of US TV products. While its nearest European rival, the UK sells 100 million dollars worth to the US. The UK's dominance in Europe is basically a result of the English language and the fact that Britain was the first European country to privatize and liberalize the frequency spectrum.

India produces more films than the US but does not compete in international markets because of its specific national language and local content. Japan, the world's third biggest film producer, has the same problem although it is somewhat more international than India. In short, language is absolutely essential to gain economies of scale.

Europe's reaction to US domination has been the imposition of quotas. Under the EU directive on film production, ironically named "TV without frontiers," 50 percent of films shown in the EU have to be produced there. Under UK pressure, the addendum "provided this is possible" was added. The directive, indeed, has proved impossible to apply.

Is there any point in limiting foreign penetration in national TV? My modest opinion is that there is not. In the first place, because it is not necessarily better for a national producer such as Silvio Berlusconi to control nearly all commercial channels in Italy, than a foreign producer such as the US citizen Rupert Murdoch to control a third of production in the UK. In the second place, the argument that media domination leads to political control is clearly not always true. Romano Prodi beat Berlusconi in the 1996 elections in Italy despite running his campaign from a bus, while Berlusconi mobilised his powerful TV and radio interests. Yeltsin then and Putin now seem to think the opposite. In the third place, it is not only more profitable but also more desirable that a TV group produces a wide range of channels with different perspectives than different groups offering the same viewpoint. Finally, digitalization is pulling down barriers to entry in these sectors at a rapid pace, allowing production to become more diversified and, above all, more closely adapted to national and local culture. Where they are allowed to and where there are no local or regional state monopolies, the big private media groups are now adapting products to local languages and culture. This means local tastes and preferences will increasingly be catered for. People now want access to global news from reliable, credible sources of information but they are mainly interested in regional and local issues. Big media groups are aware of this and are increasing national and local production in order to raise penetration rates. In that sense, digitalization, by drastically reducing costs, will allow production to be tailored to cultural preferences in each specific market rather than just imposing US culture.

On the other side of the screen, thanks to digitalization and interactive cable technologies, after all, is the viewer with a hand-held remote control who frantically zaps away in search of programs of interest. This makes it much more difficult to impose a specific point of view in news or other content. In fact, as Umberto Eco (2000) has written, "The Internet leads to the de-nationalisation of knowledge." This gives users the freedom to acquire knowledge that was previously out of reach. "The Internet is the virtual equivalent of the Universe. Everything is contained in the Net."

From culture to entertainment

So far, we have discussed how commercial, financial, and media globalization has allowed US-based news and entertainment corporations to play an increasingly dominant world role. The question that immediately arises, as a result of this situation, is whether a process of Americanization is becoming a threat to national, regional, and local cultures.

The first caveat we should make here is that culture is a concept that embraces far more than entertainment in the US sense of the word. Culture includes language, ideas, values, beliefs, and customs; codes, institutions, tools, techniques, work of art, rituals, ceremonies etc. There can be little doubt that information and entertainment will affect and modify some basic elements of each of our cultures but it is difficult to conceive of a completely homogenous culture as some suggest when they describe cultural globalization. If this were the case, at least in developed countries, it would create massive social resistance. As Daniel Bell (1977) argues, "culture for a society, a group or a person is a continual process of sustaining an identity through the coherence gained by a consistent aesthetic point of view, a moral conception of self, and a style of life which exhibits those conceptions in the objects that adorn one's home and oneself and in the taste which expresses those points of view. Culture is thus the realm of sensibility, of emotion and moral temper, and of the intelligence, which seeks to order these feelings.

This support for identity – individual or collective – is what people try hard to preserve whatever the cost in order to defend their culture from the new media avalanche. The image of a young Arab in an American bar in Cairo wearing jeans and T-shirt, smoking a cigarette, drinking coffee, listening to rap while watching the TV may seem quintessentially American. But in fact, if he is asked what he thinks of US culture, it is more than likely that he feels indifferent or even hostile. As Bernard Lewis (1995) points out, "In modern times, the dominating factor in the consciousness of most Middle Easterners has been the impact of Europe, later of the West more generally, and the transformation – some would say dislocation – which it has brought."

To what extent is the resurgence of a stricter, even fanatical, branch of Islam a reaction to the impact of globalization, described by Lewis, which is felt to threaten Muslim identity?

This is a question posed by Samuel Huntington, (1993), who strongly argues that the main source of conflict in the new globalizing world is neither ideological nor economic but, in fact, cultural. For Huntington, future wars will be waged between nations and different civilizations: Western, Confucian, Shintoist, Islamic, Hindu, Buddhist etc. and these disputes will dominate world politics in the future. Huntington (1996) believes that the West overestimates the influence if its culture on the rest of the world: "Excluding a relatively small elite, the rest of the world is unaware of or despises Western culture." Benjamin Barber (1995) agrees with Huntington that future sources of conflict will lie in the friction between local or tribal cultural values (which he calls jihad) and a new democratic, technological world based on Western values (which he calls McWorld).

Others, such as Fukuyama (1992), disagree and hold that globalization and technology will tend to homogenize, not antagonize, cultures on a world scale. The fact is that we are all capitalists now, since the disappearance of the second world, where communism ruled, and to a large extent the third world too as economies have opened up to globalization. For that reason, ideological conflicts will indeed tend to become less important, although Fukuyama (1992) probably exaggerates when he says they will disappear altogether.

Globalizing forces, however, are not basically cultural but economic; the world market is not a cultural concept but an economic one. Although it is perceived by many as a synonym for cultural, Americanization occurs because dominant products and services, which mould consumer tastes and preferences, are so often US in origin. However, as we have seen, the fact that young people's tastes throughout the world are increasingly Americanized, in terms of dress styles, music, or TV, does not mean that their own culture in the broad sense of the word is being undermined. Just because they learn English in order to communicate and get on in the new age of global knowledge and business, does not mean that they will cease to use their own languages. On the contrary, many seem to accept US culture, but, at the same time, feel that their own identity is threatened and try to avoid being buried under the avalanche. The result appears to be that while there is a superficial acceptance of the process, deep down the reaction is quite hostile. A kind of love–hate relationship develops with an instinctive desire to conserve local identity and values. In that sense, globalization may in fact have the opposite effect, leading some people to promote their local cultures as a means of distinguishing themselves from the dominant one.

Nobody, after all, wants to be the same as everybody else. They may provisionally follow fashions but perhaps only so far as these do not erode their own identity. As Umberto Eco (2000) jokes: "despite the concern about globalization imposing the English language upon the world, maybe exactly the opposite will occur and we shall see the development of multiculturalism" . . . "The role model for the millennium could be Saint Paul, born in Persia, of a Jewish family who spoke Greek, read the Tora in Hebrew and lived in Jerusalem where he spoke Aramaic and when they asked to see his passport he was Roman. The Roman empire could not impose a single language throughout its territory."

Nor do I accept the idea that globalization will generate cultural conflict and war as Huntington claims. As the volume of trade, capital, and information exchange grows, the potential for conflict will be smaller, not greater. The same applies to the growth of democracy. As Dani Rodrik (1999) points out, one of the most salient characteristics of US culture is its defense of democracy and aversion to the concentration of power. In this sense, one of globalization's problems, as Rodrik sees it, is that it is not sufficiently American. While recent financial crises have had a negative social impact, they have nevertheless toppled dictators. Greater exposure to international influence brings home the disadvantages of living without basic freedoms and hastens the fall of dictatorships and other authoritarian regimes. Trade liberalization in Spain and the growth of tourism from 1959 onwards undoubtedly led to the decline of General Franco's regime, as the Spaniards saw that life was better and freedom was greater on the other side of the Pyrenees.

Globalization aids the expansion and penetration of new ideas, technology, and knowledge and, therefore, can also have positive cultural effects. The Internet, for example, one of globalization's most important vehicles, has created a public forum for many cultures and minority identities which were previously unheard. Umberto Eco (2000) does, however, alert us to an evident danger:

> Up to now, the Church and, scientific and cultural institutions were responsible for filtering and reorganising the knowledge and information to be received by citizens. They restricted intellectual freedom but guaranteed that the community received the essential elements of knowledge. Without a filter, there is a clear risk of our sliding into intellectual anarchy. The Internet removes institutional filters however mistaken these may have been in the past. Now every individual can set up his own religion, culture, knowledge by means of his or her own personal filter.

Perhaps, the most serious problem that globalization can pose for culture is that some cultures or values may adapt better to the process than others, drastically widening inequality between some countries or cultures and others.

Culture and economy

All economic activity is immersed in a wide network of structures and cultural practices. For that reason each nation has approached economic problems and organised economic activity in its own particular way. (Granowetter and Swedberg, 1992)

The importance of culture, in the widest sense of the word, to the relative success of an economy is an object of growing interest amongst economists. Drawing on the landmark contributions of Max Weber (1905), who showed how Protestantism was a fundamental factor in the economic success of Germany or Switzerland, compared with the Catholic countries of southern Europe, cultural and institutional economists have explored the relationship between culture and economy.

Lawrence Harrison (1992) has tried to explain economic phenomena, such as inequality and income distribution, through different attitudes and cultural values. Why are Asian countries more egalitarian than Latin American and why do the former have higher savings rates? What part does culture play in forming these structural characteristics? Is Spain's traditional disdain for commerce and industry responsible for Latin America's economic failure, compared with the success of the USA or Canada? Or has climate and geography played a greater role? Behind the success of the Asian tigers, can we find Asian values based on the Confucian work ethic?

These questions are extremely difficult to answer. After all, countries as varied as Poland, the Philippines, or Italy are all Catholic and Buddhism embraces such widely different economic systems as Thailand, Mongolia, and Tibet. Weber believed that Confucianism's insistence on blind obedience and paternal authority was a disincentive to competition and innovation and so inhibited economic success. Yet Lee Kuan Yew stresses that, Confucian values of hard work, saving, and cooperation are the key to Asia's economic success. Maybe there is truth in both arguments illustrated by the experience of China, one of the most prosperous countries in the world until the mid-eighteenth century that subsequently fell victim to underdevelopment and impoverishment. In the same way, it is generally held that Islamic values run contrary to modernity, and there are reasons for it. These include the low productivity and high fertility rates generated by the lower education level of 50 percent of the labour force, the women, and of the higher cost of capital due to the prohibition of charging interest rates, much exceeded by commissions; yet they were responsible for the survival of rational thought throughout the Dark Ages and provided a bridge between Classical Greece and Rome, and the Renaissance. Cultures are so complex and multidimensional that it is impossible to establish a single relationship between them and the economy (*Economist*, 1996). At times, the cultural characteristics will favour economic growth, and at others, they will hinder its development. At the moment, and probably throughout history, hard work and a capacity to save do seem to be advantageous to economic growth. However, innovative and inventive qualities seem to be crucial too, even if they are occasionally incompatible with practices of hard work and saving. We can definitely say that the greater the role given to knowledge, information and rationality, the greater the potential long-term growth rate. Similarly, the more influence that irrational beliefs and fanaticism exert on a society, the less chance it will have of economic success.

Nevertheless, there has recently been an important development of economic research looking into the issues of culture, values, religion, and economic performance, marking a revival of the pioneer work of Max Weber. Robert Barro and Rachel McCleary (2003) have made a study about the correlation between religion and growth, with data from 59 countries, between 1980 and 2000. They come to the following conclusions: First, religiosity, that is, church attendance or the pertinence to a religion, tends to decline with the degree of urbanization and the level of economic development, mainly in Europe and other regions, but not in the US. It tends also to increase when religion is supported by governments but it tends to decline with too much government regulation or religious pressures, as is happening in Islamic countries, where there is no distinction between the religious and the political power. It also tends to increase with a higher diversity of competing religions and more pluralism, as in the US, Germany, Switzerland, the Netherlands, Australia, Malaysia, Singapore, and South Africa, but it tends to diminish with low religious pluralism, both in catholic countries (Spain, Italy, and Latin America), protestant (Nordic countries), orthodox (Russia and Greece), and Islamic countries.

Second, religious beliefs are more important than the practice or the pertinence to a religion to enhance or deter economic growth. Given a level of church attendance, an increase in religious beliefs – mainly in heaven and hell and in life beyond death – tend to increase economic growth. The fear of going to hell is even more growth enhancing than the expectation of going to heaven. As a general rule, the higher the level of economic development, the lower the level of religiosity and, the higher the religious beliefs, the higher the economic growth, because they stimulate a readiness to work with other people of the same beliefs and allow for a division of labour and trade, because they enhance honesty and therefore confidence, savings, and hard work. There are also some important exceptions because not only religious beliefs enhance gowth: In Japan there is very little fear of hell and it has grown more rapidly than in the Philippines and other catholic countries. China, which is basically atheistical, grows much faster than all Islamic countries.

In another study, Luigi Guiso, Paola Sapienzia, and Luigi Zingales (2003) using the annual World Values Survey for 66 countries, between 1981 and 1997, look at the correlation of religion and economic attitudes. They start with the basic hypothesis: First, some religions, such as

Catholicism and Islamism, tend to reduce the talent and the institutions which stimulate growth, such as trust and confidence; second, there other non-religious attitudes and institutions, which can counteract their negative economic religious influence.

They confirm some of Barro and McCleary conclusions, in the sense that, on average, religious beliefs are growth enhancing because religious people have more confidence in other citizens, in the government, in the legal system and are less inclined to disobey the law and more inclined to accept that the market is efficient and equitable. But they also find out that religious people tend to be more intolerant with women and their rights and with other religions, and that confidence tends to be more associated with religious pertinence than with religious education.

For instance, church attendance increases the confidence among Christians but much more among Protestants than among Catholics and Islamists. The relationship between religion and intolerance is present in all religions except Buddism. The least tolerant with women and other religions or other races or immigrants are the Islamists, followed by the Hindus, Jews, Catholics, and Protestants.

The most active in religiosity and church attendance tend to have a higher confidence in government and institutions in general, mainly Islamists and Hindus, but with the exception of Buddhists. The Jews are the most inclined to tax avoidance, followed by Protestants, Catholics, Hindus, and Islamists. Buddhists are more inclined to be corrupted followed by Protestants and Islamists. Protestants believe more in incentives and competition, two backbones of capitalism, and Islamists are those who believe least in them. Catholics, on the contrary believe twice as much as Protestants, in private property. Finally, most very religious people are more inclined to believe that poor people are lazy people, especially Protestants, but also Catholics. Buddhists are again the exception.

Social cohesion is also crucial in the long term since, as Fukuyama (1995) argues, it raises the level of interpersonal trust and allows for the development of more complex social institutions ranging from efficient governments to multinational corporations. Good examples are Holland, Sweden, or Switzerland where high levels of social cohesion have helped the development these institutions. However, cohesion does not appear to be a necessary condition for economic success since the US and the UK, characterized by a low level of cohesion, have also created efficient institutions.

What we can say, by way of conclusion, is that globalization and the technological revolution seem to favor one or more of these three groups:

those countries, such as Holland, Scandinavia, Canada, and Australia which have high levels of social cohesion and substantial external exposure both to the international economy and to multiculturalism; those with a tradition of entrepreneurial acumen such as the US and China, and those with greater ability for the physical sciences rather than social sciences such as China, India, and southeast Asia. Finally, religious beliefs tend to enhance growth more than religious pertinence, but with major exceptions.

CHAPTER 11

Who Wins and Who Loses in Globalization?

Some final remarks are needed on the question of who is affected positively and negatively by the increasing globalization of the world economy. These comments are prompted by the virulence of the, so far minority, protests that are taking place against this process, targeted mainly at the meetings of the international institutions created at Bretton Woods in 1945 (World Bank and IMF) and the World Trade Organization (WTO), the successor to another of these institutions: the GATT, or even the UN itself. Protests that seem to be paradoxical given that what a globalized world needs is more international organizations and not fewer, to be able to regulate and supervise those activities that produce spillovers on to the rest of the world. Globalization urgently needs international organizations to regulate international finance, intellectual property, international competition, environment, health, terrorism, arms and drugs trafficking, as well as women and children smuggling.

Unfortunately, globalization is widely perceived as increasing the gap between rich and poor, even impoverishing those who are already poor, although the empirical evidence shows that since the 1980s globalization has accelerated, world poverty has decreased substantially, that world inequality has fallen slightly, that life expectancy has improved faster than expected from increases in income alone, mainly among the poor. Thus, on the face of it, the persistence of poverty and inequality seems to be due to insufficient globalization rather than too much. But it is not an accident that some countries have been left out, nor just the result of a misguided failure to size the opportunities of integration into the world economy. Rather, it seems to be due to their lack of certain basic institutional features: a skilled labor force, a coherent and representative government, a developed civil society, which are all necessary to make globalization work (CEPR, 2002).

My intention here is to set out some general, simple, and necessarily crude, ideas about why these protests are taking place, and whether they are rooted in legitimate interests or misconceptions.

In order to do this I will first, have to make use of a simplistic classification, of countries into developed and developing, although I am aware that there are some countries classified in between these two, and of individuals into capitalists, that is, those who predominantly live off income from capital, and workers, that is, those who predominantly live off income from their labor.

Clearly, many workers today supplement their wages and pensions with earnings from capital, in the form of invested savings, so this is a very schematic distinction. Among workers I also have to distinguish between those who can be classified as skilled, because of their higher level of education and professional training, and those who can be considered unskilled, i.e., those with a low or almost non-existent level of education and training. This classification does not fully reflect reality either, because in practice there is a continuum of skills levels from high to low, within which it is impossible to make clear distinctions. Taken together, these classifications are based on the idea that individuals possess greater or lesser amounts of physical capital and greater or lesser amounts of accumulated human capital, and that countries are more or less developed, not just in terms of per capita income, but also in terms of political, judicial and social institutions and sustainable growth.

Once these distinctions are made, it is necessary to explain the effects of globalization on individuals and on countries. The driving force behind globalization is increasing competition between firms, brought about by the greater opening of the economies and larger mobility of goods and services, of capital and labor as well as new technologies, which allow firms to compete more easily, at lower cost, in many countries at the same time. This competition extends also to the capital financing these firms (either through participating in their equity, purchasing their debt, or supplying them with credits and loans), and to the individuals who work for them, either as direct employees or as external suppliers of goods and professional services.

Globalization also increases competition between countries to attract foreign capital that will top up their national savings – both in the form of foreign direct investment or of portfolio investment, loans, or debt – and to acquire larger endowments of foreign technology and human capital, factors of production essential for achieving higher growth. Obviously, those countries with consolidated, reliable democratic institutions – i.e., with political, judicial and legal systems that are fair and efficient, and which recognize and defend private property, economic freedom, the security of legal contracts, cohesion and public safety – and those with economic policies that emphasize education and training, and are open to international business, tend to acquire more foreign investment, technology and human capital, than countries which lack such democratic institutions and policies.

In this context of increasing globalization and greater competition, the first conclusion to draw is that its main winners are consumers all over the world, because the price of goods and services will tend to fall and, therefore, their buying power, or to put it another way, their real incomes, will increase as a result. The reasons are obvious. First, as the volume of trade increases, due to increasing trade liberalization and the fall in the transport costs of goods, services, and ideas, so will competition; the price of goods and services will fall, their quality will increase and there will be greater choice. Second, as the flow of capital increases, its cost will fall, and it will therefore be cheaper for families everywhere to borrow in order to consume, and to invest without a credit constraint, as long as the present segmentation of financial markets continues to disappear. Third, as technology transfers increase, due to the larger trade with and FDI flows to developing countries, to the increasing outsourcing and offshoring of parts of the production processes and the value chain to developing countries, the education and productivity of the workers in developing countries will increase, and so too will their wages, their consumption, and their exports. Fourth, the growing migration flows from developing to developed countries allows immigrants to increase their human capital and their incomes and also to send remittances to their families, increasing their purchasing power and their consumption in their countries of origin.

This is, without doubt, the most beneficial and universal aspect of globalization. Most people in the world, to the extent that they are consumers and borrowers, may benefit from lower prices for goods and services, lower levels of interest rates, easier access to education, skills and technology, and the freer option to migrate. Obviously, consumers in countries where there is a deeper rate of globalization and a higher level of competition, i.e., in the developed countries and in many developing countries that are highly open to competition, will benefit more than consumers elsewhere.

Second, capitalists in the developed countries will also benefit, except if they are shareholders or creditors of firms that do not survive in the higher competitive environment with developing countries, which globalization brings. In general, in developed countries, those who derive their income from capital will have two sorts of advantage over those who derive their income from labor. The first is that the free movement of capital allows them to invest wherever the highest returns, weighted by risk, are to be found, and, through diversification, to reduce the risk in their investments, either by delocalizing industries and services, or by investing in countries where the returns are greater because of the segmentation in their capital markets or their lower levels of domestic competition. The second is that, thanks to globalization, the new communication technologies, and the Internet, it is more difficult to tax capital than labor because the former is intangible and much more mobile than the latter.

Waged employees, by contrast, who are much less mobile, because they have deeper roots, a distinctive culture and language, as well as a family, cannot escape the tax authorities, which have the relevant information about their wages and, therefore, not only suffer the adverse effects of domestic recessions, the lack of risk diversification and the full payment of taxes, but also the partial outsourcing of the productive processes by domestic companies or even the total delocalization by foot-loose companies. This is unless, of course, workers themselves become foot-loose, which is not the case, for most of them, at least for now, except those with very high skills and often foreign immigrants.

In the third place, the large majority of the most skilled workers in developed countries will also reap the benefits of globalization, since they can adapt more quickly to the new technological revolution and to the internationalization of production and distribution, and can specialize in more competitive industries or services with greater technological inputs which allow them to increase their productivity and their relative wages.

By contrast, lower-skilled workers in developed countries will have a very high probability of being net losers, given that they encounter difficulties in adapting to new technologies and productive internationalization and will be forced to accept lower productivity and lower-wage jobs, if their labor markets are flexible. Or, alternatively, they may become unemployed if their labor markets are rigid or if they work for low skill labor-intensive firms, which have to compete with firms in developing countries that also employ low skilled workers but at much lower wage rates, longer hours, harsher and poorer working conditions and with similar, productivity rates. Or even as is recently the case, of lower and middle skilled workers affected also by outsourcing and delocalization of part of the productive processes in manufacturing or services to developing countries.

In the fourth place, capitalists in developing countries will benefit much less than those in developed countries, since most of them are operating in markets where there is little competition with lax (where not corrupt) regulatory frameworks, where they can lobby governments and obtain high profit margins. These profits, nevertheless, will be reduced or even plummet with the arrival of foreign direct investment, which can produce locally, with higher technology, productivity, and export potential, offering better conditions of quality and price, and with the increasing imports of goods and services from more competitive third countries against whom local firms can only compete by lowering margins.

Finally, the great majority of workers in developing countries will gain from globalization. Many of them will cease to be unemployed or underemployed, and those who work should receive higher earnings since, on the one hand, the companies where they work will be exporting greater volumes of goods and services to the developed countries which will increase their demand for labor, to meet the demands of a rising production and, on the other hand, they will be receiving larger flows of foreign direct investment, which will also increase the demand for labor, pay higher wages than the average national company, give better working conditions and training than the average domestic company, and benefit from the transfer of skills and technology to their local subsidiaries.

Many developing country workers will also be able to avoid emigration since they will find more local jobs as globalization intensifies, heightening the contribution of their labor content toward exported goods and services and receiving greater capital flows. They will also increase their knowledge and training, and have a greater chance of finding better jobs, not only in local companies but also abroad in other subsidiaries of the newly localized foreign firms.

Finally, globalization consists in lowering the barriers to the movement of labor and, therefore, of increasing migration flows, and giving more opportunities to many developing country workers to improve their income or their chance of finding a job in other countries. Since the 1980s, when globalization has accelerated its pace, migrant flows have also become larger, mainly in the US and in Europe, relieving some of the pressure caused by their very high ferility rate and not so high economic growth rate, in some countries of Africa, Asia, and Latin America. This trend is going to be accelerating in the coming decades, due to the aging of populations in most of the OECD countries. Historical experience shows that migration is the most powerful instrument in reducing income inequality, by lowering unemployment in developing countries, and increasing their inflows of migrant money transfers.

Therefore, an initial schematic analysis shows us that there are far more gainers from globalization than losers. Most people gain as consumers and and borrowers, and only a few lose out as productive workers in developed countries, and as capitalists in developing countries.

Why is it, then, that so many voices are raised against globalization? To answer that, we should bear in mind two empirical truths. The first is that those minorities, who are adversely affected by a phenomenon, or those who choose to protest, generally have the loudest voice, while those who benefit tend to remain silent. The second is that it is mainly the best-organized groups – those that exert most pressure on decision-makers – that lead the debate. This often leaves less organized but majority groups out of the picture.

Experience at the end of the first wave of globalization, between 1870 and 1913, bears out this thesis. During that period, countries with labor shortages such as the US and some Latin American economies experienced a massive wave of immigration from Europe (more than 60 million Europeans emigrated) leading to a fall in local wages and an increase in income inequality, while those countries whose labor supply had been plentiful, the European periphery, saw an increase in wages because of emigration to America. All this caused a convergence of income between America and Europe, and within Europe between the peripheral countries and the center. While the gainers were much more numerous than the losers, those who lost out made the most noise and were far better at defending their interests in political terms. Labor unions in the US, on the one hand, and European landowners, on the other, applied huge pressure to arrest the process, with some apparent success.

However, the political environment today is very different from then. Political systems are far more democratic, civil society is better organized both nationally and internationally in the shape of powerful NGOs, and information technology allows them to express their views freely and to be heard instantaneously around the world.

For that reason, it is crucially important to avoid becoming net losers of the increasing globalization process (that is, the difference between the gains as consumers and the possible losses as producers) or at least to help potential losers overcome their problems so that no group of people or countries is excluded from globalization and suffers the negative consequences of not reaping the benefits of globalization.

Both politicians and civil society in the developed countries must make a huge effort at cooperation and solidarity to avoid this occurring. So too must governments in developing countries who will have to make an enormous effort on all fronts, democratic, institutional, social, and economic, in order to attract the capital and investment needed to produce more, develop their external trade flows, and converge in income with the developed economies.

Who protests and why?

Globalization has become the cause of many social tensions and anxieties in developed countries that very often do not have much at all to do with globalization.

Are those people protesting in Seattle, Washington, Genoa, Cancun, Prague, Porto Alegre, or Davos against globalization really representing the actual or potential losers of such a process or are they driven by a general anti-capitalist mood? Let us have a look at who is really protesting and why.

First of all, trade unions in developed countries may be right when protesting because the new IT revolution is producing situations of increasing wage inequality. The more qualified workers are able to learn quickly and adapt to the new technological wave, improving their productivity and wages, while the less qualified ones are not able to do so and have to confine themselves to less productive jobs with lower salaries or to accept unemployment (Lommerud et al., 2005).

Globalization, by increasing competition within world producers through larger flows of trade, foreign direct investment, or more immigration, renders these less qualified workers more vulnerable to competition from workers in developing countries with similar qualification and productivity but longer hours of work and lower wages.

Recent research done in the US shows that globalization justifies on average only around 20 percent of the increase in wage inequality, while the IT revolution is responsible for around 60 percent, three times more in developed countries. Technological progress is unavoidable because it is the only way to increase productivity, incomes, and prosperity for the world as a whole; so too is the increasing volume of international trade, capital, and labor flows, which permit a reduction of poverty and inequality in the world. Therefore, it makes much more sense to help those workers which are affected by them than to try to return to a world of closed economies, recessions, conflict and violence, such as happened between 1914 and 1950.

Why do North American trade unions protest more than their European counterparts? The reason responds to the fact that US labor markets are more flexible and efficient than European ones and the US workers' adjustment to the present technological revolution and to increasing globalization has been sharper and quicker, producing a fall in the relative wages or even creating the direct unemployment of non-qualified workers who tend to have a higher share of trade union affiliation and activity.

On the contrary, European labor markers are less flexible, labor mobility is absent, firing costs and minimum wages are higher, and unemployment protection is more generous; therefore, the adjustment has been done through higher unemployment instead or higher wage dispersion. Syndicated workers or "insiders" have been affected very little by the increase in unemployment, and the bulk of the adjustment has been borne by young people and women, who have a extremely low rate of trade union affiliation.

The opposite effect is happening with the response to increasing immigration. European trade unions are much more belligerent than their US counterparts, which seems a contradiction given that the rate of immigration has been much larger in the US. There are two reasons for such a paradoxically relative response. On the one hand, the US has been by tradition a melting pot of different waves of migration from Asia, Africa, and Europe, while Europe has only recently started receiving larger inflows of foreign migrants after being a net migrating continent for more than a century. On the other hand, the present rate of unemployment is much larger in Europe than in the US.

There is another aspect, more technical, which justifies such a different reaction of the labor representatives on both sides of the Atlantic. In Europe most of the international trade among member countries of the European Union and with other OECD countries is intra-industry or intra-firm (that is, among the same sectors or companies) as a result of product differentiation, branding, and economies of scale and scope by multinationals, while a relatively higher percentage of trade in the US is inter-industry (that is, among different sectors or industries) given that it is a much larger country and diversified producer. In the latter trade pattern, increasing competition, which is based mainly on costs, prices, and wage levels, brings about more wage dispersion and more delocalization and a closing down of firms than in the intra-industry pattern, which is mainly based on product differentiation and economies of scale and not so much on relative wages and prices. Nevertheless, it is quite paradoxical that protests come mainly from the developed countries, because both the US and the EU are rather closed economies, given their very large market size, where the percentage of total trade over GDP is below 25 percent only, and where it is easier to be employed in a non-tradable service or manufacturing firm or in the government.

Why do trade unions in developing countries not protest? The reason is clear. Workers in most developing countries tend to be net winners from globalization because they are able to export more agricultural goods and low-tech high labor intensive manufactured products to the OECD countries, and at the same time, they are receiving larger capital flows. They are also less unionized and less organized in general than in developed countries. These are the reasons why many trade union and political leaders in these countries do not often feel represented by those non-governmental organizations, which try to protest on their behalf.

Second, there are other groups that protest mainly against the business concentration derived from the process of globalization of markets. It is the so-called attack on "big business." There are several reasons why "big business" is under assault. The first is that recent experience shows that big corporations have tended to be driven mainly by the objective of creating shareholder value, very often at the expense of other stakeholders of the company, like the workers themselves, the clients, and the suppliers. In order to keep creating shareholder value under increasing competition, many workers are dismissed, the quality of service to clients is reduced, and the suppliers see their margins squeezed. Meanwhile, there has been a series of cases of illicit enrichment by some CEOs of large corporations and an abuse of pay, through stock options, to the top executives in many corporations, mainly in the US. Therefore, there is an undertandable growing social reaction against the way "big business" has been conducted and an increasing revolt of stakeholders against shareholders.

During the boom and bust years, such a reaction has tended to be small because share ownership is widespread among the population of developed countries and a large percentage of the population has benefited from the large wave of mergers and acquisitions and by the shareholder value sacralization. But when stocks started taking a nosedive, the reaction has become violent. Another area where the attack on "big business" is growing is on the spread of the stock options as a system of remuneration for top executives. Today it is one of the major causes of income disparity in the US between the top and the lower decile, due to the abuse of many top executives in the amount and way they have allocated their stock options.

Third, the most important vehicle of protest is through international NGOs, which are the result of the creation of the civil society in developed countries and the growing competition that "participatory democracy," due to the increasing use and development of new communication technologies, is increasingly imposing upon the traditional "representative democracy." While the credibility and legitimacy of elected politicians is slowly decreasing, those of NGO's and other civil society organizations and associations are increasing. The new IT revolution is enhancing NGOs' "participative democracy," given that their views can be expressed freely through the Internet, and they no longer need to have their protests approved by the owners of the media in order to be able to have a voice.

The first and main economic misunderstanding with some NGOs is that many of them consider that globalization is a "zero-sum game," which is a well known fallacy. Every country in the world which participates in the increase in international competition can benefit from it, although the end result is not going to be the same for all of them. This is well confirmed in the empirical evidence of the economic history of the world. In every economic process and in every economic change which causes the world to progress, there are always some countries that do better than others and some that gain more than others in terms of prosperity and income per capita or even some that are net losers, at least temporarily, but the world as a whole gains. The roots and causes of the better or worse adaptation to change are well known: the quality of their political, social and economic institutions, productive factor endowments, levels of education, human capital and physical capital, and macro and micro economic policies applied in every country (Donges, 2004).

Globalization is not the cause of the ills of many countries, although it is blamed for them, but the main problems are usually at home: poor governance, weak institutions, or bad economic policies. These problems cannot be solved by reducing world competition or ending the globalization process; on the contrary, they may help the country with adaptation problems to change its policies and thus benefit from them.

The second misunderstanding by some NGOs and many people is that they have the perception that world inequality is growing because of globalization. The widespread view that world inequality has been rising since the late 1980s, in which globalization has accelerated, is not fully supported by the facts, as Bhalla (2002) and Sala i Martin (2002a and 2002b), among others, have demonstrated. Thus it is not so much due to the objective evolution of inequality but to changes in the perception and the conciousness of world inequality, that is, subjective inequality. Indeed it may be much harder to tolerate existing poverty and inequality, which are still too high and unacceptable, when signs of the affluence of others are all around and more visible, thanks, paradoxically, to globalization. The rapid increase in communications, broadcasting, and the Internet may make it possible today to heighten the awareness of affluence to those who are excluded from it and the awareness of poverty to those who are free from it (Bourguignon and Coyle, 2003). Even if the poor are becoming a smaller and smaller proportion of the world's total population, and even if improvements in life expectancy, child mortality and other dimensions of human capabilities mean that the objective conditions of the poor may be somewhat less terrible than they were for their predecessors, the awareness by themselves or the well-off of their deprivation relative to the rest of the world is increasing rapidly. Nevertheless, this increased awareness is positive. The more that is known by the world's population, then the more measures and policies will be taken to eradicate these terrible and humiliating situations which are clearly at odds with an increasingly prosperous world.

There are several classes of NGOs protesting at the meetings of the international organizations. These are as follows.

First, there are those which have already gained international credibility because they fulfill a service to world society, either by helping to reduce poverty, of which there are still intolerable levels, or by avoiding or denouncing environmental abuses, which are increasing, or, again, by improving consumers awareness against products of low quality or dangerous to the health, or finally, just because they are trying to achieve a better and more uniform world for all.

These reputable NGOs tend to act with a much greater degree of efficiency, transparency, and responsibility than others. Many of them are present as participants in the discussions with the World Bank and the IMF, and are helping also to shape the policies of some companies, governments, and international organizations, with regard to economic development aid, poverty reduction, debt reduction, and environmental protection.

There are, however, other issues in which the differences of view among governments, international organizations, and NGOs are still very large. Two cases are especially important in this respect. First, many NGOs would like to apply the same environmental and labor standards of developed countries to developing ones, which is considered to be very negative for the potential development of these countries, if only because they are less developed and have, in most cases, lower wage costs and a better environment that they used as comparative advantages. Second, many NGOs opposed radically, almost without discrimination, all genetically modified foods, and are thus at odds with companies and governments which consider them as a way of increasing the production of food in both developed and developing countries, and of reducing famine situations in many poor countries.

Although many of these respectable NGOs are collaborating with the World Bank in many poverty and debt reduction schemes, others totally opposed the very existence of the World Bank and the IMF because they think that some of their policies are counterproductive and do not at all help the less developed countries (Stiglitz, 2002).

There are many other NGOs and small groups of protesters, which have neither a clear objective, except to be anti-capitalist, nor any clear financing. These small organizations tend to be more aggressive and violent than those previously mentioned and are the cause of greater concern both for the institutions attacked and for most of the respectable NGOs.

Finally, there are many well-intentioned people, mostly the young, who now are able to see on TV or in the press every day that world poverty is still at intolerable levels and that inequality is still growing in many countries, although the world is becoming increasingly rich and prosperous, or who see that development aid is falling despite the increasing prosperity of the OECD countries. They are right to protest, although is not globalization per se that is the cause of these problems, but a lack of solidarity among the rich countries and the appalling political management of many developing and poor countries.

In any case, the increasing pressure from NGOs, in general, upon governments, companies, and international organizations has been positive and has helped them to focus on real issues that were not sufficiently dealt with. Companies are now showing more corporate social responsibility with stakeholders and the environment, governments are now trying to increase their levels of trade and of aid to the least developed countries, and allowing for reductions of its debt, and international organizations are much more focused on the fight to reduce poverty and to increase trade.

Therefore, it seems to be necessary to increase, where possible, collaboration with respectable NGOs and try to find practical ways of helping each other in eradicating poverty and granting more help and aid to those countries or persons which are being more negatively affected by globalization or have not been able to globalize and reap its benefits. Most poor countries are not the victims of globalization but the victims of the lack of it. Thus we should make sure that globalization more evenly extends to everybody.

The great challenge for the twenty-first century is, undoubtedly, finding a way to use the extraordinary benefits that globalization and the present technological revolution are bringing, to create institutions that enhance international solidarity and enable us to overcome the comparatively harmful effects on some economies and some peoples such as those that still exist at the moment. Only by countering these will we be able to avoid a backlash against globalization and the emergence of a period as sinister as the years between 1914 and 1945, with two world wars and a depression.

It is a daunting challenge, but one which can be met successfully. The point is to avoid curtailing the enormous potential of growth and income convergence created by globalization and the technological revolution while creating a world which is more equitable, which shows a higher degree of solidarity, and where there are no net losers.

Bibliography

Acemoglu, D. and Robinson, J. (2001) "The colonial origins of comparative development: an empirical investigation," *American Economic Review*, 91, December.

Acemoglu, D., Johnson, S., and Robinson, J. (2002) "Reversal of fortune: geography and institutions in the making of modern world income distribution," *Quarterly Journal of Economics*, 117, November.

Aghion, P. and Howitt, P. (1998) *Endogenous Growth Theory*, MIT Press, Cambridge, MA.

Aghion, P., Howitt, P., and Mayer-Foulkes, D. (2004) "The effect of financial development on convergence: theory and evidence," NBER Working Paper 10358.

Aglietta, M. (1998) "La maitrisse du risque sistemique international," Economie Internationale, 76, fourth quarter.

Aizeman, J., Pinto, B., and Radziwill, A. (2004) "Sources for financing domestic capital: is foreign saving a viable option for developing countries?," NBER Working Paper 10624.

Akerlof, G. (1970) "The market for lemons: qualitative uncertainty and the market mechanism," *Quarterly Journal of Economics*, 84.

Akerlof, G., Rose, A., Yellen, J., and Hessenius, H. (1991) "East Germany in the cold," Brookings Papers on Economic Activity, 1.

Albi, E. (2003) "Globalizacion y Estado," *Moneda y Credito*, 216, Madrid.

Alesina, A. and Perotti, R. (1995) "The political economy of budget deficits," *IMF Staff Papers*.

Alesina, A. and Spolaore, E. (1997) "On the number and size of nations," *Quarterly Journal of Economics*, November.

Alesina, A. and Summers, L. (1993) "Central Bank independence and macroeconomic performance: some comparative evidence," *Journal of Money Credit and Banking*, May.

Alesina, A. and Wacziarg, R. (1997) "Openness, country size and the government," National Bureau of Economic Research, Working Paper 6024, May.

Alesina, A., Spolaore, E., and Wacziarg, R. (1997) "Economic Integration and Political Desintegration," National Bureau of Economic Research, Working Paper 5987.

Allais, M. (1999) *La mondialisation, la destruction des emplois et de la croissance,* Clement Jutglar, Paris.

Amiti, M. and Wei, S. J. (2004) "Fear of service outsourcing: is it justified?," NBER Working Paper 10808.

Anderson, F. and Konrad, K. (2001) "Globalization and human capital formation," CEPR Discussion Paper 2657.

Anderson, N. and Breedon, F. (1996) *UK Asset Price Volatility over the Last Fifty Years in Financial Market Volatilit: Measures, Causes and Consequences,* BIS, Basel.

Antweiler, W. and Trefler, D. (1997) "Increasing returns and all that: a view from trade," University of British Columbia and University of Toronto, mimeo.

Arrow, K. (1962) "The economic implications of learning by doing," *Review of Economic Studies,* 29.

Artus, P. (1997) "Les crisis de balance de paiments peuvent-elles être autorealisatrices?," *Revue d'Economie Politique,* 107, August.

Audet, D. (1996) "Globalization in the clothing industry," in *Globalization of Industry: Overview and Sector Reports,* OECD, Paris.

Bagehot, W. [1873] (1917) *Lombard Street: A Description of the Money Market,* John Murray, London.

Baig, T. and Goldfajn, I. (1999) "Financial market contagion in the Asian crisis," *IMF Staff Papers,* 46 (2).

Bairoch, P. (1982) "International industrialisation levels from 1750 to 1980," *Journal of Economic History,* 2.

Bairoch, P. (1993) *Economics and World History,* Harvester-Wheatsheaf, London.

Bairoch, P. and Kozul-Wright, R. (1996) "Globalization myths: some historical reflections on integration, industrialisation and growth in world economy," UNC-TAD Discussion Paper 113.

Balasubramanian, V. N., Salisu, M., and Sapsford, D. (1996) "Foreign direct investment and growth in EP and IS countries," *Economic Journal,* 106, January.

Balassa, B. (1969) *The Theory of Economic Integration,* George Allen and Unwin, London.

Balassa, B. (1985) "Exports, policy choices and economic growth in developing countries after the 1973 oil shock," *Journal of Development Economics,* 18 (2).

Baldwin, R. (1989) "The growth effects of 1992," *Economic Policy,* 9, October.

Baldwin, R. (1998) "Agglomeration and endogenous capital," *European Economic Review,* 43.

Baldwin, R. and Cain, G. G. (1997) "Shifts in US relative wages: the role of trade, technology and factor endowments," *Review of Economics and Statistics,* 82 (4).

Baldwin, R. and Krugman, P. R. (2002) "Agglomeration, integration and tax harmonization," NBER Working Paper 9290.

Baldwin, R. and Martin, P. (1999) "Two waves of globalization: superficial similarities, fundamental differences," NBER Working Paper 6904.

Baldwin, R. and Martin, P. (2003) "Agglomeration and regional growth," CEPR Discussion Paper 3960.

Baldwin, R., Forslid, R., Martin, P., Ottaviano, G., and Nicoud, R. (2004) *Economic Geography and Public Policy*, Princeton University Press, Princeton, NJ.

Banerjee, A. (1992) "A simple model of herd behaviour," *Quarterly Journal of Economics*, August.

Barber, B. (1995) *Jihad versus McWorld*, Random House, New York.

Barnett, R. and Muller, R. (1974) *Global Reach: The Multinational Spread of US Enterprises*, Simon & Schuster, New York.

Barro, R. (1991) "Economic growth in a cross section of countries," *Quarterly Journal of Economics*, May.

Barro, R. (1994) "Democracy and growth," National Bureau of Economic Research Working Paper 4909.

Barro, R. (1997) *Determinants of Economic Growth*, MIT Press Cambridge, MA.

Barro, R. (1998) "Recent development in growth theory and empirics," Mimeo, Harvard University, February.

Barro, R. (1999) "Let the dollar reign from Seattle to Santiago," *Wall Street Journal Europe*, March 9.

Barro, R. and McCleary, R. M. (2003) "International determinants of religiosity," NBER Working Paper 10147.

Barro, R. and Sala I Martin, X. (1991) "Convergence across states and regions," Brookings Papers on Economic Activity, Washington.

Barro, R. and Sala I Martin, X. (1992) "Convergence," *Journal of Political Economy*, 1000.

Barro, R. and Sala I Martin, X. (1995) *Economic Growth*, McGraw Hill, New York.

Baumol, W. J. (1986) "Productivity growth, convergence, and welfare: what the long run data show," *American Economic Review*, December.

Baumol, W. J., Nelson, R., and Wolff, E. N. (1994) *Convergence of Productivity: Cross-national Studies and Historical Evidence*, Oxford University Press, New York.

Beckaert, G., Harvey, C. R., and Lundblad, C. (2005) "Does financial liberalization spur economic growth?," *Journal of Financial Economics*.

Bell, D. (1977) *Las contradicciones culturales del capitalismo*, Alianza Universidad, Madrid.

Bell, D. (1987) "The world and the United States in 2013," *Daedalus*, summer.

Ben David, D. (1993) "Equalizing exchange: trade liberalization and income convergence," *Quarterly Journal of Economics*, 108, August.

Ben David, D. (1996) "Trade and convergence among countries," *Journal of International Economics*, May.

Ben David, D. and Lowrey, M. (1997a) "Knowledge discrimination, capital accumulation, trade and endogenous growth" Sackler Institute Working Paper 38.

Ben David, D. and Lowrey, M. (1997b) "Free trade, growth and convergence," NBER Working Paper 6095.

Ben David, D. and Papell, D. (1996) "International trade and structural change," CEPR Discussion Paper 1568.

Bencivenga, V. and Smith, B. (1991) "Financial Intermediation and endogenous growth," *Review of Economic Studies*, 58, April.

Bergsten, F. Horst, T., and Moran, T. (1978) *American multinationals and American Interests*, Brookings Institution, Washington, DC.

Berman, E., Bound, J., and Griliches, Z. (1994) "Changes in the demand for skilled labor within US manufacturing industries," *Quarterly Journal of Economics*, 109 (2).

Bernanke, B. and Gertler, M. (1989) "Agency costs, collateral and business fluctuations," *American Economic Review*, 79, March.

Bernatzi, S. and Thaler, R. (1995) "Myopic loss aversion and the equity premium puzzle," *Quarterly Journal of Economics*, 110.

Bertola, G. (1999) *Convergence: An Overview on Market Integration, Rgionalism and the Gobal Eonomy*, edited by Richard Baldwin, Daniel Cohen, André Sapir, and Anthony Venalbles, CEPR and Cambridge University Press.

Bhagwati, J. (1998) "The capital myth: the difference between trade in widgets and trade in dollars," *Foreign Affairs*, May–June.

Bhagwati, J. (2000) "Free trade today: three lectures," Stockholm School of Economics, Stockholm University, November 23–5.

Bhagwati, J. (2004) *In Defense of Globalization*, Oxford University Press, Oxford.

Bhagwati, J. and Dehejia, V. (1994) "Free trade and wages of the unskilled: Is Marx striking again?," in Bhagwati and Kosters (eds.), *Trade and Wages*, American Enterprise Institute, Washington, DC.

Bhalla, S. (2002) *Imagine There Is No Country: Poverty, Inequality and Growth in the Era of Globalization*, Institute for International Economics, September, Washington, DC.

Blanchard, O. (1997) *Macroeconomics*, Prentice-Hall, New Jersey.

Blanchard, O. and Watson, M. W. (1982) "Bubbles, rational expectations and financial markets," in Paul Wachtel (ed.), *Crisis in the Economic and Financial Structure*, Heath, Lexington, MA.

Blomstrom, M., Lipsey, R., and Zejan, M. (1993) "Is fixed investment the key to economic growth?" NBER Working Paper 4436, August.

Blomstrom, M. Lipsey, R. and Zejan, M. (1994) "What explains growth in developing countries," NBER Working Papers 1924.

Bloomenstein, H. (1999) "The global financial landscape under stress," OECD Development Centre, November.

Bordo, M. D. and Murshid, A. P. (1999) "The international transmission of financial crises before World War II: was there contagion?" Prepared for the ADB/IMF/World Bank Conference on International Financial Contagion, February 2000, Washington, DC.

Bordo, M. and Murshid, A. P. (2000) "Are financial crises becoming increasingly more contagious? What is the historical evidence of contagion?," NBER Working Paper 7900.

Bordo, M. D., Eichengreen, B., and Irwin, D. A. (1999) "Is globalization today really different from globalization a hundred years ago?," in S. Collins and R. Lawrence (eds.), *Brookings Trade Policy Forum*, Brookings Institution, Washington, DC.

Borensztein, E., De Gregorio, J., and Lee, J. W. (1995) "How does foreign investment affect growth?," NBER Working Paper 5057.

Borjas, G. and Ramey, V. (1994) "The relationship between wage inequality and international trade," in Jeffrey Bergstrand (ed.), *The iChanging Distribution of Income in an Open US Economy*, North Holland, Amsterdam.

Borjas, G., Freeman, R., and Katz, L. (1997) "How much do inmigration and trade affect labour market outcomes?" Brookings Papers on Economic Activity 1.

Bound, J. and Johnson, G. (1992) "Changes in the structure of wages in the 1980's: an evaluation of alternative explanations," *American Economic Review*, 82.

Bosworth, B., Collins, S., and Yu-Chin, C. (1995) *Accounting for Differences in Economic Growth in Structural Adjustment Policies in the 1990's: Experience and Prospects*, Institute of Development Economics, Tokyo.

Bradford, C. and Chakwin, N. (1993) "Alternative explanation of the trade-output correlation in East Asian economies," OECD Development Centre Technical Papers 87.

Bourguignon, F. and Coyle, D. Inequality, public perception and the institutional responses to globalization," *Moneda y Credito*, 216, Madrid.

Braga de Macedo, G., Cohen, D., and Reisen, H. (2001) *Don't Fix, Don't Float*, Development Centre Studies, OECD, Paris.

Brainard, L. (1997) "An empirical assessment of the proximity-concentration trade-off between multinational sales and trade," *American Economic Review*, 87.

Braudel, F. (1984) "Civilisation and capitalism, 15th–18th centuries," in *The Perspective of the World*, vol. 3, Harper and Row, New York.

Bresnahan, T. (1999) "Computerisation and wage dispersion: an analitical reinterpretation," *Economic Journal*, June.

Brown, R. and Julius, D. A. (1993) "Is manufacturing still special in the New World order?," *Amex Bank Review*, First Prize, London.

Buchanan, J. (1975) *The Limits of Liberty*, University of Chicago Press, Chicago.

Buchanan, J. and Tullock, G. (1962) *The Calculus of Consent*, University of Michigan Press, Ann Arbor.

Buchanan, J. and Wagner, R. (1977) *Democracy in the Deficit: The Political Legacy of Lord Keynes*, Academic Press, New York.

Buckley, P. and Casson, M. (1976) *The Future of the Multinational Enterprise*, Macmillan, London.

Burnside, C., Eichenbaum, M., and Rebelo, S. (2001) "Prospective deficits and the Asian currency crisis," *Journal of Political Economy*, 109.

Caballero, R. (2003) "On the international financial architecture: insuring emerging markets" NBER Working Paper 9570, March.

Calomiris, C. and Gorton, G. (1991) "The origin of banking panics: models, facts, and bank regulation," in G. Hubbard (ed.), *Financial Markets and Financial Crisis*, Chicago University Press.

Calomiris, C. W. and Hubbard, G. (1989) "Price flexibility, credit availability and economic fluctuations: evidence from the USA 1894–1909," *Quarterly Journal of Economics*, 54, August.

Calvo, G. (1999) "On dollarization," *Economics of Transition Journal*, available on line: http//www.bsos.umd.edu/econ/ciecpns/pdf.

Calvo, G. A. and Mendoza, E. G. (1999) "Rational contagion and the globalization of securities markets," NBER Working Paper 7153.

Calvo, G. A. and Mishkin, F. (2003) "The mirage of exchange rates regimes for emerging market countries," NBER Working Paper 9808.

Calvo, S. and Reinhart, C. (1995) "Capital flows to Latin America is there evidence of contagion effects?," Institute for International Economics. Vienna, September, session 5.

Calvo, G. A. and Reinhart, C. (2000) "Fear of floating," NBER Working Paper 7993.

Calvo, G. A. and Reinhart, C. (2001) "When capital flows come to a sudden stop: consequences and policy options," in Kenen and Swoboda (eds.), *Key Issues in Reform of the International Monetary System*, IMF, Washington, DC.

Calvo, G. A., Izquierdo, A., and Mejia, L. F. (2004) "On the empirics of sudden stops: the relevance of balance-sheets effects," NBER Working Paper 10520.

Calvo, G. and Talvi, E. (2004) "Sudden stop, financial factors and economic collapse: a view from the Latin American frontlines," paper prepared for the conference, From the Washington Consensus towards a new global governance," mimeo, Barcelona, September.

Cameron, D. (1978) "The expansion of the public economy," *American Political Science Review*, 72.

Caprio, G. and Klingebiel, D. (1996) *Bank Insolvencies: Cross-country Experience*, World Bank. Washington, DC.

Cavallo, D. (1999) "The quality of money," Mimeo, March.

Caves, R. (1982) *Multinational Enterprises and Economic Analysis*, Harvard University Press, MA.

Caves, R. (1998) "Industrial organization and new findings on the turnover and mobility of firms," *Journal of Economic Literature*, December.

CEPR, Centre for Economic Policy Research (2002) "Making sense of globalization: a guide to economic issues," CEPR Policy Paper 8, London.

Chang, R. and Velasco, A. (1998) "The Asian liquidity crisis," NBER Working Paper 6796, November.

Chang, R. and Velasco, A. (1999) "Liquidity crisis in emerging markets: theory and policy," NBER Working Paper 7272, July.

Chenery, H. and Bruno, M. (1962) "Development alternatives in an open economy," *Economic Journal*, 57.

Chibber, A. (1997) "El Estado en un mundo en transformación," *Finance and Development*, IMF, September.

Chui, M., Levine, P., and Pearlman, J. (1999) "Winners and losers in a North–South model of growth, innovation and product cycles," CEPR Discussion Paper 2291.

Cline, W. (1997) *Trade and Income Distribution*, Institute for International Economics, Washington, DC.

Coase, R. (1937) "The nature of the firm," *Economica New Series*, 4.

Coe, D. and Helpman, E. (1995) "International R & D spill overs," *European Economic Review*, 39.

Cohen, D. (1993) "Foreign finance and economic growth, an empirical analysis," in Leonardo Leiderman and Assaf, Razin (eds.), *Capital Mobility*, CEPR and Cambridge University Press, London and Cambridge.

Cohen, D. (1997) *Richesse du monde, pauvreté des Nations*, Paris, Flammarion.

Cohen, D. (1999) *Nos temps modernes*, Flammarion, París.

Cohen, D. and Portes, R. (2003) "Crise souveraine: entre prevention et resolution," Conseil D'analyse Economique, *Rapport*, 43, La Documentation Française, Paris.

Cohen, D. and Portes, R. (2004a) "Dealing with destabilizing market discipline," NBER Working Paper 10533.

Cohen, D. and Portes, R. (2004b) "Towards a lender of first resort," CEPR Discussion Paper 4615.

Collins, S. (1996) "On becoming more flexible: exchange rate regimen in Latin America and the Caribbean," *Journal of Development Economics*, 51.

Cooper, R. (1994) "Foreign trade, wages and unemployment," Harvard University, mimeo.

Cooper, R. (1999) *Key Currencies after the Euro*, Basil Blackwell, Oxford.

Cooper, R. and John, A. (1993) "Coordinating coordination failures in Keynesian models," in G. Mankiw and D. Romer (eds.), *New Keynesian Economics*, vol. 2, MIT Press, Harvard, MA.

Corsetti, G., Guimaraes, B., and Roubini, N. (2004) "International lender of last resort and moral hazard: a model of IMF's catalytic finance," NBER Working Paper 10125.

Corsetti, G., Pesenti, P., and Roubini, N. (1998) "What caused the Asian currency crisis?," CEPR–World Bank Conference, Financial Crisis, Contagion and Market Volatility, London, May 8–9, and NBER Working Papers 6833 and 6834, December.

Crafts, N. (1984) "Patterns of development in the nineteenth-century Europe," *Oxford Economic Papers*, 36.

Crafts, N. (1989) "British Industrialization in an international context," *Journal of Interdisciplinary History*, 19 (3).

Crafts, N. (1995) "Exogenous or endogenous growth?: the Industrial Revolution reconsidered," *Journal of Economic History*, 55 (4).

Deardoff, A. (1974) "A geometry of growth and trade," *Canadian Journal of Economics*, 7, May.

Deardoff, A. and Hakura, D. (1994) "Trade and wages: what are the questions in trade and wages: levelling wages donks?," mimeo.

De Bondt, W. F. M. and Thaler, R. (1985) "Does the stock market overreact?," *Journal of Finance*, 40.

De La Dehesa, G. (1992a) "Politica industrial, comercio exterior e inversión directa extranjera," in *Política industrial: teoría y práctica*, Colegio de Economistas de Madrid.

De La Dehesa, G. (1992b) "¿Se repite la historia? Tendencias económicas y sociales en el siglo XXI," *Claves*, 148.

De La Dehesa, G. (1994) "Coste laboral y dumping social," *Economía y Sociología del Trabajo*, 25–6, Madrid.

De La Dehesa, G. (1995) "Convergencia real y movilidad de factores de producción," *Papeles de Economía Española*, FIES, Madrid.

De La Dehesa, G. (1997) "España y la economía internacional," in Ramón Febrero (ed.), *Qué es la economía*, Pirámide. Madrid.

De La Dehesa, G. (1998a) "Lecciones de una crisis financiera inacabada en Asia," *El País*, March 24.

De La Dehesa, G. (1998b) "Estabilidad y crecimiento de una Unión Económica y Monetaria," in *El reto de la Unión Económica y Monetaria, Instituto de Estudios Económicos de Galicia*, Pedro Barrié de la Maza, La Coruña.

De La Dehesa, G. (1998c) "¿Porqué se autoalimentan las crisis financieras?," *El País*, September 21.

De La Dehesa, G. (1999a) "Los paradigmas financieros en tiempos de crisis, *El País*, January 30.

De La Dehesa, G. (1999b) "Lecturas de Política Económica Española," Instituto de Estudios Económicos de Galicia, Pedro Barrié de la Maza, La Coruña.

De La Dehesa, G. (1999c) "Globalization, exchange rates and dollarization," *Financial Mail*, March 22, Johannesburg.

De La Dehesa, G. (1999d) "Las tendencias demográficas y las pensiones futuras," *El País*, July 19.

De La Dehesa, G. (1999e) "Globalización y mercados laborales" in *Estudios económicos del mercado de trabajo en España*, Instituto de Estudios Económicos, Madrid.

De La Dehesa, G. (2000) "El desafío de la convergencia," in *El Libro Marrón del Círculo de Empresarios*, Madrid.

De La Dehesa, G. (2003) "The international role of the euro," Briefing Paper to the Economic and Monetary Committee of the European Parliament, fall, Strasbourg.

De La Dehesa, G. and Krugman, P. (1992) "EMU and the regions," Occasional Paper 39, Group of Thirty, Washington, DC.

De La Dehesa, G. and Snower, D. (1996) *Unemployment Policy: Governments Options for the Labour Market*, Cambridge University Press for CEPR, Cambridge.

De La Dehesa, G., Ruiz, J. J., and Torres, A. (1991) "Trade liberalisation in Spain," in Michaely, Papagoergiou, and Choski, (eds.), *Liberalising Foreign Trade*, vol. 6, Blackwell, Oxford.

De Long, J. B. and Summers, L. H. (1991) "Equipment investment and economic growth," *Quarterly Journal of Economics*, 56 (2).

De Long, J. B., Shleifer, A., Summers, L. H., and Waldman, R. J. (1989) "The size and incidence of losses from noise trading," *Journal of Finance*, 44.

De Long, J. B., Shleifer, A., Summers, L. H., and Waldman, R. J. (1990) "Positive feedback investment strategies and destabilizing rational speculation," *Journal of Finance*, 45.

De Mello, L. R. (1997) "Foreign direct investment in developing countries and growth: a selected survey," *Journal of Development Economics*, 34, October.

Demirgüç-Kunt, A. and Levine, R. (2001) *Financial Structures and Economic Growth: A Cross-country Comparison of Banks, Markets and Development*, MIT Press, Cambridge, MA.

Denison, E. (1962) *The Sources of Economic Growth in the U.S. and the Alternatives before Us*, Committee for Economic Development, New York.

Diamond, D. and Dybvig, P. (1983) "Bank runs, deposit insurance and Liquidity," *Journal of Political Economy*, 91.

Diwan, I. and Hoekman, B. (1999) "Competition, complementarity and contagion in East Asia," CEPR Discussion Paper 2112, March.

Dicken, P. (1998) *Global Shift*, Paul Chapman Publishing, London.

Dicken, P. and Lloyd, P. (1990) *Location in Space*, Harper and Row, New York.

Dixit, A. and Norman, V. (1980) *Theory of International Ttrade*, Cambridge University Press, Cambridge.

Dobson, W. and Hufbauer, G. C. (2001) *World capital markets: Challenge to the G10*, Institute for International Economics, Washington, DC.

Dobson, W. and Jacquet, P. (1998) *Financial Services Liberalization in the WTO*, Institute of International Economics, Washington, DC.

Dollar, D. (1992) "Outward-orientated developing economies really do grow more rapidly: evidence from 15 LDC's: 1976–1985," *Economic Development and Cultural Change*, 40.

Dollar, D. and Kray, A. (2000) "Growth is good for the poor," IMF Seminar Series 35, Washington, DC.

Dollar, D. and Kray, A. (2001) *Trade Growth and Poverty*, World Bank, Washington, DC.

Dollar, D., Wolf, E. and Baumol, W. (1988) "The factor price equalization, model and industry labour productivity: an empirical test across countries," in C. Robert (ed.), *Empirical Methods for International Trade*, MIT Press, Cambridge, MA.

Donges, J. B. (2004) *Las criticas contra la globalizacion economica a examen*, Instituto de Investigaciones Economicas y Sociales "Francisco de Vitoria," Union Editorial, Madrid.

Dooley, M. P. (1996) "A survey of literature on controls over international capital transactions," *IMF Staff Papers*, 43, December.

Dornbusch, R. (1997) "Argentina's monetary policy lesson for México," *World Economy Laboratory*, April.

Dornbusch, R. (2000) "When funny money is no joke," *Financial Times*, January 3.

Drazen, A. (1999) "Political contagion in currency crisis," NBER Working Paper 7211.

Drucker, P. (1999) "Interview in *L'Expansion*," September 22 and October 6, París.

Dunning, J. (1958) *American Investment in British Manufacturing Industry*, George Allen and Unwin, London.

Dunning, J. (1974) *Economic Analysis and the Multinational Enterprise*, G. Allen and Unwin, London.

Easterly, W. (1993) "How much do distortions affect growth?," *Journal of Monetary Economics*, 32.

Eco, U. (2000) "Interview by Florent Latrive y Annick Rivoire," in *Liberation*, reproduced by El Periódico de Cataluña, January 7.

Economist (1996) "Cultural explanations," November 9.

Economist (1997a) "The future of the state: a survey of the world economy," September 20.

Economist (1997b) "Series on globalisation," fall, several editions.

Economist (2000) "A survey of globalisation and tax," January 29.

Economist (2003) "Executive pay," October 11.

Edwards, S. (1992) "Trade orientation, distortions and growth in developing countries," *Journal of Developing Economics*, 39.

Edwards, S. (1993) "Openness, trade liberalization and growth in developing countries," *Journal of Economic Literature*, 31, September.

Edwards, S. (1996) "The determinants of the choice between fixed and flexible exchange rate regimes," NBER Working Paper 5756.

Edwards, S. (1997) "Openness, productivity and growth: what do we really know?," NBER Working Paper 5978.

Edwards, S. (1998) "Interest rate volatility, capital controls and contagion," NBER Working Paper 6756, October.

Edwards, S. (1999) "A capital idea?: Reconsidering a financial quick fix," *Foreign Affairs*, May–June.

Edwards, S. and Savastano, M. (1999) "Exchange rates in emerging economies: What do we know? What do we need to know?," NBER Working Paper 7228.

Eichengreen, B. (1996) *Globalizing Capital: A History of International Monetary Systems*, Princeton University Press, Princeton, NJ.

Eichengreen, B. (1999a) *Toward a New International Financial Architecture*, Institute of International Economics, Washington, DC.

Eichengreen, B. (1999b) "Kicking the habit: moving from pegged rates to greater exchange rate flexibility," *Economic Journal*, 109, March.

Eichengreen, B. and Hausmann, R. (1999) "Exchange rates and financial fragility," NBER Working Paper 7418.

Eichengreen, B. and Hausmann, R. (2003) "Original sin, the road to redemption," Kennedy School of Government, Harvard University, mimeo, October.

Eichengreen, B. and Mussa, M. (1998) "Capital account liberalization: theoretical and practical aspects," IMF Occasional Paper 172.

Eichengreen, B. and Portes, R. (1995) *Crisis?, What Crisis? Orderly Workouts for Sovereign Debtors*, CEPR, London.

Eichengreen, B., Hausmann, R., and Panizza, U. (2003) "Currency mismatches, debt intolerance and original sin: why they are not the same and why it matters," NBER Working Paper 10036.

Eichengreen, B., Kletzer, K., and Mody, A. (2005) "The IMF in a world of private capital markets," NBER Working Paper 11198.

Eichengreen, B., Rose, A., and Wyplosz, C. (1996) "Contagious currency crisis," NBER Working Paper 5681, July.

Engels, F. (1845) *Die Lage der arbeitenden klasse in England*, Leipzig.

Engerman, S. and Sokoloff, K. (2000) "Institutions, factor endowments and paths of development among new world economies," *Economia*, 3, fall.

Engerman, S. and Sokoloff, K. (2005) "Colonialism, inequality and long-run paths of development," NBER Working Paper 11057.

Ethier, W. (1982) "National and international returns to scale in the modern theory of international trade," *American Economic Review*, 72.

Ethier, W. (1986) "The multinational firm," *Quarterly Journal of Economics*, 101.

Fabricio, S. and Lopez, H. (1996) "Domestic, Foreign or Common shocks?," IMF, Working Paper 96/107.

Fama, E. (1970) "Efficient capital markets: a review of theory and empirical work," *Journal of Finance*, 25, May.

Feder, G. (1983) "On exports and economic growth," *Journal of Developing Economics*, 59.

Feenstra, R. (1998) "Integration of trade and desintegration of production in a global economy," *Journal of Economic Perspectives*, 12 (4).

Feenstra, R. and Hanson, G. (1996a) "Globalization, outsourcing and wage inequality," *American Economic Review*, 86, May.

Feenstra, R. and Hanson, G. (1996b) "Foreign Investment, outsourcing and relative wages," in *Political Economy of Trade Policy*, Papers in Honour of Jagdish Bhagwati, MIT Press. Cambridge, MA.

Feenstra, R. and Hanson, G. (1998) "Productivity measurement and the impact of trade and technology on wages: estimates for the US 1972–1990," NBER Working Paper 6052, June.

Feldstein, M. (1999) "A self-help guide for emerging markets," *Foreign Affairs*, March–April.

Feldstein, M. and Horioka, C. (1980) "Domestic savings and international capital flows," *Economic Journal*, 90.

Fernandez Arias, E. and Hausmann, R. (1999) "Getting it right; what to reform in international financial markets," *InterAmerican Development Bank IADB*, November, Washington, DC.

Fidler, S. (1999) "Dollarize or die," *Financial Times*, January 19.

Fiekele, N. (1994) "Is global competition making the poor even poorer?," *New England Economic Review*, 3.

Financial Times (2004) "F.T. Global 500," May 27.

Findlay, R. (1995) *Factor Proportions, Trade and Growth*, MIT Press, Cambridge, MA.

Fischer, S. (1997) "Capital account liberalization and the role of the IMF," speech made at the IMF Annual Meetings seminar on "Asia and the IMF," Washington, DC.

Fischer, S. (1999a) "On the need of an international lender of last resort," *Journal of Economic Perspectives*, 13, fall.

Fischer, S. (1999b) "Reforming the International monetary system," *Economic Journal*, 109.

Fischer, S. (2001) "Exchange rate regimes: is the bipolar view correct?," *Journal of Economic Perspectives*, 15 (2).

Fischer, S. (2002) "Financial crises and reform of the international financial system," NBER Working Paper 9297, Cambridge, MA.

Fisher, I. (1933) "The debt deflation theory of a Great Depression," *Econometrica*, 1.

Fitoussi, J. P. (1997) "Mondialisation et innegalités," *Futuribles*, October.

Flamm, K. and Grunwald, J. (1985) *The Global Factory*, Brookings Institution, Washington, DC.

Francois, J. F. and Schuknecht, L. (1999) "Trade in financial services: precompetitive effects and growth performance," CEPR Discussion Paper 2144.

Francois, J. F., Grier, K., and Nelson, D. (2004) "Globalization, roundaboutness and relative wages," CEPR Discussion Paper 4406.

Frankel, J. (1995) "Monetary regime choice for a semi-open country," in S. Edwards (ed.), *Capital Controls, Exchange Rates and Monetary Policy in the World Economy*, Cambridge University Press, New York.

Frankel, J. (2003) "Experience of and lessons from exchange rate regimes in emerging economies," NBER Working Paper 10032.

Frankel, J. (2004) "The world trading system and implications of external opening," in "From the Washington consensus towards a new global governance," Barcelona, mimeo.

Frankel, J. and Romer, D. (1999) "Does trade cause growth?," *American Economic Review*, 89, 3.

Freeman, R. (1991) "How much has de-unization contributed to the rise in male earnings inequality," NBER Working Paper 3826.

Freeman, R. (1995) "Will globalization dominate US labour market outcomes?," mimeo.

Freeman, R. (1996) "When earnings diverge: causes, consecuences and cures for the new inequality in the US," mimeo, Chicago University.

Freeman, R. and Katz, L. (1996) *Differences and Changes in Wage Structures*, University of Chicago Press, Chicago.

Freeman, R. and Oostendorp, R. H. (2000) "Wages around the world: pay across occupations and countries," NBER Working Paper 8058.

Friedberg, R. and Hunt, J. (1995) "The impact of inmigrants on host country wages, employment and growth," *Journal of Economic Perspectives*, 9, spring.

Friedman, M. and Schwartz, A. (1963) "A monetary history of the United States," Princeton University Press, Princeton, NJ.

Friedman, T. (1999) *The Lexus and the Olive Tree*, Farrar, Strauss, and Giroux, New York.

Froot, K. A. and Obstfeldt, M. (1991) "Intrinsic bubbles: the case of stock prices," *American Economic Review*.

Froot, K. A., O'Connell, P. G. J., and Seasholes, M. S. (1998) "The portfolio flows of international investors," NBER Working Paper 6687.

Fujita, M. and Thisse, J. F. (2003) "Globalization and the evolution of the supply chain: who losses and who gains?," CEPR Discussion Paper 4152.

Fujita, M., Krugman, P. R., and Venables, A. (1999) *The Spatial Economy: Cities, Regions and International Trade*, MIT Press, Cambridge, MA.

Fukuyama, F. (1992) *The End of History and the Last Man*, Free Press, New York.

Fukuyama, F. (1995) *Trust: The Social Virtues and the Creation of Prosperity*, Free Press, New York.

Gallup, J. L. and Sachs, J. (1998) "Geography and economic growth," Annual World Bank Conference on Development Economics, World Bank, Washington, DC.

Gertler, M. and Rose, A. K. (1996) "Finance, public policy and growth," in Gerard Caprio, Iza Atiyas, and James Hanson (eds.), *Financial Reform, Theory and Experience*, Cambridge University Press, Cambridge.

Giannini, C. (1999) "Enemy of none but a common friend of all?: an International perspective of the lender of last resort function," *Essays in International Finance*, 214, Princeton University.

Gilpin, R. (1975) *US Power and the Multinational Corporation*, Basic Books, New York.

Glick, R. and Rose, A. K. (1998) "Contagion and trade: why are currency crisis regional?," NBER Working Paper 6806, November.

Goldfajn, I. and Valdes, R. (1997) "Capital flows and the twin crisis: the role of liquidity," IMF Working Paper WP/97/87, July.

Goldsmith, R. (1969) *Financial Structure and Development*, Yale University Press, New Haven, CT.

Goldstein, M. (1998) "The Asian financial crisis, causes, cures and systemic impications," *Institute for International Economics*, 55, July.

Goldstein, M. and Turner, P. (1996) "Banking crises in emerging economies: origins and policy options," *BIS Economic Papers*, 46. October.

Goldstein, M. and Turner, P. (2003) "Currency mismatches in emerging market economies: an alternative to the original sin hypothesis," *Institute of International Economics*, August.

Gosh, A., Gulde, A. M., and Wolf, H. (2000) "Currency boards: the ultimate fix?," IMF Occasional Paper, and "Currency boards: more than a quick fix?," *Economic Policy*, 31.

Graham, E. (1996) *Global Corporations and National Governments*, Institute for International Economics, Washington, DC.

Graham, E. and RICHARDSON, D. (1997) *Competition Policies for the Global Economy*, Institute for International Economics, Washington, DC.

Granowetter, M. and Swedberg, R. (1992) *The Sociology of Economic Life*, Westview Press, Boulder, CO.

Greenaway, D. (1998) "Does trade liberalization promote economic development?," *Scottish Journal of Political Economy*, 45 (5).

Greenspan, A. (1998a) "Testimony at the House Banking Committee," September 18, Federal Reserve Board, Washington, DC.

Greenspan, A. (1998b) "Testimony at the House Banking Committee, October 1, Federal Reserve Board, Washington, DC.

Greenspan, A. (2001) "The Euro as an international currency," paper delivered to the Euro Group 50, mimeo, November 30, Washington, DC.

Greenwald, B. (1999) "International adjustment in the face of imperfect financial markets," Annual World Bank Conference on Development Economics, Washington, DC.

Greenwald, B. and Stiglitz, J. E. (1988) "Information, financial constraints and business fluctuations," in Meier Kahn and S. C. Tsiang (eds.), *Expectations in Macroeconomics*, Oxford University Press.

Group of Thirty (1999) "The evolving corporation: global imperatives and national responses," A Study Group, Washington, DC.

Grossman, S. and Hart, O. (1986) "The costs and benefits of ownership," *Journal of Political Economy*, 94.

Grossman, G. and Helpman, E. (1991a) *Innovation and Growth in the Global Economy*, MIT Press, Cambridge, MA.

Grossman, G. and Helpman, E. (1991b) "Trade, knowledge spillovers and growth," *European Economic Review*, 35.

Grossman, G. and Helpman, E. (1995) "Trade wars and trade talks," *Journal of Political Economy*, 103.

Grossman, G. and Helpman, E. (2002) "Outsourcing versus FDI in industry equilibrium," CEPR Discussion Paper 3647.

Grossman, G. and Helpman, E. (2004) "Outsourcing in a global economy," *Review of Economic Studies*.

Grossman, S. and Stiglitz, J. E. (1980) "On the impossibility of informationably efficient markets," *American Economic Review*, 70, June.

Gurley, J. and Shaw, E. (1995) "Financial aspects of economic development," *American Economic Review*, 45.

Guiso, L., Sapienzia, P., and Zingales, L. (2003) "People's opium?: religion and economic attitudes," NBER Working Paper 9237.

Guttentag, J. M. and Herring, R. J. (1986) "Disaster myopia in international banking," *Essays in International Finance*, 164. Princeton University Department of Economics.

Gwyne, S. (1986) *Selling Money*, Weidenfeld & Nicolson, New York.

Hanke, S. and Walters, A. (1992) "Currency boards," *New Palgrave Dictionary of Money and Finance*, Macmillan, London.

Hanson, G. H. (1995) "The effects of offshore assembly on industry location: evidence from US border cities," NBER Working Paper 5400, December.

Hanson, G. H. (1996) "Economic integration, intraindustry trade and frontier regions," *European Economic Review*, 40.

Hanson, G. H. (1998) "Market potential, increasing returns and geographic concentration," NBER Working Paper 6429.

Harrison, L. (1992) *Who Prospers?: How Cultural Values Shape Economic and Political Success*, Basic Books, New York.

Harrison, S. A. (1995) "Openness and growth: a time-series cross-country analysis for developing countries," NBER Working Paper 5221, August.

Haskel, J. E. and Slaughter, M. (1998) "Does the sector bias of skill biased technical change explain changing skill differentials?," NBER Working Paper 6565.

Hausmann, R., Gavin, M., Pages-Serra, C., and Stein E. (1999) "New Initiatives to tackle international financial turmoil," InterAmerican Development Bank, Washington, DC, March.

Hausmann, R. and Panizza, U. (2002) "The mystery of the original sin: the case of the missing apple," mimeo, July 16.

Hausmann, R. and Rigobon, R. (2003) "On the benefits of changing currency denomination in concessional lending to low income countries," mimeo.

Hayek, F. A. (1945) "The use of knowledge in society," *American Economic Review*, 35, September.

Helpman, E. (1984) "A simple theory of trade with multinational corporations," *Journal of Political Economy*, 92.

Helpman, E. and Krugman, P. (1985) "Trade and market structure," MIT Press, Cambridge.

Hemming, R., Kell, M., and Schimmelphennig, A. (2003) "Fiscal vulnerability and financial crises in emerging economies," IMF Occasional Paper 218, Washington, DC.

Heston, A., Summers, R., and Aten, B. (2002) "Penn World Tables, Version 6,0, CICUP, Penn University, PA.

Hildebrand, P. and Reggling, K. (1999) "Should Argentina dollarize?: absolutely," *International Economy*, May–June.

Honohan, P. (1996) *Financial System Failures in Developing Countries: Diagnosis and Prediction*, IMF, Washington.

Hufbauer, G. C. (1994) "The coming boom in services trade: what will it do to wages?," *Law and Policy in International Business*, 25, winter.

Hufbauer, G. C. and Wada, E. (1999) "Hazards and precautions: tales of international finance," Institute of International Finance Working Paper 99/11, Washington, DC.

Hugill, P. (1993) *World Trade since 1431*, Johns Hopkins University Press, Baltimore, MD.

Hummels, D., Rapaport, D., and Yi, K. M. (1997) "Globalization and the changing nature of world trade," Federal Reserve Bank of New York. December.

Huntington, S. (1993) "The clash of civilisations," *Foreign Affairs*, 72.

Huntington, S. (1996) *The Clash of Civilizations and the Remaking of World Order*, Simon & Schuster, New York.

Hymer, S. (1976) *The International Operations of National Firms*, MIT Press, Cambridge, MA.

IMF (1993) "Foreign trade, engine of growth," *World Economic Outlook*, May.

IMF (1997) "Globalization opportunities and challenges," *World Economic Outlook*, May.

IMF (2005) "Globalization and external imbalances," *World Economic Outlook*, April.

IMF and World Bank (2002) "Market access for developing country exports: selected issues," Special Paper for the Annual Meetings, September, Washington, DC.

Jeanne, O. (2003) "Why do emerging economies borrow in foreign currency?," CEPR Discussion Paper 4030.

Jeanne, O. and Wyplosz, C. (2001) "The international lender of last resort: how large is large enough?," NBER Working Paper 3831.

Jones, C. (1997) "On the evolution of world income distribution," *Journal of Economic Perspectives*, 11 (3).

Kahneman, D. and Tversky, A. (1979) "Prospect theory: an analysis of decision under risk," *Econometrica*, 46.

Kahneman, D., Slovic, P., and Tversky, A. (1982) *Judgement under Uncertainty: Heuristics and Biases*, Cambridge University Press, Cambridge.

Kaldor, N. (1961) "Capital accumulation and economic growth" in F. A. Lutz and D. C. Hague (eds.), *The Theory of Capital*, St. Martin Press, New York.

Kamin, S. B. (1988) "Devaluation, exchange control and black markets for foreign exchange in developing countries," Federal Reserve Board Occasional Paper 334, October.

Kaminsky, G. and Schmukler, S. (2003) "Short run pain and long run gain: the effects of financial liberalization," NBER Working Paper 9787.

Kaminsky, G., Reinhart, C., and Vegh, C. (2003) "The unholy trinity of financial contagion," NBER Working Paper 10061.

Kane, E. J. (1998) "Capital movements, asset values and banking policy in globalized markets," NBER Working Paper 6633, July.

Karoly, L. and Klerman, J. A. (1994) "Using regional data to reexamine the contribution of demographic and sectoral change to increasing wage inequality in the changing distribution of income in an open US Economy," Jeffrey Bergstrand (ed.), North Holland, Amsterdam.

Katz, L. and Krueger, A. (1998) "Computing inequality: have computers changed the labour market?," *Quarterly Journal of Economics*.

Keller, W. (1997) "Trade and transmission of technology," NBER Working Paper 6113.

Keynes, J. M. (1936) *The General Theory of Employment, Interest and Money*, Macmillan, London.

Kim, W. and Wei, S. J. (1999) "Offshore investment funds: monsters in emerging markets?," NBER Working Paper 7133, May.

Kindleberger, C. (1978) *Manias, Panics, and Crashes*, Basic Books, New York.

King, M. (1996) "Tax systems in the 21st Century," Fiftieth Congress of the International Fiscal Associations, Geneva.

King, R. and Levine, R. (1993) "Finance and growth: Schumpeter might be right," *Quarterly Journal of Economics*, 108.

Kose, M. A., Prassad, E., and Terrones, M. (2003) "Financial integration and macroeconomic volatility," *IMF Staff Papers*, 50, Washington, DC.

Kremer, M. (1993) "The o-ring theory of economic development," *Quarterly Journal of Economics*, August.

Krueger, A. (1978) *Foreign Trade Regimes and Economic Development: Liberalization Attempts and Consequences*, Ballinger, for NBER.

Krueger, A. (1998) "Why trade liberalization is good for growth?," *Economic Journal*, 108.

Krueger, A. (2002) *New Approaches to Sovereign Debt Restructuring*, International Monetary Fund, Washington, DC.

Krugman, P. R. (1991a) "Increasing returns and economic geography," *Journal of Political Economy*, 99.

Krugman, P. R. (1991b) *Geography and Trade*, MIT Press, Cambridge, MA.

Krugman, P. R. (1992) "International finance and economic development," in Giovannini, A. (ed.), *Finance and Development: Issues and Experience*, CEPR and Cambridge University Press, London and Cambridge.

Krugman, P. R. (1994) "The myth of Asia's miracle," *Foreign Affairs*, November–December.

Krugman, P. R. (1995a) "Technology, trade and factor prices," Stanford University, Department of Economics, October.

Krugman, P. R. (1995b) "Growing world trade: causes and consequences," Brookings Papers on Economic Activity, Washington, DC.

Krugman, P. R. (1996a) "Does third world growth hurt first world prosperity?," *Harvard Business Review*, 72.

Krugman, P. R. (1996b) "Are currency crisis self-fulfilling?," *NBER Macroeconomics Annual*.

Krugman, P. R. (1996c) *Pop Internationalism*, MIT Press, Cambridge, MA.

Krugman, P. R. (1997a) "In praise of cheap labor," World Economic Laboratory, MIT, Cambridge, MA.

Krugman, P. R. (1997b) *The Age of Diminished Expectations*, MIT Press, Cambridge, MA.

Krugman, P. R. (1998a) "The role of geography in development," Annual World Bank Conference on Development Economics, Washington, DC.

Krugman, P. R. (1998b) "What happened to Asia?," MIT, January, mimeo.

Krugman, P. R. (1998c) "Will Asia bounce back?," MIT, March, mimeo.

Krugman, P. R. (1998d) "Paradigms of panic," *Slate*, March 12.

Krugman, P. R. (1998e) "Saving Asia, it's time to get radical," *Fortune*, September 7.

Krugman, P. R. (1999a) "Monetary crises and is there a way out?," Lecciones Pedro Barrié de la Maza. Fundación Barrié.

Krugman, P. R. (1999b) "Introduction," NBER Conference on Currency Crisis, Cambridge, MA.

Krugman, P. R. (1999c) "Balance sheets, the transfer problem, and financial crisis," MIT, mimeo.

Krugman, P. R. (1999d) *The Return of Depression Economics*, N. W. Norton. New York.

Krugman, P. R. and Lawrence, R. Z. (1993) "Trade, jobs and wages," NBER Working Paper 4478.

Krugman, P. R. and Lawrence, R. Z. (1994) "Trade, jobs and wages," *Scientific American*, 270, April.

Krugman, P. R. and Obstfeldt, M. (1991) *International Economics: Theory and Politics*, Harper Collins, New York.

Kumar, M. and Prasad, E. (1997) "International trade and the business cycle," IMF Working Paper.

Kumar, K., Rajan, R., and Zingales, L. (1999) "What determines firm size?," NBER Working Paper 7208.

Kuznets, S. (1965) *Economic Growth and Structure: Selected Essays*, Heinemann Educational Books, London.

Kydland, F. and Prescott, E. (1977) "Rules rather than discretion: the inconsistency of optimal plans," *Journal of Political Economy*, 85 (3).

Lakonishok, J., Shleifer, A., and vishny, R. (1992) "The impact of institutional trading on stock prices," *Journal of Financial Economics*, 32.

Lall, S. (1980) "Vertical firm linkages: an empirical study," *Oxford Bulletin of Economics and Statistics*, 42.

Lawrence, R. (1994) *The Impact of Trade on OECD's Labor Markets*, Group of Thirty, Washington, DC.

Lawrence, R. and Slaughter, M. (1993) "Trade and US wages; great sucking sound of small hiccup?," Brookings Papers on Economic Activity, 2.

Lazear, E. (1999) "Globalisation and the market for team-mates," *Economic Journal*, 109, March.

Leamer, E. (1984) *Sources of International Comparative Advantage*, MIT Press, Cambridge, MA.

Leamer, E. (1994) "Trade, wages and revolving door ideas," NBER Working Paper 4716.

Leamer, E. (1995) "The Heckscher–Ohlin model in theory and in practice," *Princeton Essays in International Finance*, 77.

Leamer, E. (1996) "In search of Stolper–Samuelson effects on US wages," NBER Working Paper 5427, January.

Leamer, E. (1998) "Measure of openness," in Richard Baldwin (ed.), *Trade Policy and Empirical Analysis*, University of Chicago Press. Chicago.

Leamer, E. and Levinsohn, J. (1995) "International trade theory: the evidence," in G. Grossman and K. Rogoff (eds.), *Handbook of International Economics*, vol. 3, Elsevier, Amsterdam.

Lee, J. W. (1993) "International trade, distortions and long run economic growth," IMF Staff papers, 40, July.

Lee, J. W. (1995) "Capital goods imports and long-run growth," *Journal of Development Economics*, 48, October.

Lee, H. Y., Ricci, L. A., and Rigobon, R. (2004) "Once again, is openness good for growth?," NBER Working Paper 10749.

Leontief, W. (1953) "Domestic production and foreign trade: the American capital position reexamined," *Proceedings of the American Philosophical Society*, 97.

Levine, R. (1996) "Foreign banks, financial development and economic growth" in Claude Barfield (ed.), *International Financial Markets: Harmonization versus Competition*, American Enterprise Institute, Washington, DC.

Levine, R. (1997) "Financial Development and Economic Growth: views and agenda," *Journal of Economic Literature*, 35, June.

Levine, R. (2004) "Finance and economic growth: theory and evidence," NBER Working Paper 10766.

Levine, R. and Renelt, D. (1992) "A sensitivity analysis of cross-country growth regressions," *American Economic Review*, 82.

Levitt, T. (1983) "The globalization of markets," *Harvard Business Review*, May–June.

Levy-Yeyati, E. and Ubide, A. (1998) "Crisis, contagion and the close end country fund puzzle," IMF Working Paper WP/98/143.

Levy-Yeyati, E. and Sturzenegger, F. (2001) "To float or to trail: evidence on the impact of exchange rate regimes," NBER Summer Institute at the Torcuato di Tella University, Buenos Aires.

Lewis, B. (1995) *The Middle East*, Weidenfeld & Nicolson, London.

Lipsey, R. (1984) "Foreign production and exports of individual firms," *Review of Economics and Statistics*, 63.

Lipsey, R. (2002) "Home and host country effects of FDI," NBER Working Paper 9293.

Lommerud, K. E., Meland, F., and Straume, O. R. (2005) "Globalization and union opposition to technological change," CEPR Discussion Paper 4836.

Longin, F. (1999) "From value at risk to stress testing: the extreme value approach," CEPR Discussion Paper 2161, May.

Lucas, R. E. (1977) "Understanding business cycles in stabilization of the domestic and the insternational economy," Carnegie Rochester Conference Series in Public Policy, vol. 5, eds. Karl Brunner and Alan Meltzer, North Holland, Amsterdam.

Lucas, R. E. (1978) "On the size and distribution of business firms," *Bell Journal of Economics*, 9.

Lucas, R. E. (1988) "On the mechanics of economic development," *Journal of Monetary Economics*, 22.

Lucas, R. E. (1990) "Why does not capital flow from rich to poor countries," *American Economic Review, Papers and Proceedings*, 80.

Lucas, R. E. (2000) "Some macroeconomics for the 21st century," *Journal of Economic Perspectives*, 14 (1).

Lucas, R. E. (2002) *Lectures on Economic Growth*, Harvard University Press, Cambridge, MA.

Lucas, R. E. and Sargent, T. (1978) "After Keynesian economics," in *After the Phillips Curve: Persistence of High Inflation and High Unemployment*, Federal Reserve Bank of Boston.

Lumsdaine, R. and Prasad, E. (1996) "Identifying the common component in international economic fluctuations," IMF Working Paper, December.

Mackay, C. [1852] (1932) *Memoirs of Extraordinary Popular Delusions and the Madness of Crowds*, L. C. Page, Boston.

Maddison, A. (1983) "A comparison of levels of GDP per capita in developed and developing countries, 1700–1980," *Journal of Economic History*, March.

Maddison, A. (1991) *Dynamic Forces in Capitalist Development: A Long-run Comparative View*, Oxford University Press, Oxford.

Maddison, A. (2001) *The World Economy: A Millennium Perspective*, OECD, Paris.

Magee, S. (1977) "Multinational corporations, the industry technology cycle and development," *Journal of World Trade Law*, 2 (4).

Mankiw, G. N. (1986) "The allocation of credit and financial collapse," *Quarterly Journal of Economics*, 101, August.

Mankiw, G. N., Romer, D., and Weil, D. (1992) "A contribution to the empirics of economic growth," *Quarterly Journal of Economics*, 107, May.

Markusen, J. (1984) "Multinationals, multiplant economies and gains from trade," *Journal of International Economics*, 16.

Markusen, J. and Maskus, K. (1995) "Discriminating among alternative theories of the multinational enterprise," NBER Working Paper 7164.

Markusen, J. and Maskus, K. (1999) "Multinational firms: reonciling theory and evidence," NBER Working Paper 7163.

Martin, P. (1996) "Economic aspects of International immigration," IMF Working Paper, Washington, DC.

Martin, P. and Rey, H. (2002) "Financial globalization and emerging markets: with or without crash?," CEPR Discussion Paper 3378.

Masson, P. (1998) "Contagion: moonsoonal effects, spillovers and jumps between multiple equilibria," IMF Working Paper 98-42, September.

Masson, P. and Mussa, M. (1995) "The role of the IMF: financing and its interactions with adjustment and surveillance," Pamphlet Series, 50.

Matin, K. (1992) "Openness and economic performance in Subsaharan Africa: evidence from time-series cross-country analysis," World Bank, Working Paper 1025.

Mayer, M. (1999) "Is everything too big to fail?," International Economy, January–February.

McKinnon, R. (1964) "Foreign exchange constraints in economic development and efficient aid allocation," Economic Journal, 74.

McKinnon, R. (1973) Money and Capital in Economic Development, Brookings Institution, Washington, DC.

McKinnon, R. (1996) The Rules of the Game: International Money and Exchange Rates, MIT Press, Cambridge, MA.

McKinnon, R. (1998) "Exchange rate coordination for surmounting the East Asia currency," mimeo, Stanford University.

McKinnon, R. (1999) "The euro threat is exaggerated," International Economy, May–June.

Mehra, R. and Prescott, E. C. (1985) "The equity premium: a puzzle," Journal of Monetary Economics, 15.

Meltzer Commission (2000) http://www.bicusa.org/usgovtoversight/meltzer.htm.

Messerlin, P. (1999) Measuring the Costs of Protection in Europe, Institute for International Economics, Washington, DC.

Michaely, M. (1977) "Exports and growth: an empirical investigation," Journal Development Economics, 4.

Miller, M. H. (1988) "Financial markets and Economic growth" Journal of Applied Corporate Finance, 11.

Mincer, J. (1991) "Human capital, technology and the wage structure, what time series show?," NBER Working Paper 3581.

Minford, P., Riley, J., and Novell, E. (1996) "The elixir of growth: trade, non-traded goods and development," CEPR Discussion Paper 1165.

Minsky, H. (1986) Stabilizing an Unstable Economy: A Twentieth-century Fund Report, Yale University Press, New Haven, CT.

Mishkin, F. (1991) "Asymmetric information and financial crisis: a historical perspective," in G. Hubbard (ed.), Financial Markets and Financial Crisis, Chicago University Press, Chicago.

Mishkin, F. (1996) "Understanding financial crises: a developing country perspective," NBER Working Paper 5600, May.

Mundell, R. (1957) "International trade and factor mobility," American Economic Review, 47, June.

Mundell, R. (1961) "A theory of optimum currency areas," *American Economic Review*, 51.

Neary, P. (2002) "Globalization and market structure," CEPR Discussion Paper.

Neven, D. (1990) "EEC integration towards 1992: some distributional aspects," *Economic Policy*, 10.

Neven, D. and Wyplosz, C. (1996) "Relative prices, trade and reestructuring in European industry," Centre for economic Policy Research Discussion Paper 1451, August.

Niskanen, W. (1992) "The case for a new fiscal constitution," *Journal of Economic Perspectives*, spring.

Obstfeld, M. (1996) "Models of currency crises with self-fulfilling features," *European Economic Review*, 40.

Obstfeldt, M. (1998) "The global capital market: benefactor or menace?," *Journal of Economic Perspectives*, fall.

Obstfeld, M. and Rogoff, K. (1996) *Foundations of International Macroeconomics*, MIT Press, Cambridge, MA.

Obstfeld, M. and Rogoff, K. (1998) "The mirage of fixed exchange rates," *Journal of Economic Perspectives*, 9, fall.

Obstfeldt, M. and Taylor, A. (1998) "The Great Depression as a wathershed: international capital mobility over the long run" in Bordo, Goldin, and White (eds.), *The Defining Moment: The Great Depression and the American Economy in the Twentieth Century*, Chicago University Press, Chicago.

Obstfeldt, M. and Taylor, A. M. (2004) *Global Capital Markets: Integration, Crisis and Growth*, Cambridge University Press, Cambridge, MA.

Obstfeldt, M., Shambaugh, J. C., and Taylor, A. M. (2004) "The trilemma in history: trade-offs among exchange rates, monetary policies and capital mobility," CEPR Discussion Paper 4352.

OECD (1996) *Economic Outlook*, 60, December, Paris.

OECD (1998a) "Ageing in OECD Countries: a critical policy challenge," *Social Policy Studies*, 20, Paris.

OECD (1998b) *Open Markets Matter: The Benefits of Trade and Investment Liberalization*, Paris.

OECD (1999a) *OECD in Figures*, Paris.

OECD (1999b) *Benchmarking Knowledge-based Economies*, Paris.

Ohlin, B. (1933) *Interregional and International Trade*, Harvard University Press, Cambridge, MA.

Ohmae, K. (1990) *Borderless World: Power and Strategy in the Interlinked Economy*, Harper Business, New York.

Ozkan, F. G. and Sutherland, A. (1993) "A model of ERM crisis," CEPR Discussion Paper 874.

Pagano, M. (1993) "Financial markets and growth: an overview," *European Economic Review*, 37.

Pagano, M., Panetta, F., and Zingales, L. (1998) "Why do companies go public," *Journal of Finance*, 50.

Pastor, A. (1999) "El euro frente al dólar," *Management Review*, 10, Barcelona.

Phelps, E. (1997) *Rewarding Work*, Harvard University Press, Cambridge, MA.

Porter, M. (1990) *The Competitive Advantage of Nations*, Free Press, New York.

Portes, R. and Rey, H. (1998) "The emergence of the euro as international currency," *Economic Policy*, 26, April.

Prassad, E. (1999) "International trade and the business cycle," IMF Working Paper 99/56.

Proudman, J., Redding, S., and Bianchi, M. (1997) "Is international openness associated with faster economic growth?," Bank of England Working Paper 63, June.

Quah, D. T. (1996) "Twin Peaks: growth and convergence in models of distribution dynamics," *Economic Journal*, July.

Quah, D. T. (1999) "Convergence as distribution dynamics (with or without growth)," in Richard Baldwin, Daniel Cohen, André Sapir, and Anthony Venables (eds.), *Market Integration, Regionalism and the Global Economy*, CEPR and Cambridge University Press, London and Cambridge.

Radelet, S. and Sachs, J. (1998) "The East Asian financial crisis: diagnosis, remedies and prospects," Brooking Papers on Economic Activity 1, spring.

Rajan, R. and Zingales, L. (1998) "Financial dependence and growth," *American Economic Review*, 88.

Ram, R. (1985) "Exports and economic growth: some additional evidence," *Economic Development and Cultural Change*, 33.

Ramaswamy, R. and Rowthorn, R. (1991) "Efficency, wages and wage dispersion," *Economica*, 58, November.

Rassekh, F. and Thompson, H. (1998) "Micro convergence and macro convergence: factor price equalization and per capita income," *Pacific Economic Review*, 3, February.

Razin, A. and Chi-Wa, Y. (1993) "Convergence in growth rates: the role of capital mobility and international taxation," Leonard Leiderman and Assaf Razin (eds.), *Capital Mobility*, CEPR and Cambridge University Press, London and Cambridge.

Rebelo, S. (1991) "Long run policy analysis and long run growth," *Journal of Political Economy*, 99, June.

Redding, S. and Schott, P. K. (2003) "Distance, skill deepening and development: will peripheral countries ever get rich?," NBER Working Paper 9447.

Redding, S. and Venables, A. (2001) "Economic geography and international inequality," CEPR Discussion Paper 2568.

Reich, R. (1991) *The Work of Nations*, Vintage Books, New York.

Reinhart, C. and Rogoff, K. (2000) "The miracle of floating excahage rates," *American Economic Review*, 104.

Reinhart, C., Rogoff, K., and Savastano, M. (2003) "Debt intolerance," Brookings Papers on Economic Activity 1, Washington, DC.

Revenga, A. (1992) "Exporting jobs?: The impact of import competition on employment and wages in US manufacturing," *Quarterly Journal of Economics*, February.

Rigobon, R. (1999) "On the measurements of the international propagation of shocks," NBER Working Paper 7354.

Robbins, D. (1996) "Evidence on trade and wages in the developing world," OECD Development Centre Technical Paper 119, December.

Robinson, J. (1952) "The generalization of the General Theory," in *The Rate of Interest and Other Essays*, Macmillan, London.

Rodríguez, F. and Rodrik, D. (1999 and 2001) "Trade policy and economic growth: a skeptic's guide to the cross national evidence," NBER Working Paper 7081, and *NBER Macroeconomics Annual*, 2001, Cambridge, MA.

Rodrik, D. (1992) "The rush to free trade in the developing world: why so late, why now, will it last?," NBER Working Paper 3947.

Rodrik, D. (1993) "Trade and industrial policy reforms in developing countries: a review of recent theory and evidence," NBER Working Paper 4417.

Rodrik, D. (1996) "Why do more open countries have bigger governments?," NBER Working Paper 5537, April.

Rodrik, D. (1997) *Has Globalization Gone Too Far?*, Institute for International Economics, Washington, DC.

Rodrik, D. (1999) "The new global economy and developing countries: making openness work," Overseas Development Council, *Policy Essay*, 24, Washington.

Rodrik, D., Subramanian, A., and Trebbi, F. (2002) "Institutions rule: the primacy of institutions over geography and integration in economic development," CID Working Paper 97, October.

Rogoff, K. (1996) "The purchasing power parity puzzle," *Journal of Economic Literature*, June.

Rogoff, K. (1999) "International institutions for reducing global financial instability," NBER Working Paper 7265, June.

Romer, P. (1986) "Increasing returns and long run growth," *Journal of Political Economy*, 94.

Romer, P. (1989) "Capital accumulation in the theory of long run growth," in Robert Barro (ed.), *Modern Business Cycle Theory*, Harvard University Press and Oxford University Press, Cambridge, MA, and Oxford.

Romer, P. (1990) "Endogenous technological change," *Journal of Political Economy*, 98, October.

Rosen, S. (1982) "Authority, control and the distribution of earnings," *Bell Journal of Economics*, fall.

Rosenberg, N. (1980) "Inside the black box," Cambridge University Press, Cambridge.

Rowthorn, R. and Ramaswamsy, R. (1997) "Deindustrialization, causes and implications," *IMF Staff Papers*, Washington, DC.

Sachs, J. (1997) "The limits of convergence," *Economist*, June 14.

Sachs, J. (1999) "Crear problemas," *El País*, Madrid. Project Syndicate.

Sachs, J. (2000) "Tropical underdevelopment," NBER Working Paper 8119, February.

Sachs, J. and Shatz, H. (1994) "Trade and jobs in US manufacturing," Brookings Papers on Economic Activity 1.

Sachs, J. and Warner, A. (1995) "Economic reform and the process of global integration," Brookings Papers on Economic Activity 1.

Sachs, J., Tornell, A., and Velasco, A. (1996) "Financial crisis in emerging markets: the lessons from 1995," NBER Working Paper 5576, May.

Saeger, S. (1996) "Globalization and economic structure in the OCDE," mimeo, Harvard University, May.

Saint-Paul, G. (1992) "Technological choice, financial markets and economic growth," *European Economic Review*, 36.

Sala i Martín, X. (2002a) "The disturbing rise in global income inequality," NBER Working Paper 8904, April.

Sala i Martín, X. (2002b) "The world distribution of income estimated from individual country distributions," NBER Working Paper 8933, April.

Samuelson, P. (1948) "International trade and the equalisation of factor prices," *Economic Journal*, 58.

Samuelson, P. (1949) "International factor-price equalization once again," *Economic Journal*, 59.

Scharfstein, D. and Stein J. C. (1990) "Herd behavior and investment," *American Economic Review*, 80 (3).

Scheve, K. and Slaughter, M. (2002) "Economic insecurity and the globalization of production," NBER Working Paper 9339.

Schultze, C. (1992) "Is there a bias towards excess in US government budgets or deficits?," *Journal of Economic Perspectives*, spring.

Schumpeter, J. A. (1911) *The Theory of Economic Development*, Harvard University Press, Cambridge, MA.

Sharpe, W. (1964) "Capital asset prices: a theory of market equilibrium unders conditions of risk," *Journal of Finance*, 19, September.

Shaw, E. (1973) *Financial Deepening in Economic Development*, Oxford University Press, New York.

Shiller, R. (1981) "Do stock prices move too much to be justified by subsequent changes in dividens?," *American Economic Review*, 71.

Shiller, R. (1995) "Conversation, information and herd behavior," American Economic Association Papers and Procedings, May.

Shiller, R. (2003) *The New Financial Order: Risk in the 21st Century*, Princeton University Press, Princeton, NJ.

Shrefin, H. and Statman, M. (1984) "Explaining investor preference for dividends," *Journal of Financial Economics*, 3 (2).

Shrefin, H. and Statman, M. (1985) "The disposition to sell winners too early and to ride losers too long," *Journal of Finance*, 40.

Siebert, H. (1997) "Labour market rigidities; at the root of unemployment in Europe," *Journal of Economic Perspectives*, 11 summer.

Siegel J. and Thaler, R. (1997) "The equity premium puzzle," *Journal of Economic Perspectives*, 2 (1).

Sinn, H. W. (2004) "Migration, social standards and replacement incomes," NBER Working Paper 10798.

Slaughter, M. (1995a) "Multinational corporations, outsourcing and American wages," NBER Working Paper 5252, September.

Slaughter, M. (1995b) "The antebellum transportation revolution and factor price convergence," NBER Working Paper 5303, October.

Slaughter, M. (1997) "Per capita income convergence and the role of international trade," NBER Working Paper 5897.

Slaughter, M. (1999) *Globalization and Wages: A Tale of Two Perspectives*, Blackwell, Oxford.

Slaughter, M. and Swagel, P. (1997) "The effect of globalization on wages in advanced economies," IMF Working Paper, April.

Smithin, J. (1999) "Money and national sovereignty in the global economy," *Eastern Economic Journal*, 25 (1).

Smith, A. (1984) "Capital theory and trade theory," in Ronald Jones and Peter Kenen (eds.), *Handbook of International Economics*, vol. 1, North Holland, Amsterdam.

Solow, R. (1956) "A contribution to the theory of economic growth," *Quarterly Journal of Economics*, 70, February.

Solow, R. (1957) "Technical change and the aggregate production function," *Review of Economics and Statistics*, 39, August.

Sorensen, P. (1993) "Coordination of capital income taxes in the Economic and Monetary Union: what needs to be done?," in Torres and Giavazzi (eds.), *Adjustment and Growth in the European Monetary Union*, CEPR and Cambridge University Press, London and Cambridge.

Srinivasan, T. N. (1999) "Trade orientation, trade liberalization and economic growth," in P. van Dijck and G. Faber (eds.), *Challenges to the WTO*, Kluwer, The Netherlands.

Stolper, W. and Samuelson, R. (1941) "Protection and real wages," *Review of Economic Studies*, 9.

Stern, N. (1989) "The economics of development: a survey," *Economic Journal*, 99.

Stern, N. and Stiglitz, J. E. (1998) "New role for government," in Edmond Malinvaud et al. (eds.), *Development Strategy and Management of the Market Economy*, Oxford University Press, Oxford.

Stiglitz, J. E. (1998) "Towards a new paradigm for development: strategies, policies and processes," Prebisch Lecture at UNCTAD, Geneva, October.

Stiglitz, J. E. (2000) "Capital account liberalization, economic growth and instability," *World Development*, 28(5).

Stiglitz, J. E. (2003) *Globalization and Its Discontents*, W. W. Norton, New York.

Stiglitz, J. E. and Weiss, A. (1981) "Credit rationing in markets with imperfect information," *American Economic Review*, 71.

Straubhaar, T. (1988) *On the Economics of International Labor Migration*, Paul Haupt, Stuttgart.

Stulz, R. (1999) "Globalization of equity markets and the cost of capital," NBER Working Paper 7021.

Sutton, J. (1997) "Gibrat's legacy," *Journal of Economic Literature*, 35.

Swan, T. (1965) "Economic growth and capital accumulation," *Economic Record*, 32, November.

Swenson, D. (2004) "Overseas assembly and country sourcing choices," NBER Working Paper 10697.

Syrquin, M. and Chenery, H. (1989) "Three decades of industrialization," *World Bank Economic Review*, 3.

Talvi, E. and Vegh, C. (2000) "Tax base variability and procyclical fiscal policy," NBER Working Paper 7499.

Tanzi, V. (1996) "Globalization, tax competition and the future of tax systems," IMF Working Paper, 96.

Tempest, R. (1996) "Barbie and the world economy," *Los Angeles Times*, September 22.

Thomson Financial (2004) Statistics on M&A's.

Tisdale, S. (1994) "Shoe and Tell," *The New Republic*, September 12.

Tobin, J. (1978) "A proposal for internationbal monetary reform," *Eastern Economic Journal*, 4.

Tolchin, M. and Tolchin, S. (1988) *Buying into America*, New York Times Books, New York.

Tolchin, M. and Tolchin, S. (1992) *Selling Our Security: The Erosion of America's Assets*, Alfred A. Knopf, New York.

Tornell, A. (1999) "Common fundamentals in the Tequila and Asian crisis," NBER Working Paper 7139, May.

Tufte, E. (1978) *Political Control of the Economy*, Princeton University Press, Princeton, NJ.

Tversky, A. and Kahneman, D. (1981) "The framing of decisions and the psichology of choice," *Science*, 211.

Tytell, I. and Wei, S. J. (2004) "Does financial globalization induce better macroeconomic policies?", paper presented to the Fifth Annual IMF Research Conference, November 14, Washington, DC.

UNCTAD (1999) *World Investment Report*, Geneva.

UNCTAD (2004) *World Investment Report*, Geneva.

UNDP, United Nations Development Programme (1999) *Human Development Report*, United Nations, New York.

United Nations (2001) *World Population Prospects: The 2000 Review*, New York.

United Nations (2005) *World Population Prospects: The 2002 Revision*, New York.

Venables, A. and Limao, N. (1999) "Geographical disadvantage: a Hechscher–Ohlin–Von Thunen model of international specialization," CEPR Discussion Paper 2305.

Vernon, R. (1966) "International trade and international investment in product cycle," *Quarterly Journal of Economics*, 83 (1).

Vernon, R. (1971) *Sovereignty at Bay*, Basic Books, New York.

Vernon, R. (1974) "The location of economic activity" in John Dunning (ed.), *Economic Analysis and Multinational Enterprise*, G. Allen and Unwin, London.

Von Thunen, J. H. (1826) *The Isolated State*, translated by C. M. Wartenberg (1966), Pergamon Press, Oxford.

Wacziarg, R. (2001) "Measuring the dynamic gains from trade," *World Bank Economic Review*, 15 (3).

Wacziarg, R. and Horn-Welch, K. (2003) "Trade liberalization and growth: new evidence," NBER Working Paper 10152.

Weber, M. [1904] (1930) *The Protestant Ethic and the Spirit of Capitalism*, Allen and Unwin, London.

Williamson, J. (1996) "Globalization and inequality, then and now," NBER Working Paper 5491.

Williamson, J. (1998) "Globalization, labor markets and policy backlash in the past," *Journal of Economic Perspectives*, fall.

Williamson, J. (2000) *Exchange Rate Regimes for Emerging Markets: Reviving the Intermediate Option*, Institute of International Economics, Washington, DC.

Williamson, J. and Mahar, M. (1998) "A survey of financial liberalisation," *Princeton Essays in International Finance*, 21.

Williamson, O. (1975) *Markets and Hierarchies: Analysis and Antitrust Implications*, Free Press, New York.

Wolf, M. (1999) "Capital punishment," *Financial Times*, May 5.

Wolf, M. (2004) *Why Globalization Works*, Yale University Press, New Haven, CN.

Wood, A. (1994) *North–South Trade, Employment and Inequality: Changing Fortunes in a Skill Driven World*, Oxford University Press, New York.

Wood, A. (1995) "How trade hurt unskilled workers," *Journal of Economic Perspectives*, 9, summer.

World Bank (1987) *World Development Report 1987*, Washington DC.

World Trade Organization (1999) *World Trade Report*, Geneva.

Wyplosz, C. (1998) "Currency crisis contagion and containment: a framework," in *Financial Crisis in Asia*, CEPR Conference Report 6, March.

Young, A. (1994) "The tyranny of numbers: confronting the statistical realities of the East Asian growth experience," NBER Working Paper 4680, March.

Zimmerman, K. (1995) "Tackling the European migration problem," *Journal of Economic Perspectives*, 9, spring.

Index